FALLING SKIES™

Created by
ROBERT RODAT

FALLING SKIES ™

Story **PAUL TOBIN**

Art **JUAN FERREYRA**

Colors **ANDREW DALHOUSE**

Letters **NATE PIEKOS OF BLAMBOT®**

Cover **STEVE MORRIS**

Editor **SCOTT ALLIE**

Assistant Editor **DANIEL CHABON**

Designer **DAVID NESTELLE**

Publisher **MIKE RICHARDSON**

DARK HORSE BOOKS

Mike Richardson President and Publisher • Neil Hankerson Executive Vice President • Tom Weddle
Chief Financial Officer • Randy Stradley Vice President of Publishing • Michael Martens Vice Presi-
dent of Book Trade Sales • Anita Nelson Vice President of Business Affairs • Micha Hershman Vice
President of Marketing • David Scroggy Vice President of Product Development • Dale LaFountain Vice
President of Information Technology • Darlene Vogel Senior Director of Print, Design, and Production
• Ken Lizzi General Counsel • Davey Estrada Editorial Director • Scott Allie Senior Managing Editor
• Chris Warner Senior Books Editor • Diana Schutz Executive Editor • Cary Grazzini Director of Print
and Development • Lia Ribacchi Art Director • Cara Niece Director of Scheduling

Special thanks to Ashley Smith, Whitney Melancon, Melinda Hsu Taylor, and Mark Verheiden

This volume collects the Falling Skies custom comic and the Falling Skies webcomic.

Published by Dark Horse Books
A division of Dark Horse Comics, Inc.
10956 SE Main Street
Milwaukie, OR 97222

DarkHorse.com   TNT.tv

To find a comics shop in your area, call the Comic Shop Locator Service toll-free at (888) 266-4226.

First edition: July 2011
ISBN 978-1-59582-737-1

10 9 8 7 6 5 4 3 2
Printed at Midas Printing International, Ltd., Huizhou, China

INTRODUCTION MARK VERHEIDEN

IT BEGINS when the skies over Earth fill with alien spacecraft. For weeks they hover in silence, mystery compounding mystery, until our initial fear is replaced by curiosity and even complacency. Then, without warning, the visitors attack, and all at once the world is irrevocably changed. Human armies fall, and mankind is left virtually defenseless.

How those left alive adapt to this new world—how we survive, defend ourselves, and even find hope—is the story of *Falling Skies*.

As conceived by Robert Rodat, the television series begins several months after the first devastating attack. The initial shock has worn off, and the survivors are coping with a world turned upside down. There are no computers and no communications, as virtually all our posttransistor technology has been destroyed. Major cities lie deserted, while the aliens gather materials to build massive structures for reasons unknown. At the same time, the aliens continue to make strategic strikes on human enclaves, and a dark plan involving the Earth's children unfolds. In Massachusetts, home to history professor Tom Mason and his three boys, survivors have formed makeshift militia units, hoping to find strength in numbers—and a way to strike back.

But what about those long months before the formation of the Second Mass? How did these militias actually come together? When did our characters first meet? And will Captain Weaver ever crack a smile? To explore these arenas, the folks at TNT turned to the crack team at Dark Horse Comics.

It was an excellent decision, and I'm not just saying that because I've known and worked with Dark Horse publisher/president Mike Richardson for many years, or because he is one of the few people in the media business taller than me—even though both are true! The exciting part of this collaboration was knowing Dark Horse's long history of picking up the creative ball on movie and television-related works. They don't just rehash the original story; they expand and amplify and make something special happen on the page. This collection is no exception. Writer Paul Tobin and artist Juan Ferreyra have taken the framework of the television series and produced a rock 'em, sock 'em adventure that stands on its own, but also introduces the reader to the *Falling Skies* world. Of course, they didn't do it alone. Special mention should also go to *Falling Skies* supervising producer Melinda Hsu Taylor for her ever-watchful story eye, Dark Horse editor Scott Allie, and TNT's great creative group, including Ashley Smith and Whitney Melancon.

And now? The skitters have arrived and the mechs are out for blood, but mankind still has a few tricks up its collective sleeve. Settle back and prepare yourself for *Falling Skies*.

Mark Verheiden is the co-executive producer of Falling Skies.

CHAPTER ONE

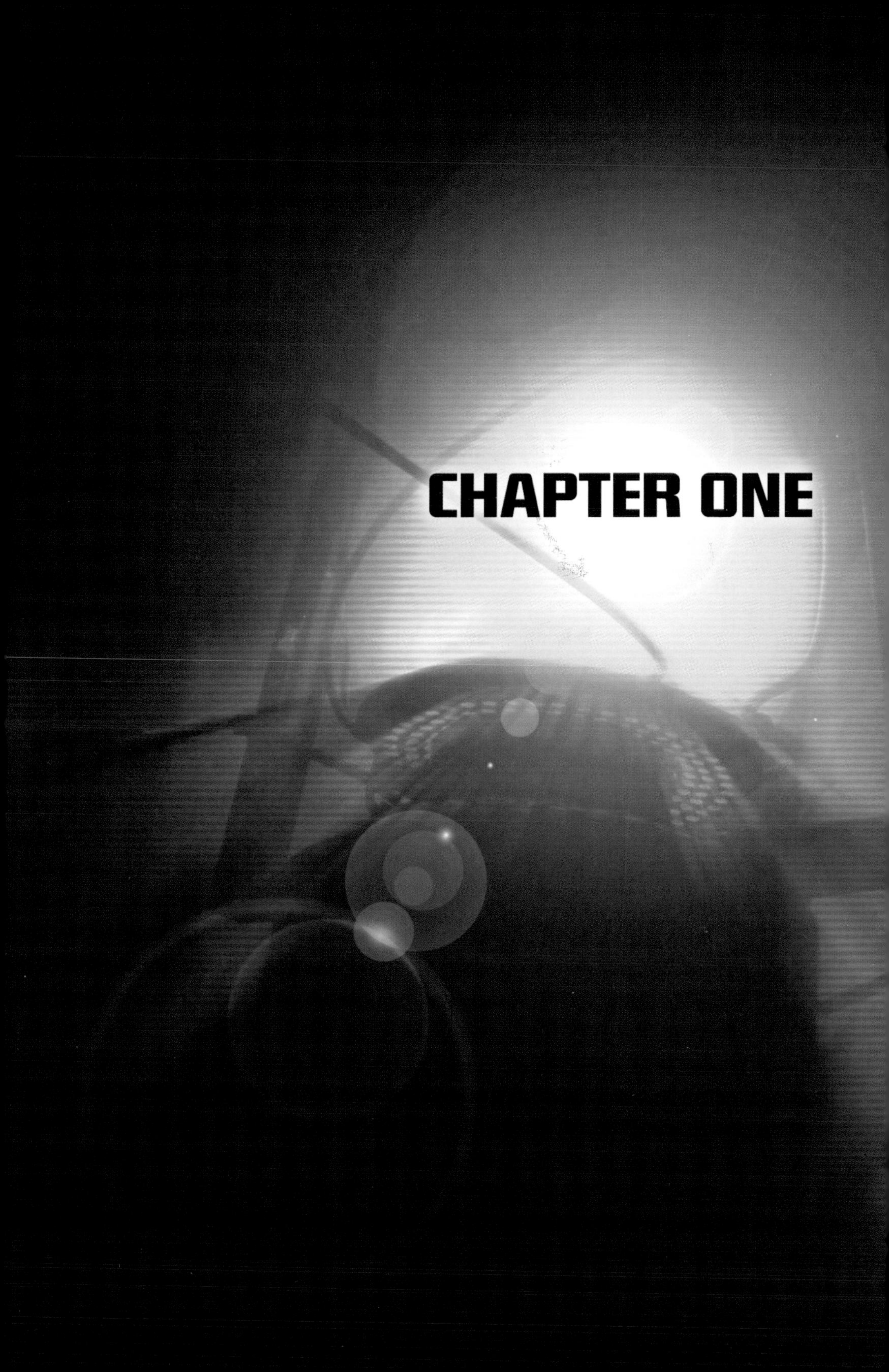

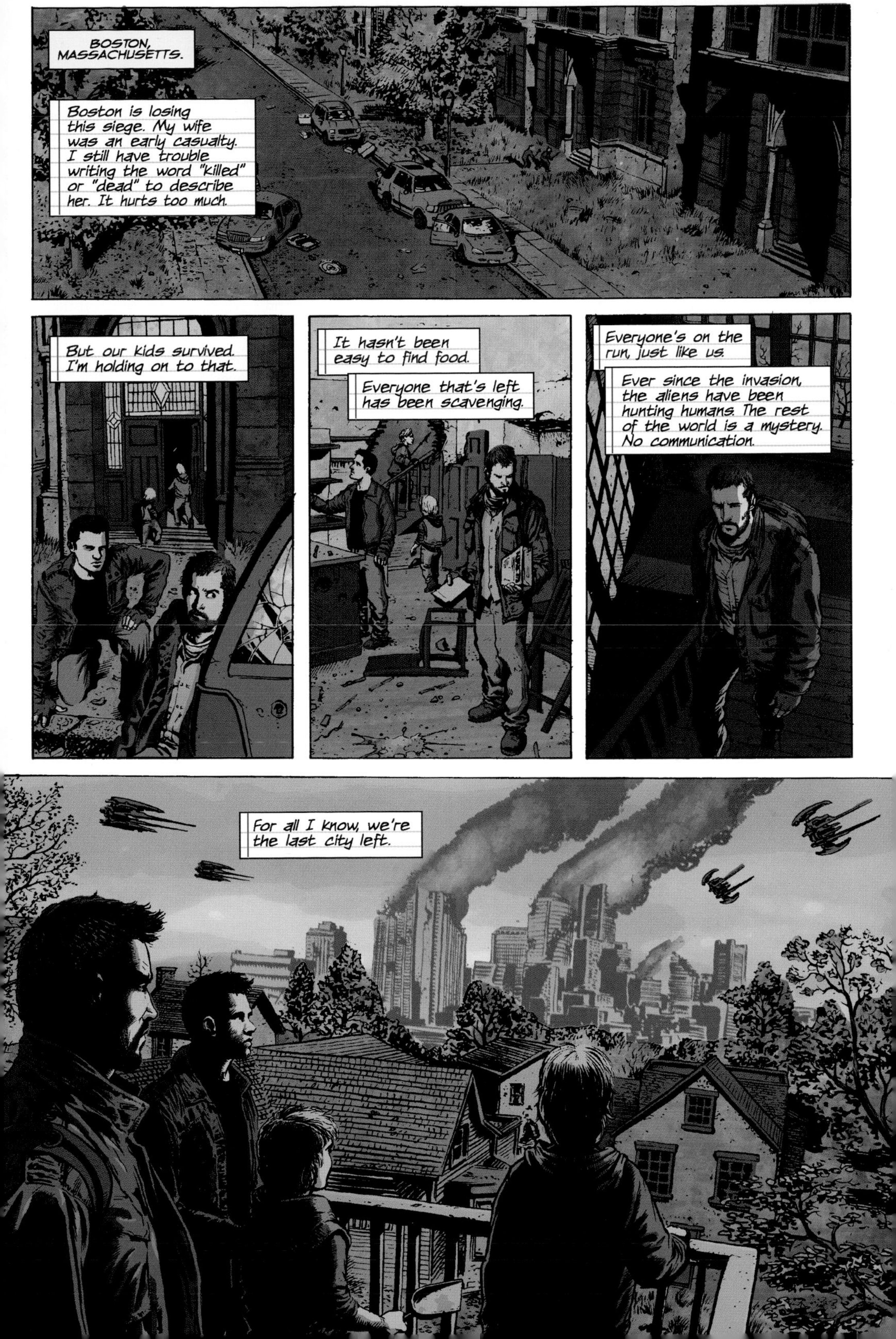
BOSTON, MASSACHUSETTS.
Boston is losing this siege. My wife was an early casualty. I still have trouble writing the word "killed" or "dead" to describe her. It hurts too much.
But our kids survived. I'm holding on to that.
It hasn't been easy to find food.
Everyone that's left has been scavenging.
Everyone's on the run, just like us.
Ever since the invasion, the aliens have been hunting humans. The rest of the world is a mystery. No communication.
For all I know, we're the last city left.

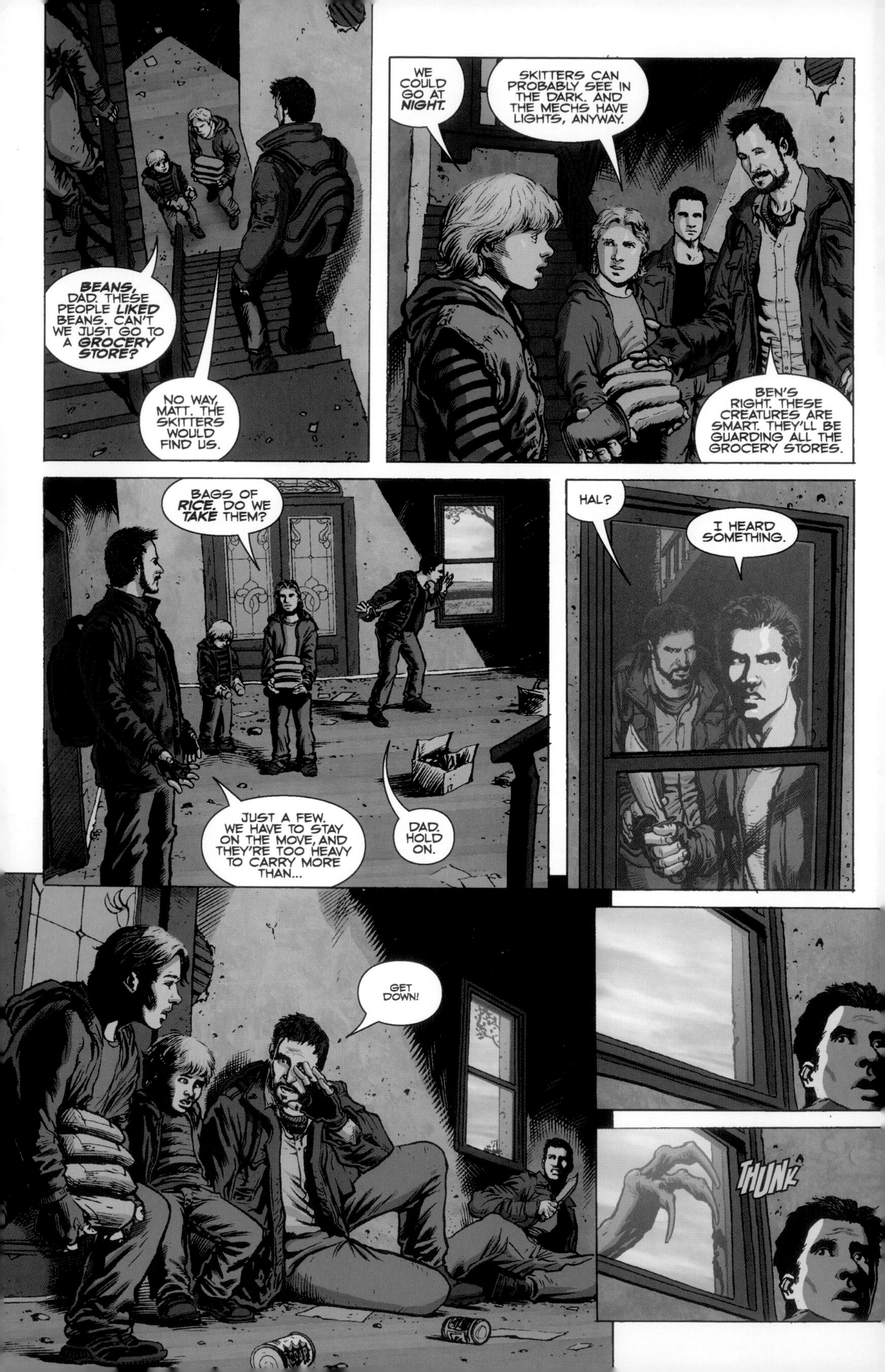
BEANS, DAD. THESE PEOPLE LIKED BEANS. CAN'T WE JUST GO TO A GROCERY STORE?
NO WAY, MATT. THE SKITTERS WOULD FIND US.
WE COULD GO AT NIGHT.
SKITTERS CAN PROBABLY SEE IN THE DARK. AND THE MECHS HAVE LIGHTS, ANYWAY.
BEN'S RIGHT. THESE CREATURES ARE SMART. THEY'LL BE GUARDING ALL THE GROCERY STORES.
BAGS OF RICE. DO WE TAKE THEM?
JUST A FEW. WE HAVE TO STAY ON THE MOVE, AND THEY'RE TOO HEAVY TO CARRY MORE THAN...
DAD. HOLD ON.
HAL?
I HEARD SOMETHING.
GET DOWN!
THUNK

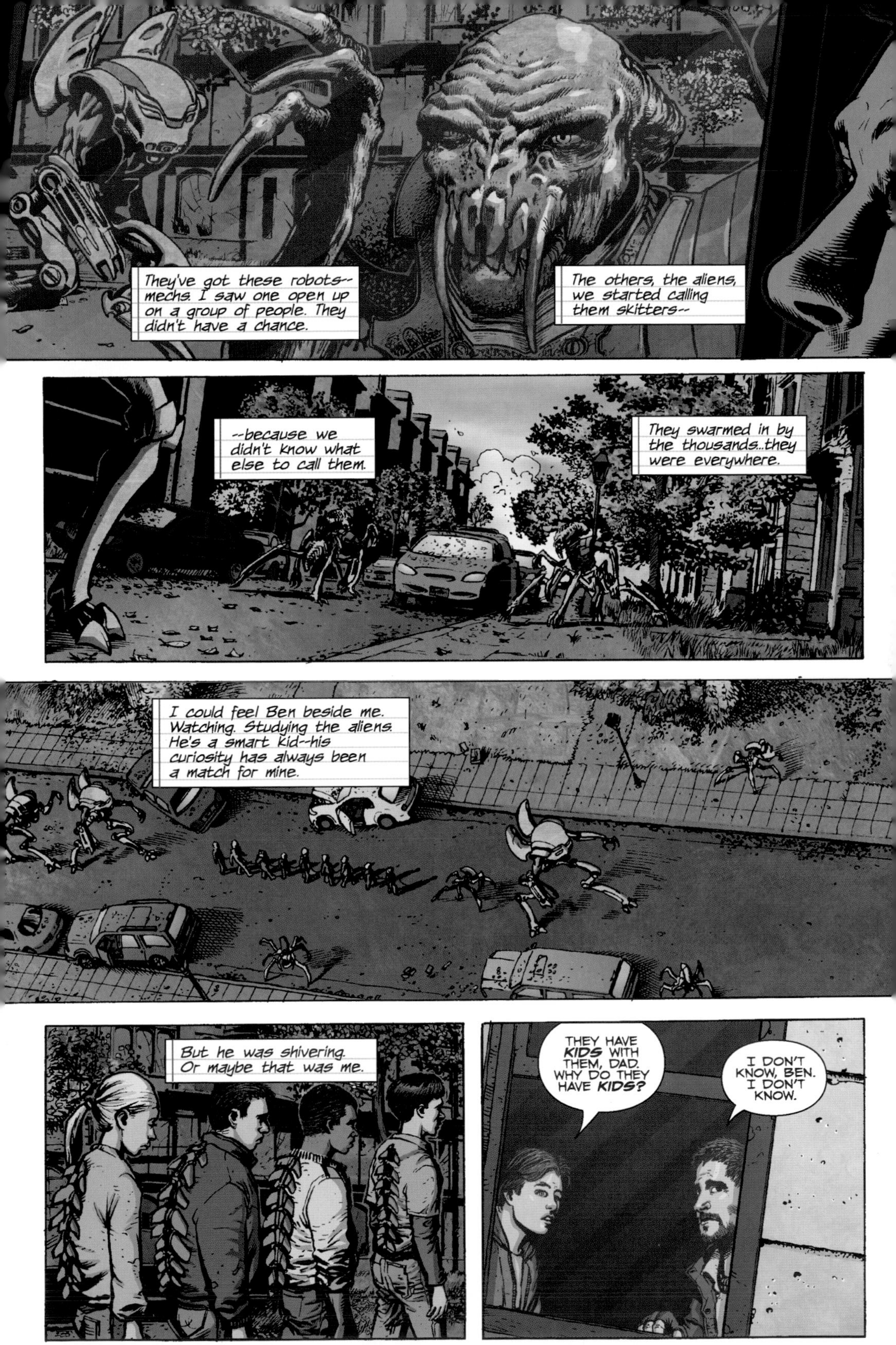

They've got these robots--mechs. I saw one open up on a group of people. They didn't have a chance.
The others, the aliens, we started calling them skitters--
--because we didn't know what else to call them.
They swarmed in by the thousands..they were everywhere.
I could feel Ben beside me. Watching. Studying the aliens. He's a smart kid--his curiosity has always been a match for mine.
But he was shivering. Or maybe that was me.
THEY HAVE KIDS WITH THEM, DAD. WHY DO THEY HAVE KIDS?
I DON'T KNOW, BEN. I DON'T KNOW.

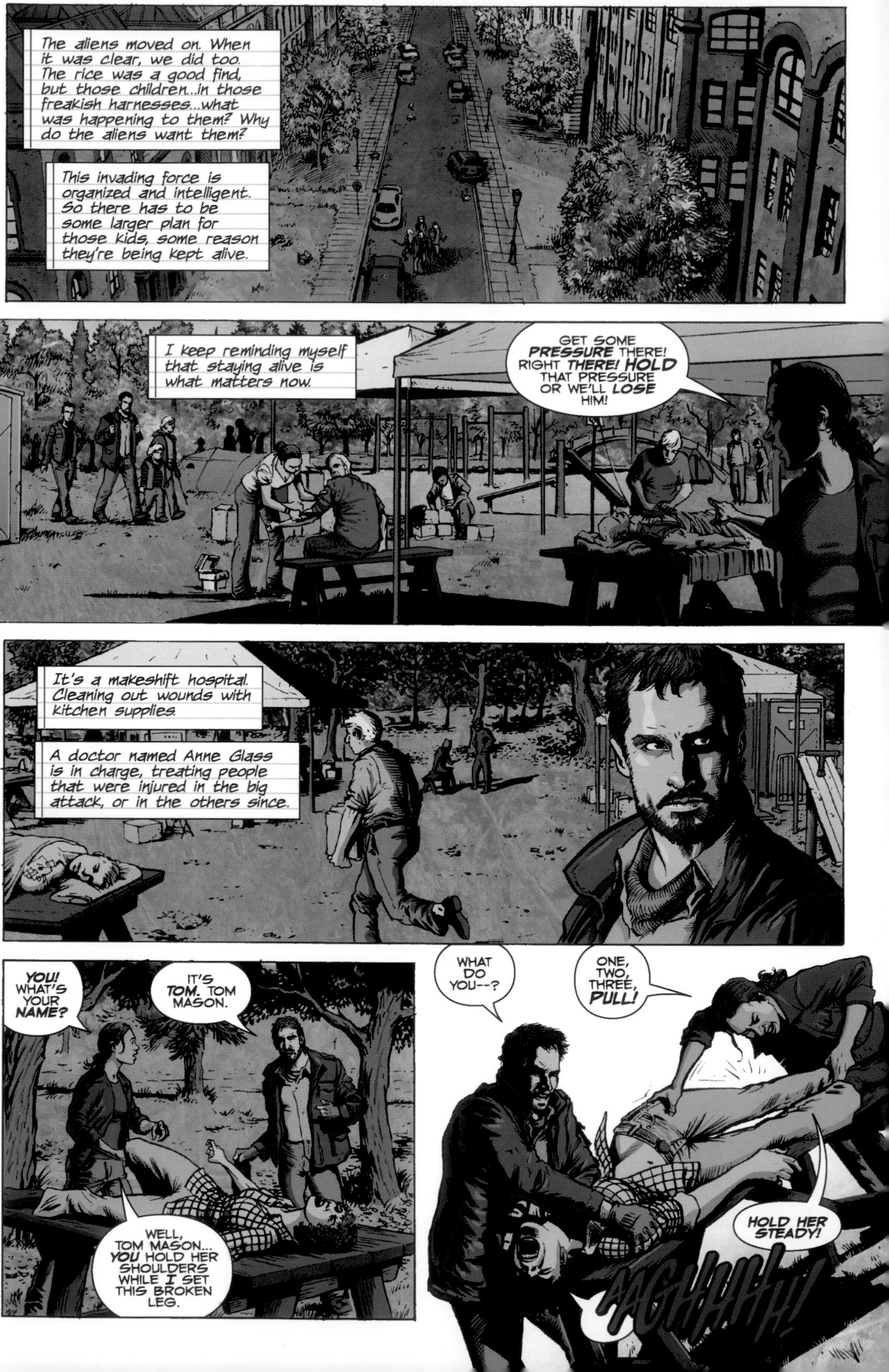
The aliens moved on. When it was clear, we did too. The rice was a good find, but those children...in those freakish harnesses...what was happening to them? Why do the aliens want them?
This invading force is organized and intelligent. So there has to be some larger plan for those kids, some reason they're being kept alive.
I keep reminding myself that staying alive is what matters now.
GET SOME PRESSURE THERE! RIGHT THERE! HOLD THAT PRESSURE OR WE'LL LOSE HIM!
It's a makeshift hospital. Cleaning out wounds with kitchen supplies.
A doctor named Anne Glass is in charge, treating people that were injured in the big attack, or in the others since.
YOU! WHAT'S YOUR NAME?
IT'S TOM. TOM MASON.
WELL, TOM MASON... YOU HOLD HER SHOULDERS WHILE I SET THIS BROKEN LEG.
WHAT DO YOU--?
ONE, TWO, THREE, PULL!
HOLD HER STEADY!
AAGHHHH!

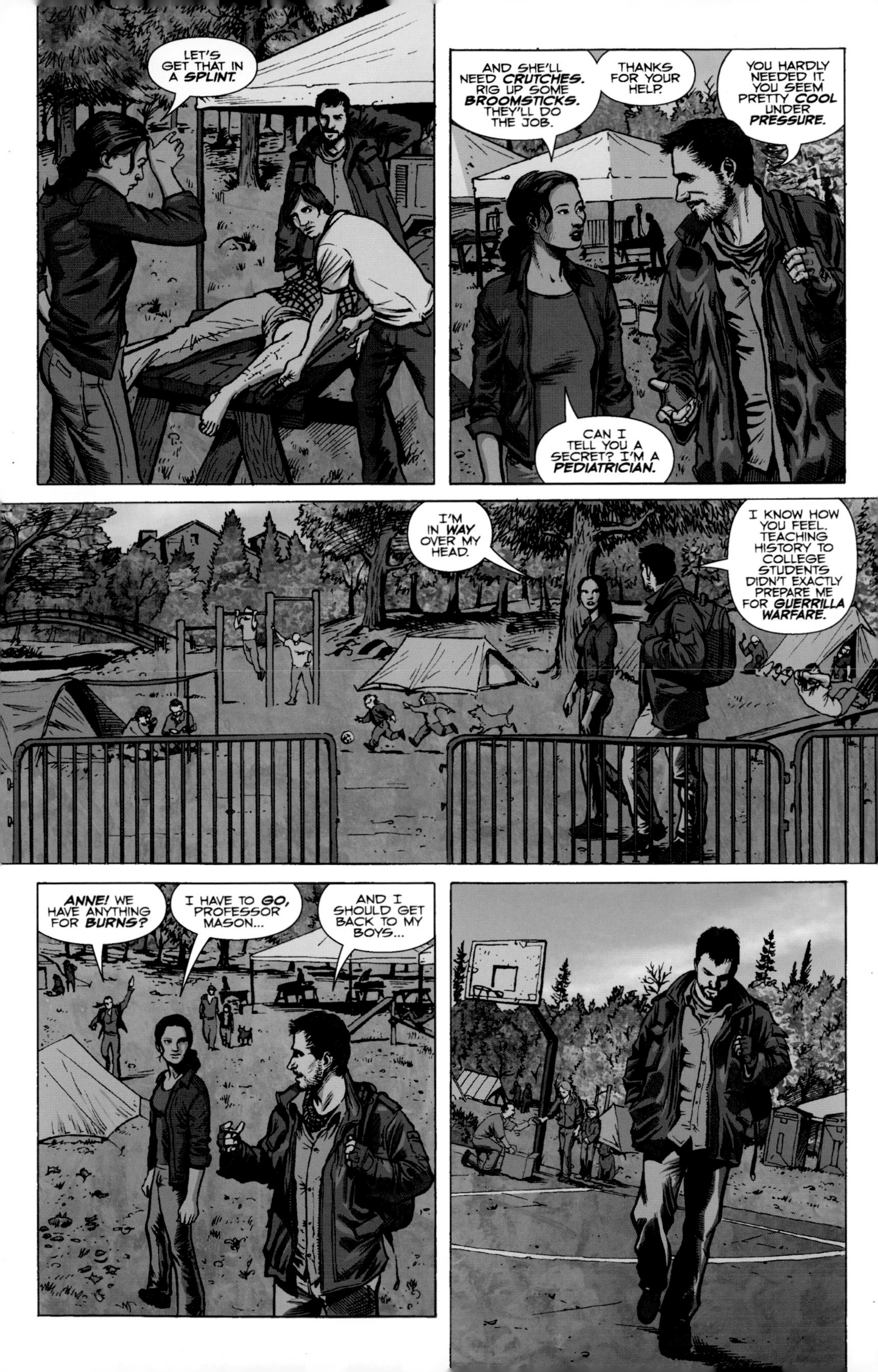
LET'S GET THAT IN A SPLINT.
AND SHE'LL NEED CRUTCHES. RIG UP SOME BROOMSTICKS. THEY'LL DO THE JOB.
THANKS FOR YOUR HELP.
YOU HARDLY NEEDED IT. YOU SEEM PRETTY COOL UNDER PRESSURE.
CAN I TELL YOU A SECRET? I'M A PEDIATRICIAN.
I'M IN WAY OVER MY HEAD.
I KNOW HOW YOU FEEL. TEACHING HISTORY TO COLLEGE STUDENTS DIDN'T EXACTLY PREPARE ME FOR GUERRILLA WARFARE.
ANNE! WE HAVE ANYTHING FOR BURNS?
I HAVE TO GO, PROFESSOR MASON...
AND I SHOULD GET BACK TO MY BOYS...

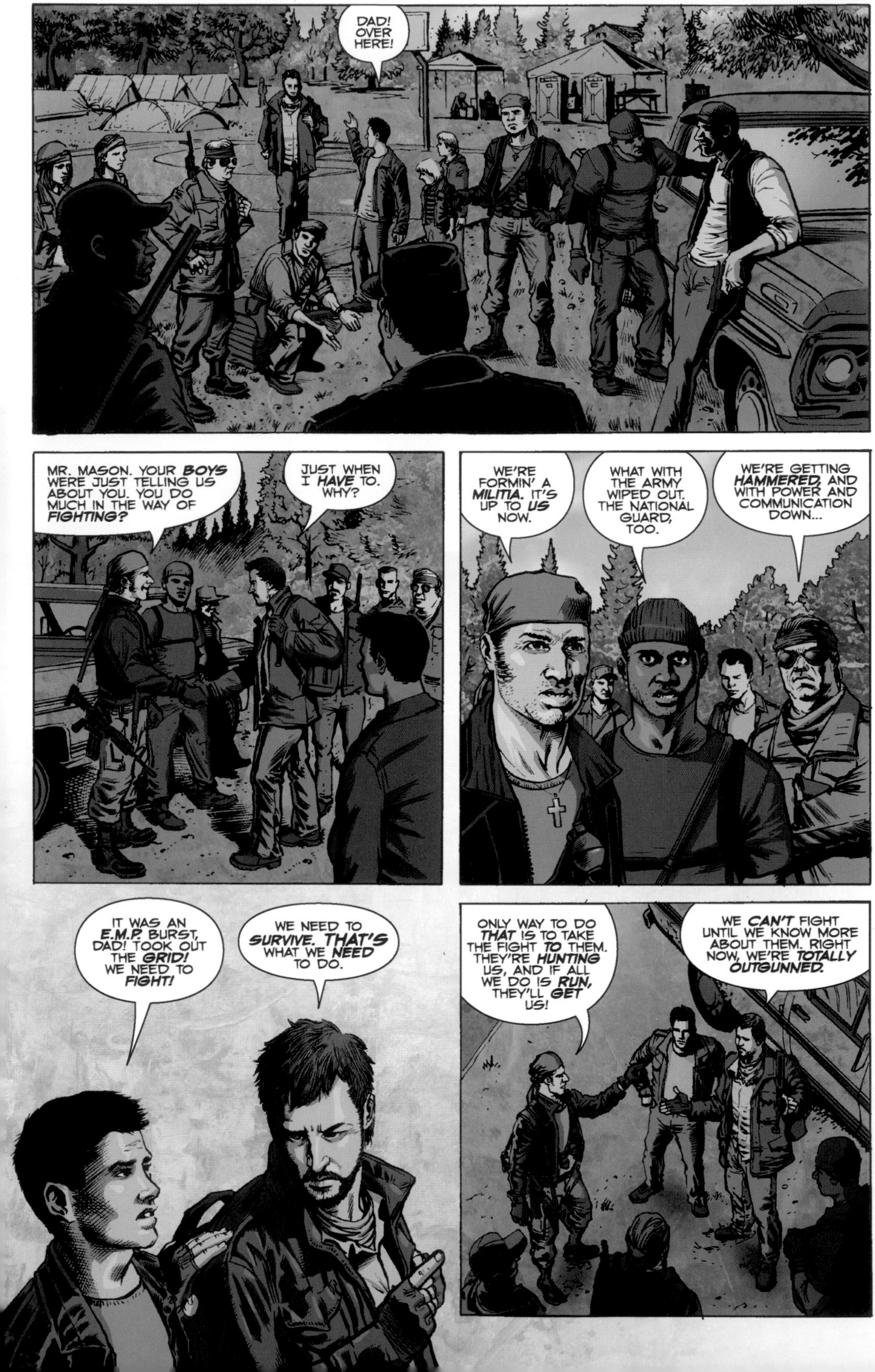
DAD! OVER HERE!
MR. MASON. YOUR BOYS WERE JUST TELLING US ABOUT YOU. YOU DO MUCH IN THE WAY OF FIGHTING?
JUST WHEN I HAVE TO. WHY?
WE'RE FORMIN' A MILITIA. IT'S UP TO US NOW.
WHAT WITH THE ARMY WIPED OUT. THE NATIONAL GUARD, TOO.
WE'RE GETTING HAMMERED, AND WITH POWER AND COMMUNICATION DOWN...
IT WAS AN E.M.P. BURST, DAD! TOOK OUT THE GRID! WE NEED TO FIGHT!
WE NEED TO SURVIVE. THAT'S WHAT WE NEED TO DO.
ONLY WAY TO DO THAT IS TO TAKE THE FIGHT TO THEM. THEY'RE HUNTING US, AND IF ALL WE DO IS RUN, THEY'LL GET US!
WE CAN'T FIGHT UNTIL WE KNOW MORE ABOUT THEM. RIGHT NOW, WE'RE TOTALLY OUTGUNNED.

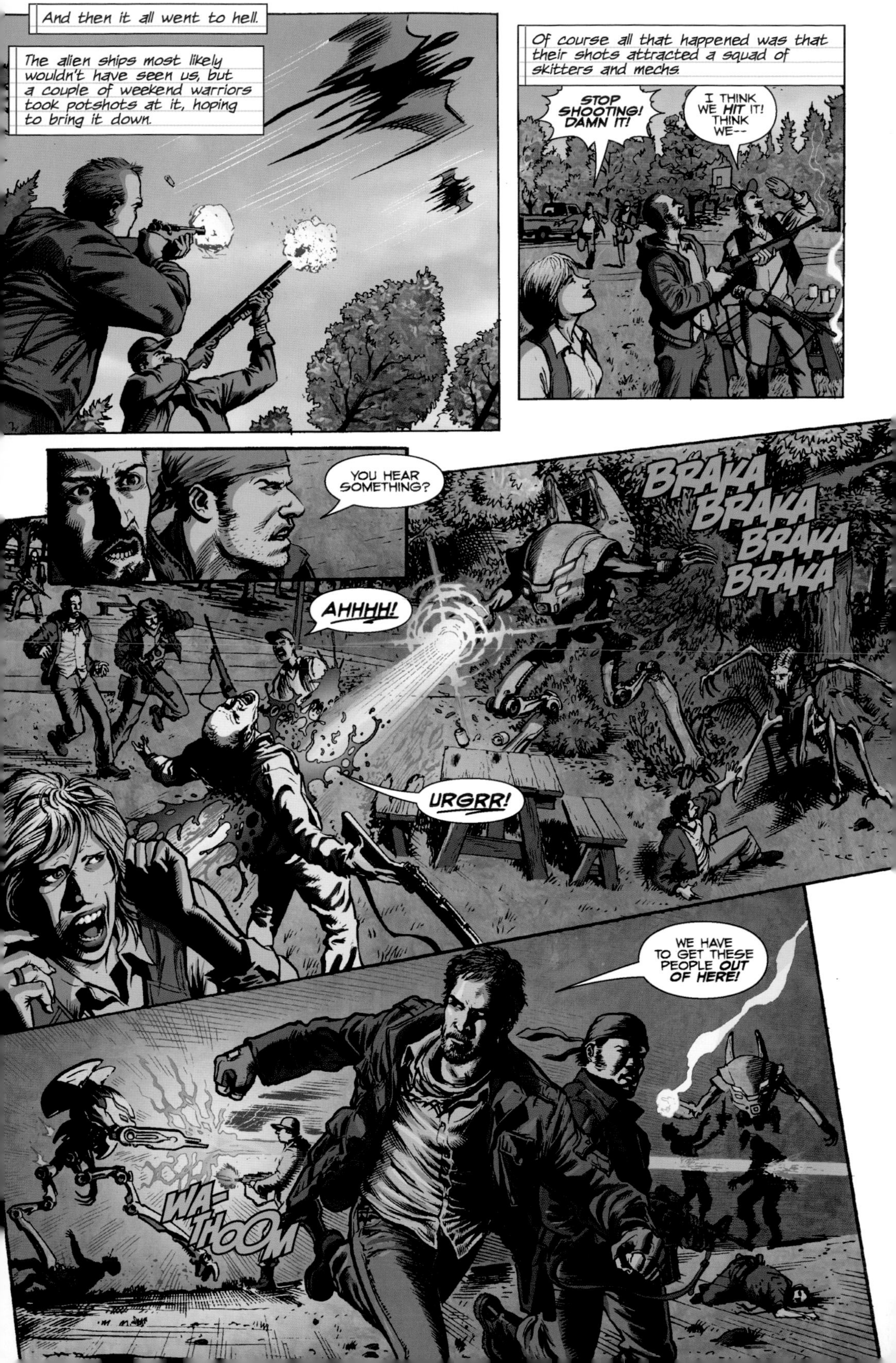

And then it all went to hell.
The alien ships most likely wouldn't have seen us, but a couple of weekend warriors took potshots at it, hoping to bring it down.
Of course all that happened was that their shots attracted a squad of skitters and mechs.
STOP SHOOTING! DAMN IT!
I THINK WE HIT IT! THINK WE--
YOU HEAR SOMETHING?
BRAKA BRAKA BRAKA BRAKA
AHHHH!
URGRR!
WE HAVE TO GET THESE PEOPLE OUT OF HERE!
WA-THOOM

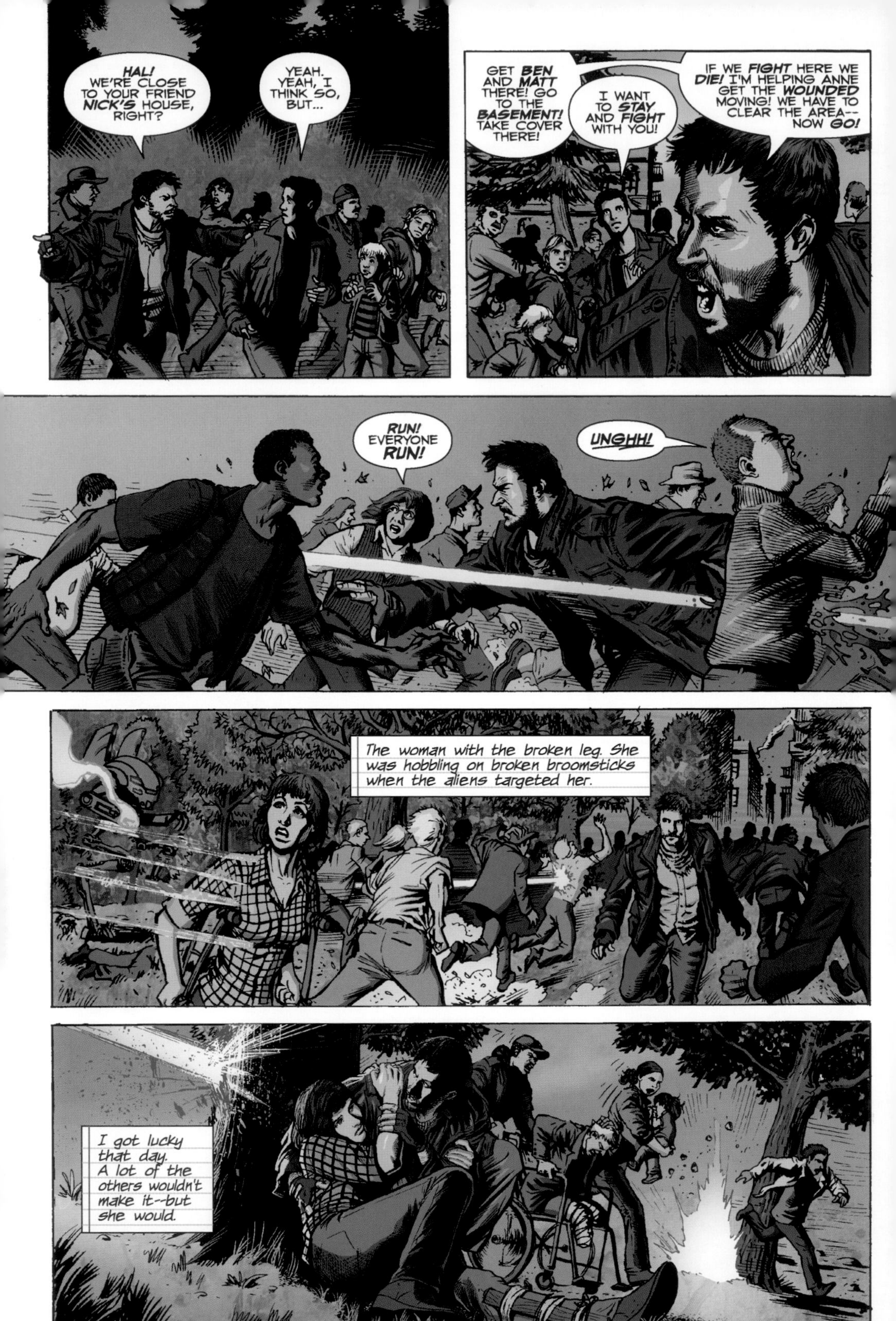
HAL! WE'RE CLOSE TO YOUR FRIEND NICK'S HOUSE, RIGHT?
YEAH. YEAH, I THINK SO, BUT...
GET BEN AND MATT THERE! GO TO THE BASEMENT! TAKE COVER THERE!
I WANT TO STAY AND FIGHT WITH YOU!
IF WE FIGHT HERE WE DIE! I'M HELPING ANNE GET THE WOUNDED MOVING! WE HAVE TO CLEAR THE AREA-- NOW GO!
RUN! EVERYONE RUN!
UNGHH!
The woman with the broken leg. She was hobbling on broken broomsticks when the aliens targeted her.
I got lucky that day. A lot of the others wouldn't make it--but she would.

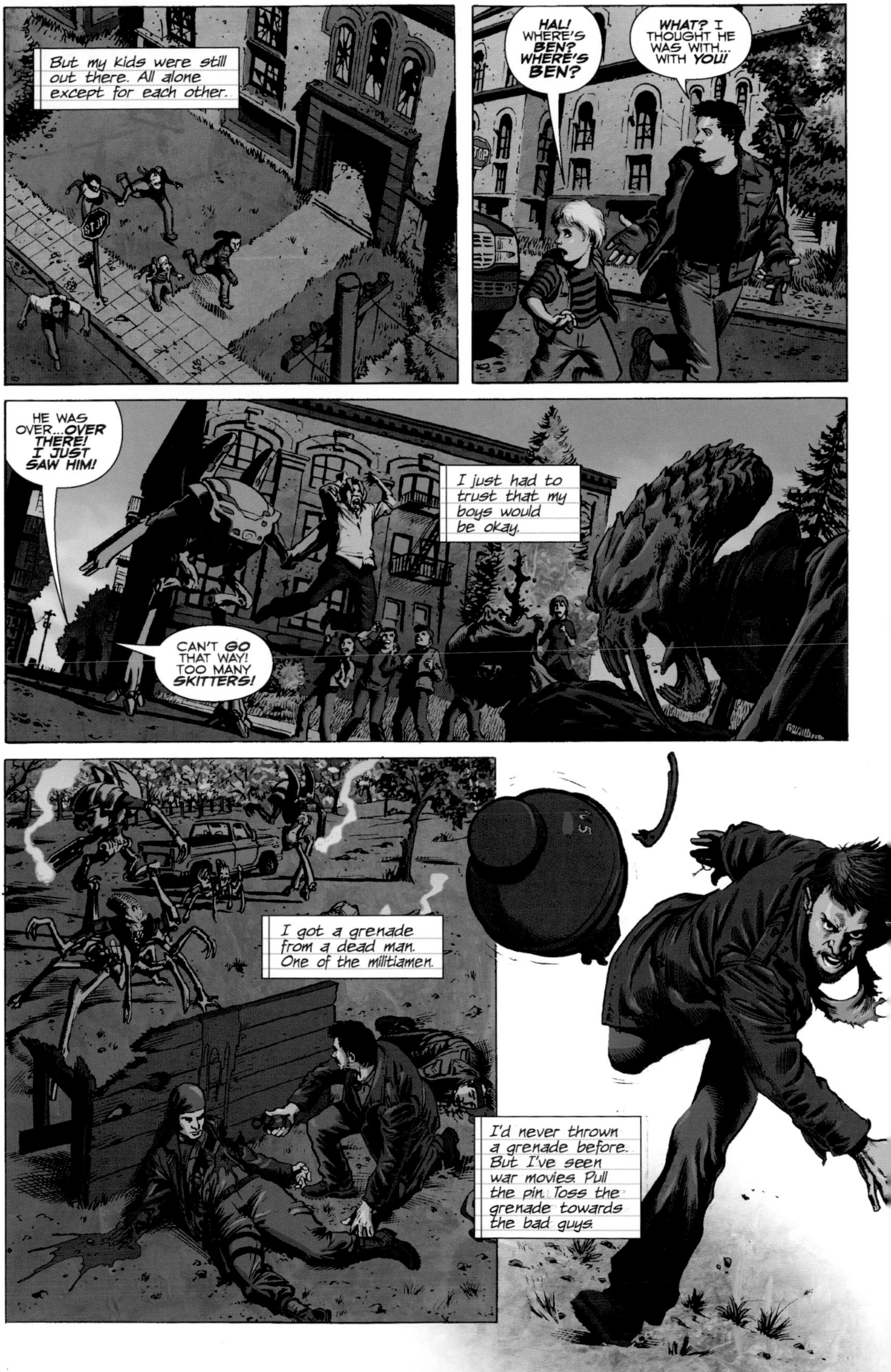
But my kids were still out there. All alone except for each other.
STOP
HAL! WHERE'S BEN? WHERE'S BEN?
WHAT? I THOUGHT HE WAS WITH... WITH YOU!
STOP
HE WAS OVER...OVER THERE! I JUST SAW HIM!
I just had to trust that my boys would be okay.
CAN'T GO THAT WAY! TOO MANY SKITTERS!
I got a grenade from a dead man. One of the militiamen.
I'd never thrown a grenade before. But I've seen war movies. Pull the pin. Toss the grenade towards the bad guys.

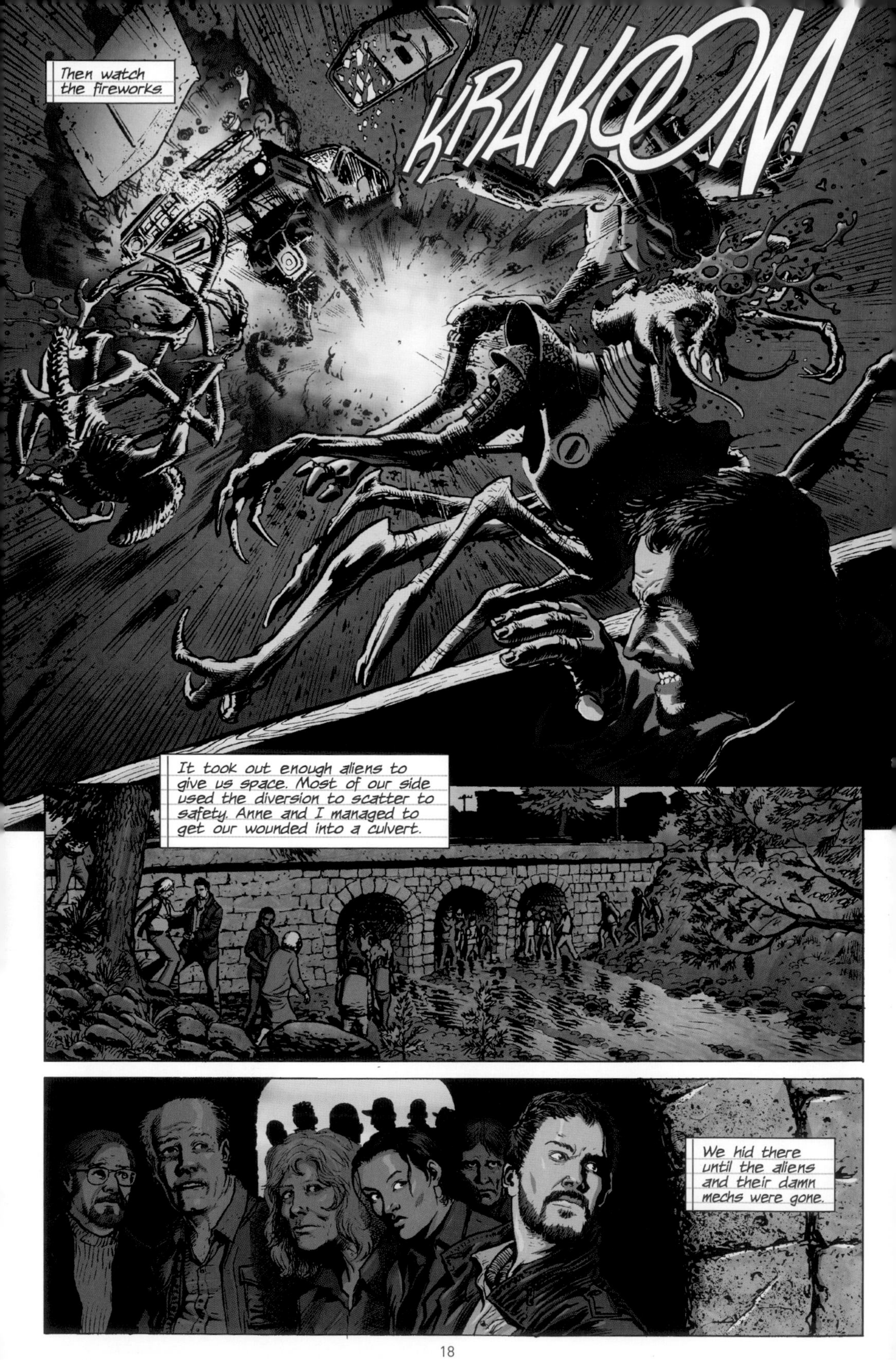
Then watch the fireworks.
KRAKOOM
It took out enough aliens to give us space. Most of our side used the diversion to scatter to safety. Anne and I managed to get our wounded into a culvert.
We hid there until the aliens and their damn mechs were gone.

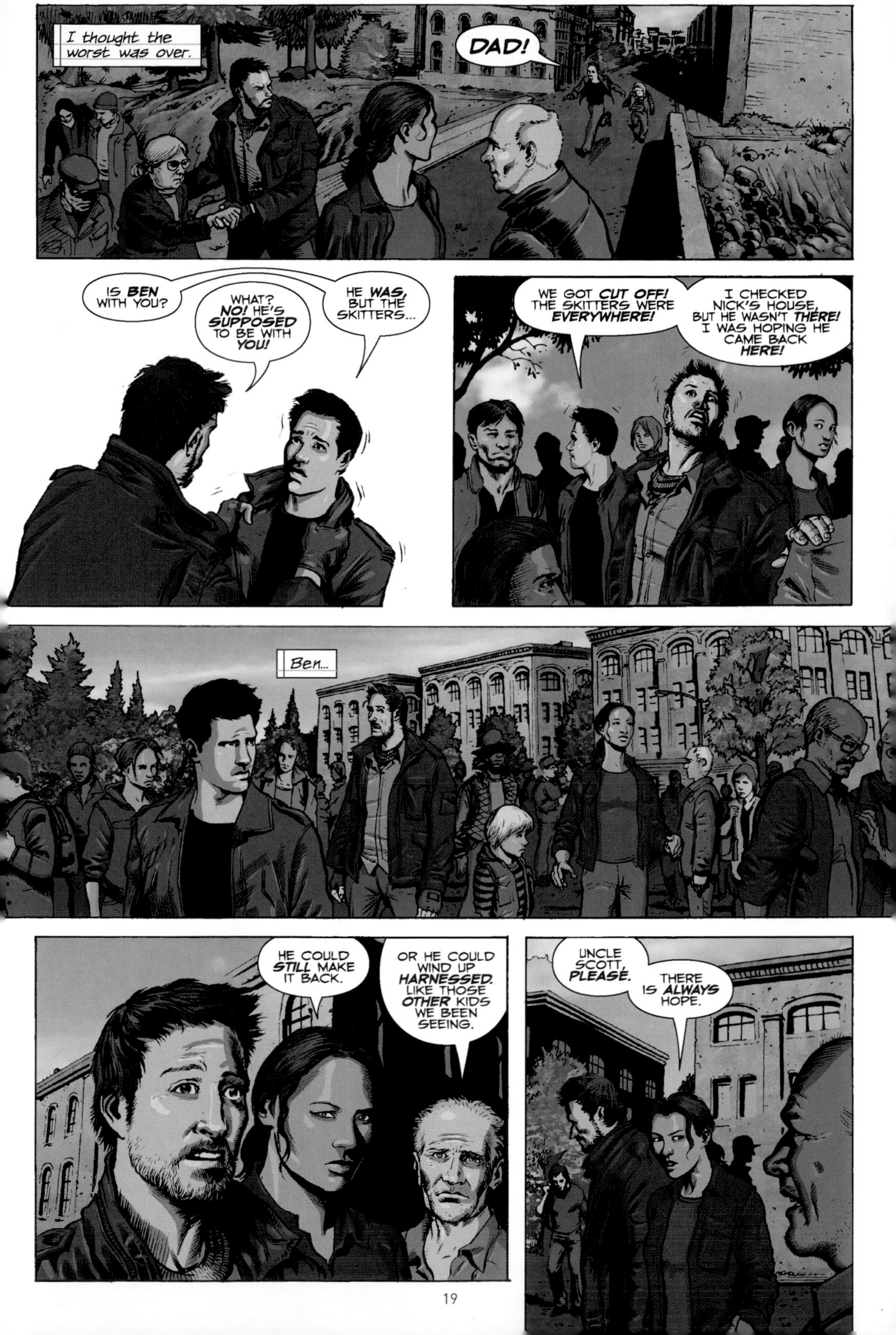
I thought the worst was over.
DAD!
IS BEN WITH YOU?
WHAT? NO! HE'S SUPPOSED TO BE WITH YOU!
HE WAS, BUT THE SKITTERS...
WE GOT CUT OFF! THE SKITTERS WERE EVERYWHERE!
I CHECKED NICK'S HOUSE, BUT HE WASN'T THERE! I WAS HOPING HE CAME BACK HERE!
Ben...
HE COULD STILL MAKE IT BACK.
OR HE COULD WIND UP HARNESSED. LIKE THOSE OTHER KIDS WE BEEN SEEING.
UNCLE SCOTT, PLEASE.
THERE IS ALWAYS HOPE.

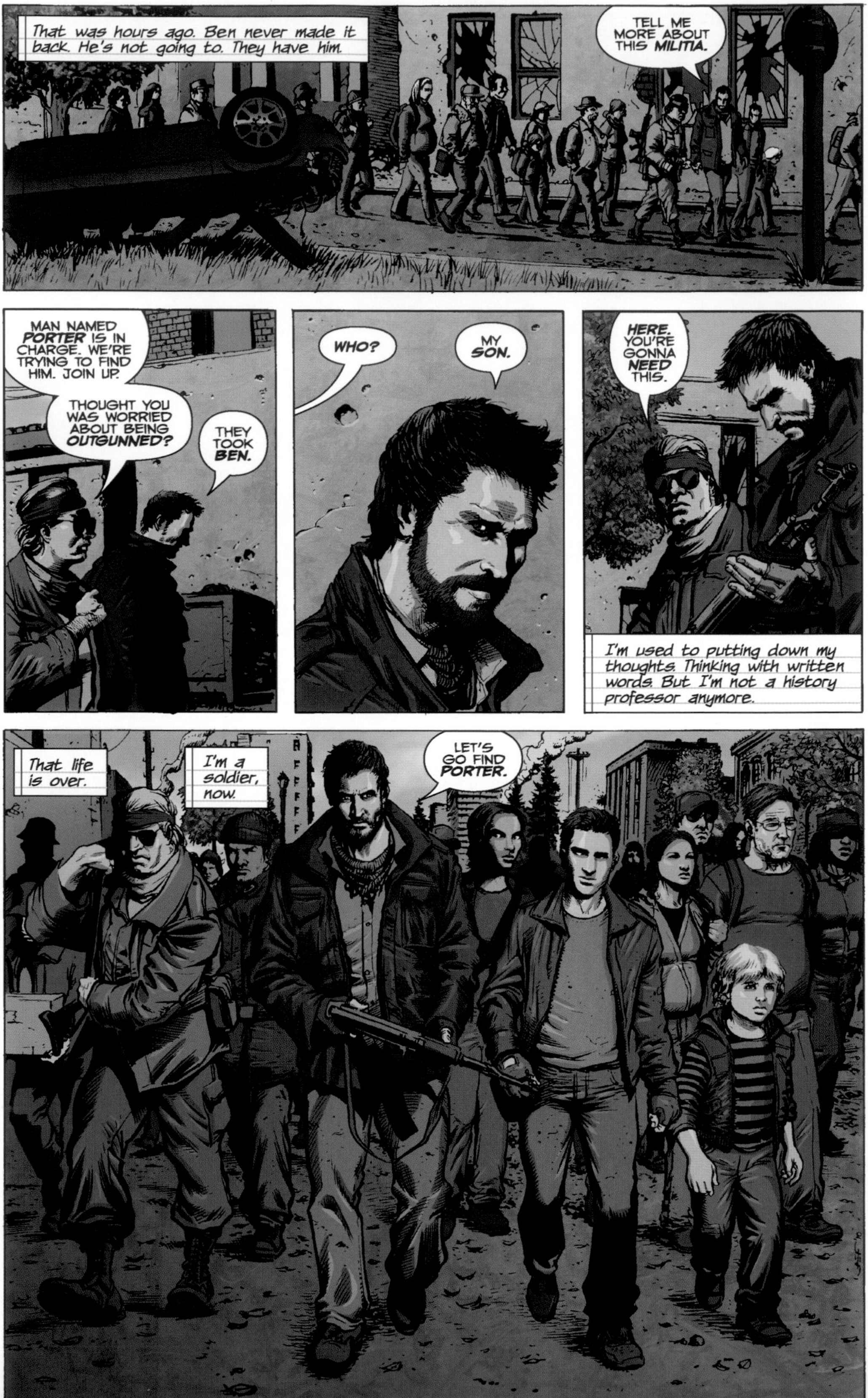

That was hours ago. Ben never made it back. He's not going to. They have him.
TELL ME MORE ABOUT THIS MILITIA.
MAN NAMED PORTER IS IN CHARGE. WE'RE TRYING TO FIND HIM. JOIN UP.
THOUGHT YOU WAS WORRIED ABOUT BEING OUTGUNNED?
THEY TOOK BEN.
WHO?
MY SON.
HERE. YOU'RE GONNA NEED THIS.
I'm used to putting down my thoughts. Thinking with written words. But I'm not a history professor anymore.
That life is over.
I'm a soldier, now.
LET'S GO FIND PORTER.

CHAPTER TWO

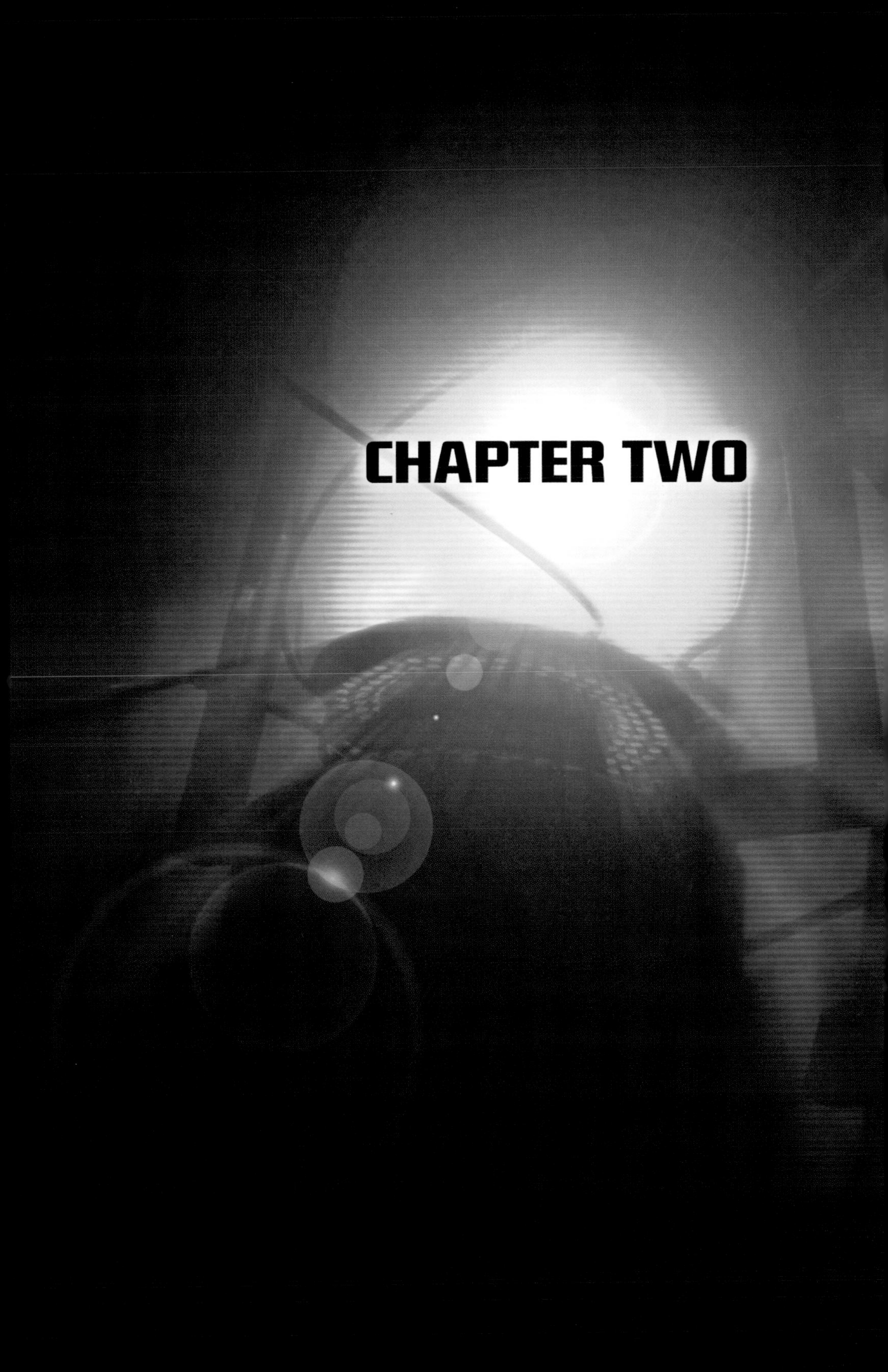

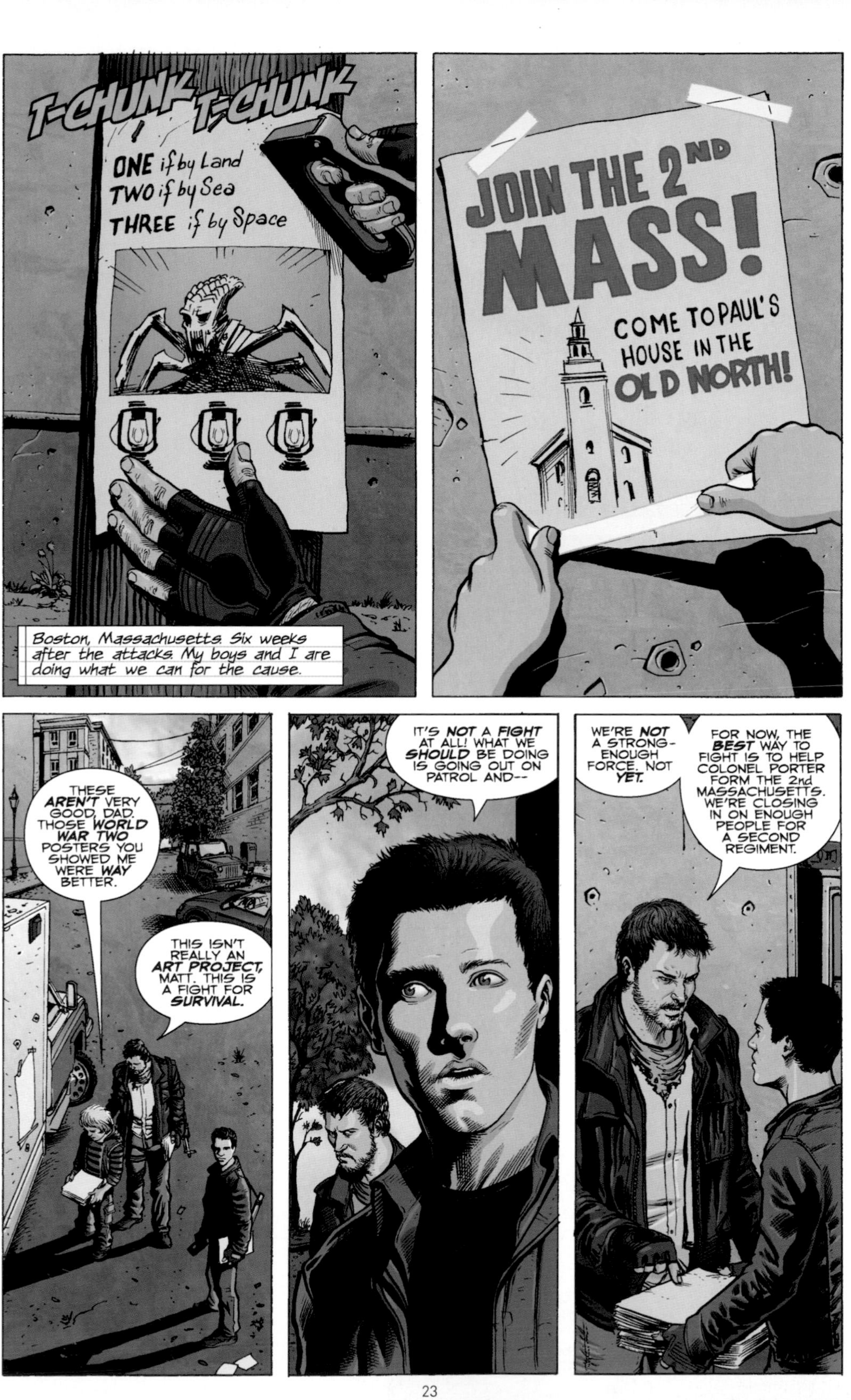
T-CHUNK T-CHUNK
ONE if by Land
TWO if by Sea
THREE if by Space
Boston, Massachusetts. Six weeks after the attacks. My boys and I are doing what we can for the cause.
JOIN THE 2ND MASS!
COME TO PAUL'S HOUSE IN THE OLD NORTH!
THESE AREN'T VERY GOOD, DAD. THOSE WORLD WAR TWO POSTERS YOU SHOWED ME WERE WAY BETTER.
THIS ISN'T REALLY AN ART PROJECT, MATT. THIS IS A FIGHT FOR SURVIVAL.
IT'S NOT A FIGHT AT ALL! WHAT WE SHOULD BE DOING IS GOING OUT ON PATROL AND--
WE'RE NOT A STRONG-ENOUGH FORCE. NOT YET.
FOR NOW, THE BEST WAY TO FIGHT IS TO HELP COLONEL PORTER FORM THE 2nd MASSACHUSETTS. WE'RE CLOSING IN ON ENOUGH PEOPLE FOR A SECOND REGIMENT.

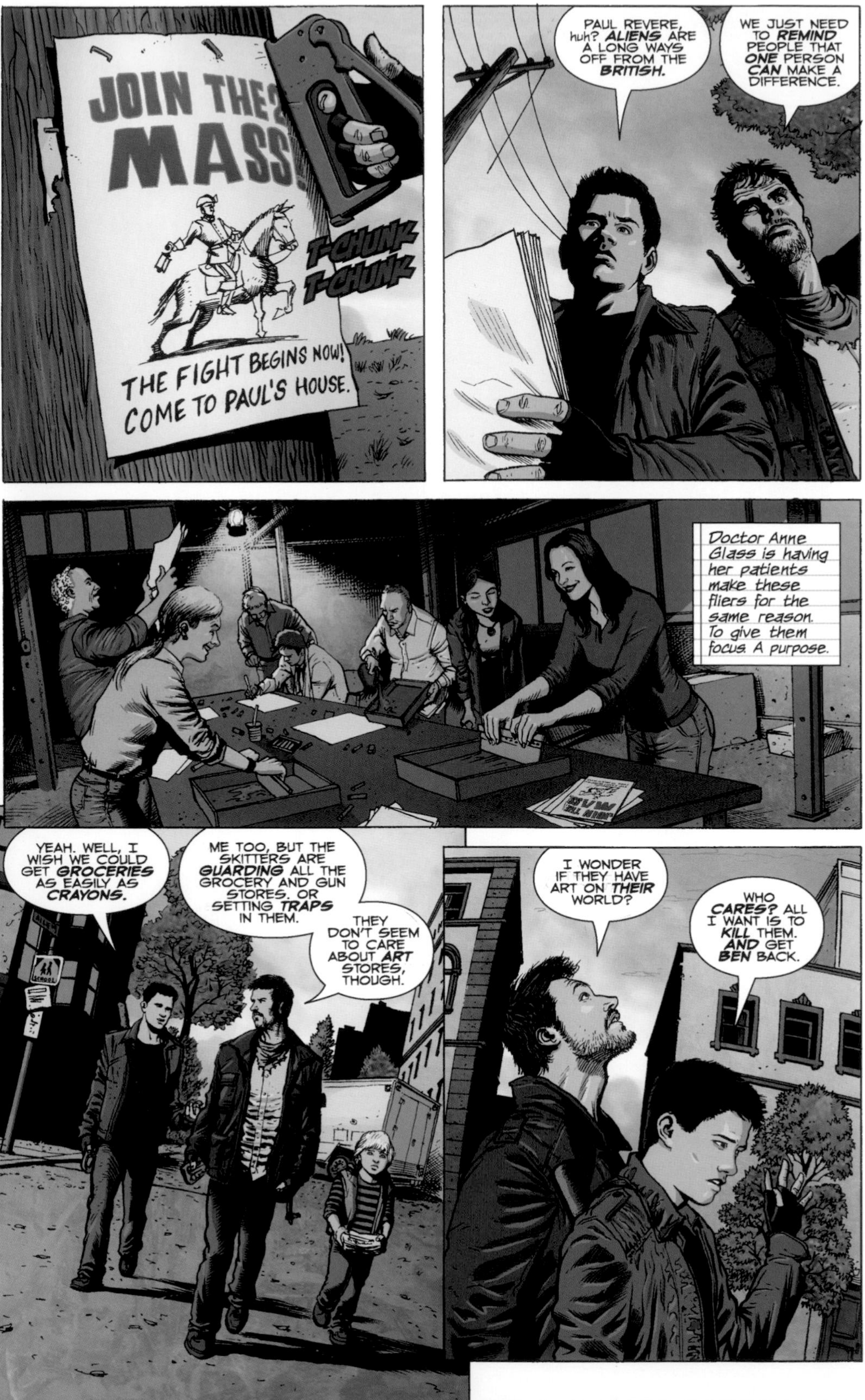
JOIN THE 2nd MASS!
T-CHUNK
T-CHUNK
THE FIGHT BEGINS NOW!
COME TO PAUL'S HOUSE.
PAUL REVERE, huh? ALIENS ARE A LONG WAYS OFF FROM THE BRITISH.
WE JUST NEED TO REMIND PEOPLE THAT ONE PERSON CAN MAKE A DIFFERENCE.
Doctor Anne Glass is having her patients make these fliers for the same reason. To give them focus. A purpose.
YEAH. WELL, I WISH WE COULD GET GROCERIES AS EASILY AS CRAYONS.
ME TOO, BUT THE SKITTERS ARE GUARDING ALL THE GROCERY AND GUN STORES. OR SETTING TRAPS IN THEM.
THEY DON'T SEEM TO CARE ABOUT ART STORES, THOUGH.
I WONDER IF THEY HAVE ART ON THEIR WORLD?
WHO CARES? ALL I WANT IS TO KILL THEM. AND GET BEN BACK.

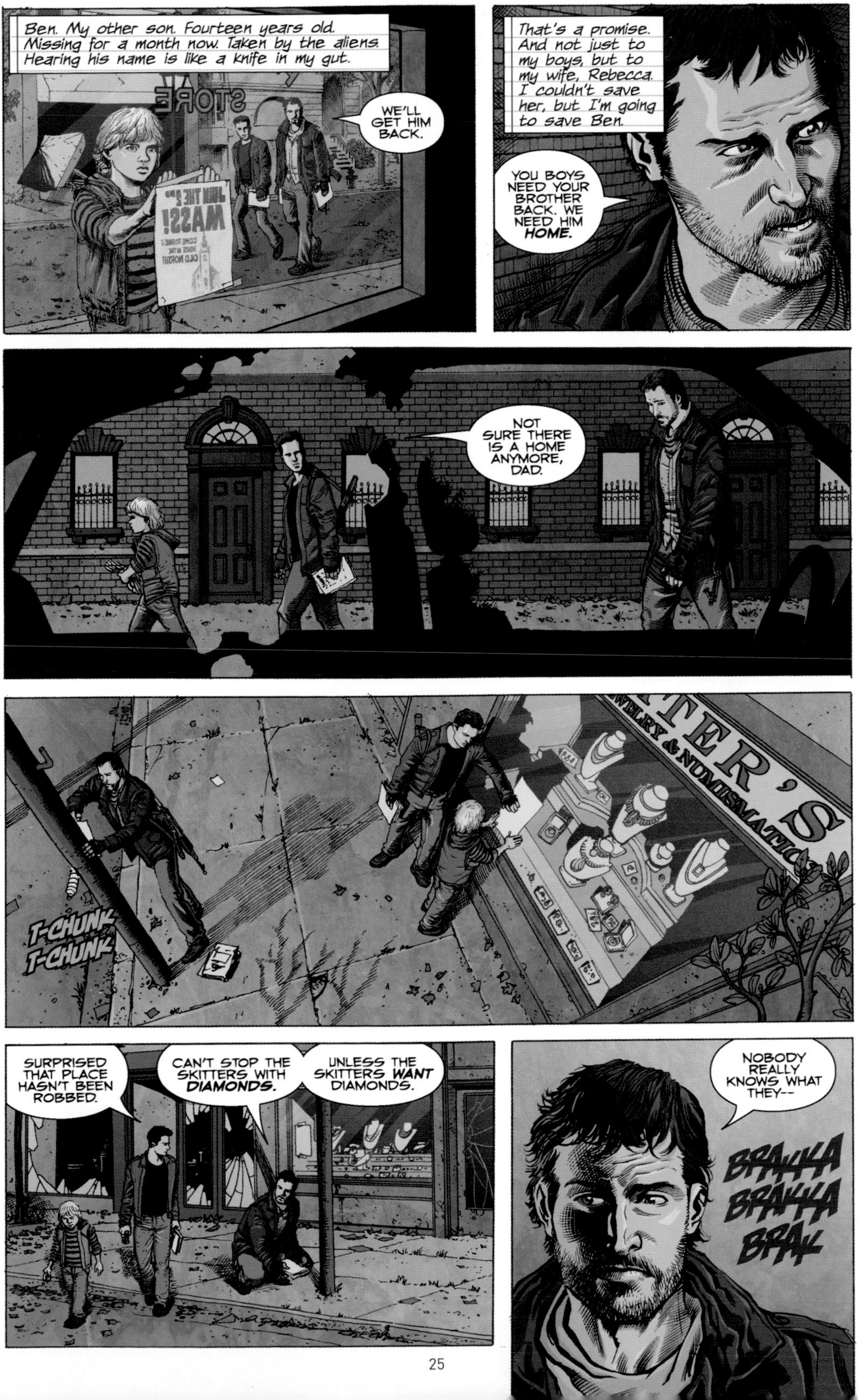

Ben. My other son. Fourteen years old. Missing for a month now. Taken by the aliens. Hearing his name is like a knife in my gut.
STORE
WE'LL GET HIM BACK.
JOIN THE 2ND MASS!
That's a promise. And not just to my boys, but to my wife, Rebecca. I couldn't save her, but I'm going to save Ben.
YOU BOYS NEED YOUR BROTHER BACK. WE NEED HIM HOME.
NOT SURE THERE IS A HOME ANYMORE, DAD.
JEWELRY & NUMISMATICS
T-CHUNK T-CHUNK
SURPRISED THAT PLACE HASN'T BEEN ROBBED.
CAN'T STOP THE SKITTERS WITH DIAMONDS.
UNLESS THE SKITTERS WANT DIAMONDS.
NOBODY REALLY KNOWS WHAT THEY--
BRAKKA BRAKKA BRAK

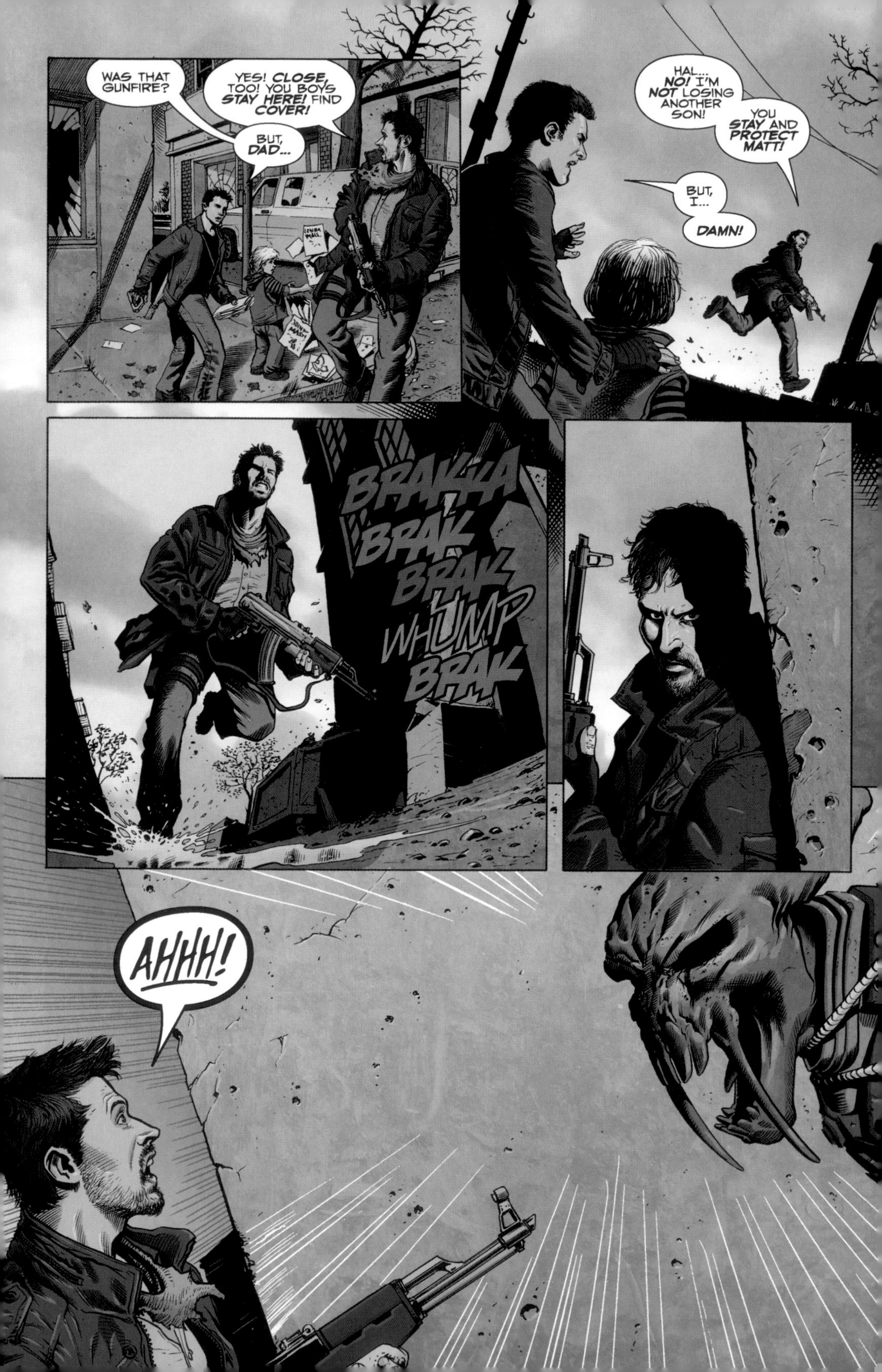
WAS THAT GUNFIRE?
YES! CLOSE, TOO! YOU BOYS STAY HERE! FIND COVER!
BUT, DAD...
HAL... NO! I'M NOT LOSING ANOTHER SON!
YOU STAY AND PROTECT MATT!
BUT, I...
DAMN!
BRAKKA
BRAK
BRAK
WHUMP
BRAK
AHHH!

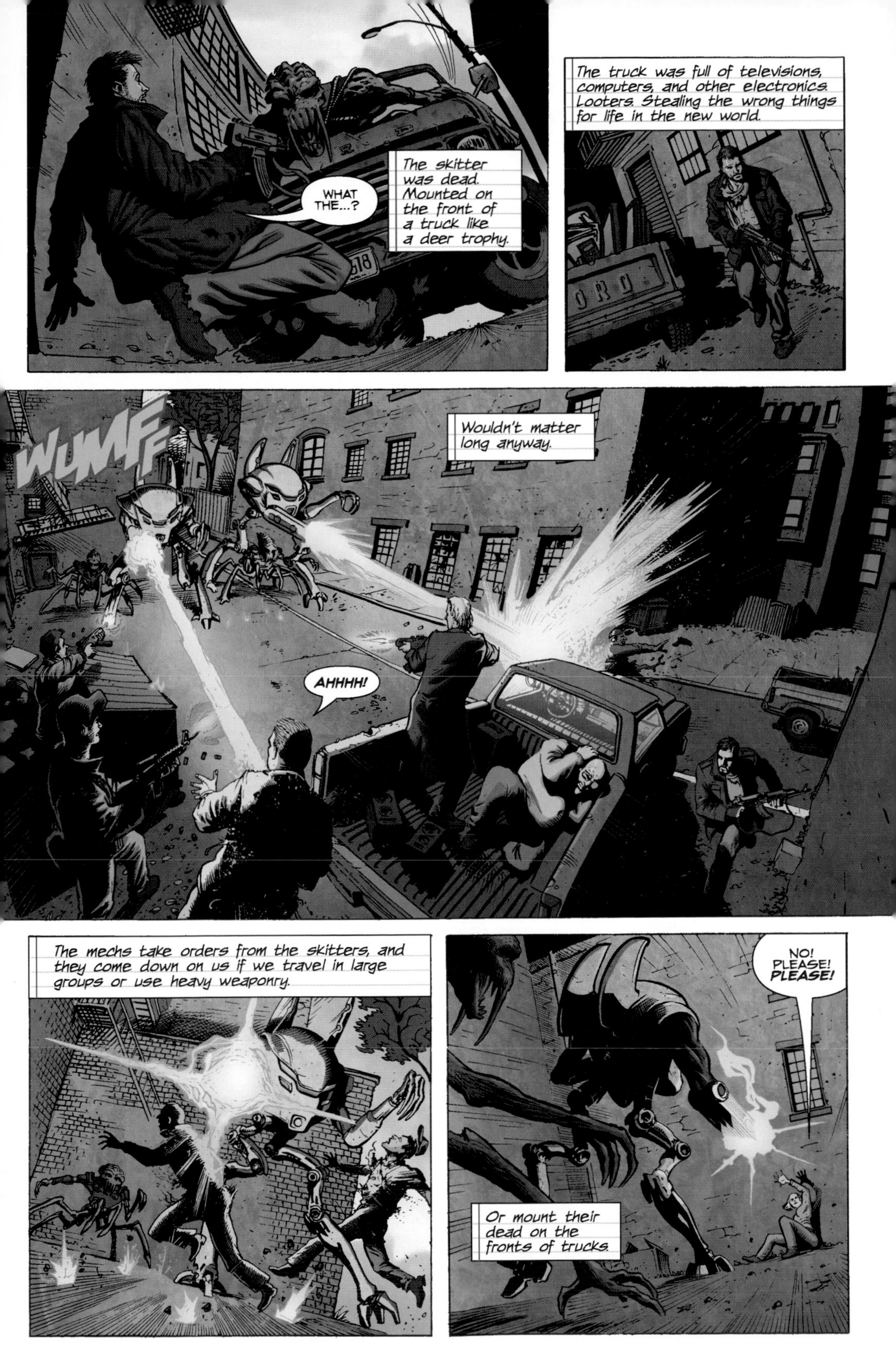
WHAT THE...?
The skitter was dead. Mounted on the front of a truck like a deer trophy.
The truck was full of televisions, computers, and other electronics. Looters. Stealing the wrong things for life in the new world.
WUMFF
Wouldn't matter long anyway.
AHHHH!
The mechs take orders from the skitters, and they come down on us if we travel in large groups or use heavy weaponry.
NO! PLEASE! PLEASE!
Or mount their dead on the fronts of trucks.

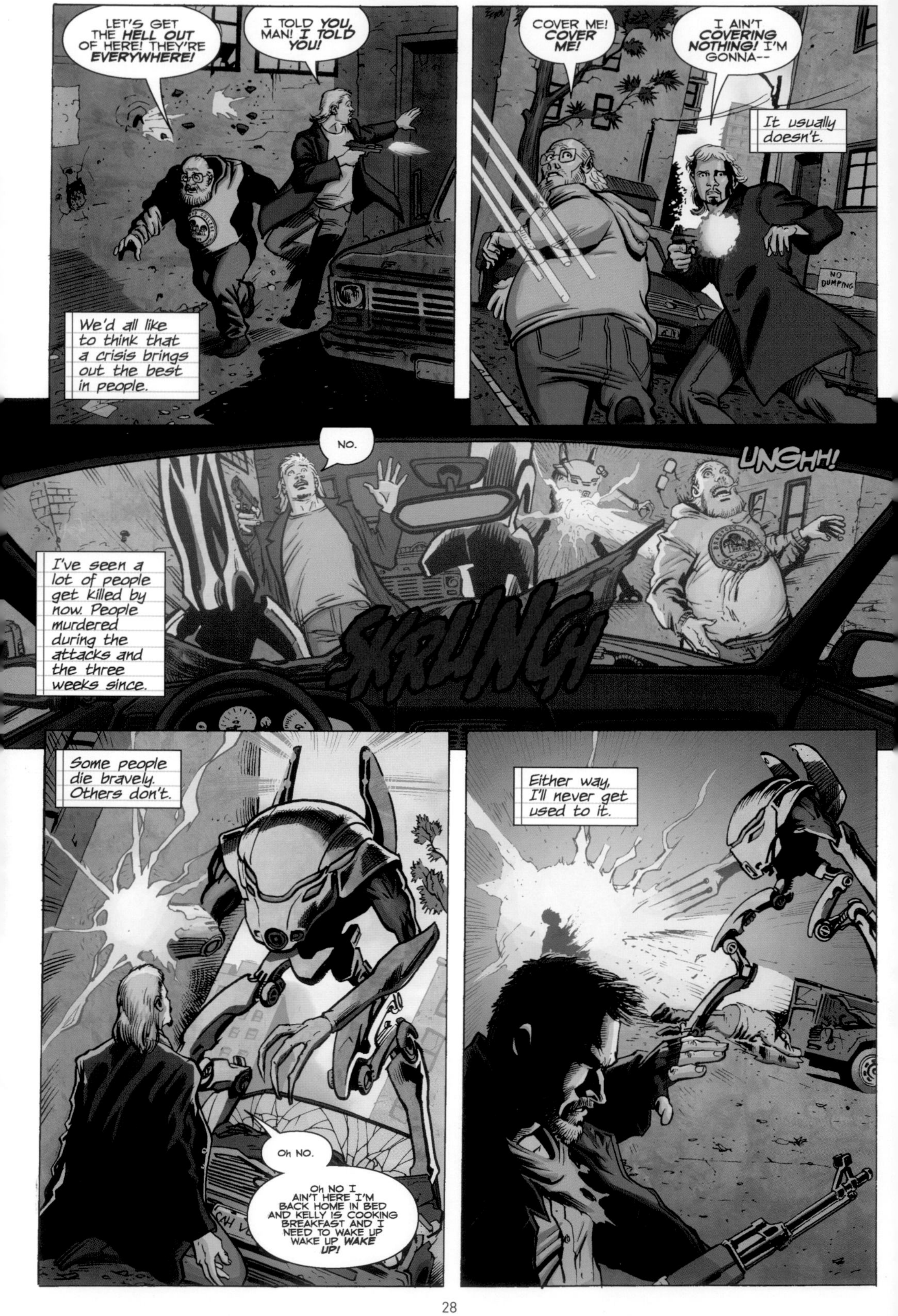
LET'S GET THE **HELL OUT** OF HERE! THEY'RE **EVERYWHERE!**
I TOLD **YOU,** MAN! **I TOLD YOU!**
We'd all like to think that a crisis brings out the best in people.
COVER ME! **COVER ME!**
I AIN'T **COVERING NOTHING!** I'M GONNA--
It usually doesn't.
NO DUMPING
NO.
UNGHH!
I've seen a lot of people get killed by now. People murdered during the attacks and the three weeks since.
SKRUNCH
Some people die bravely. Others don't.
Oh NO.
Oh NO I AIN'T HERE I'M BACK HOME IN BED AND KELLY IS COOKING BREAKFAST AND I NEED TO WAKE UP WAKE UP **WAKE UP!**
Either way, I'll never get used to it.

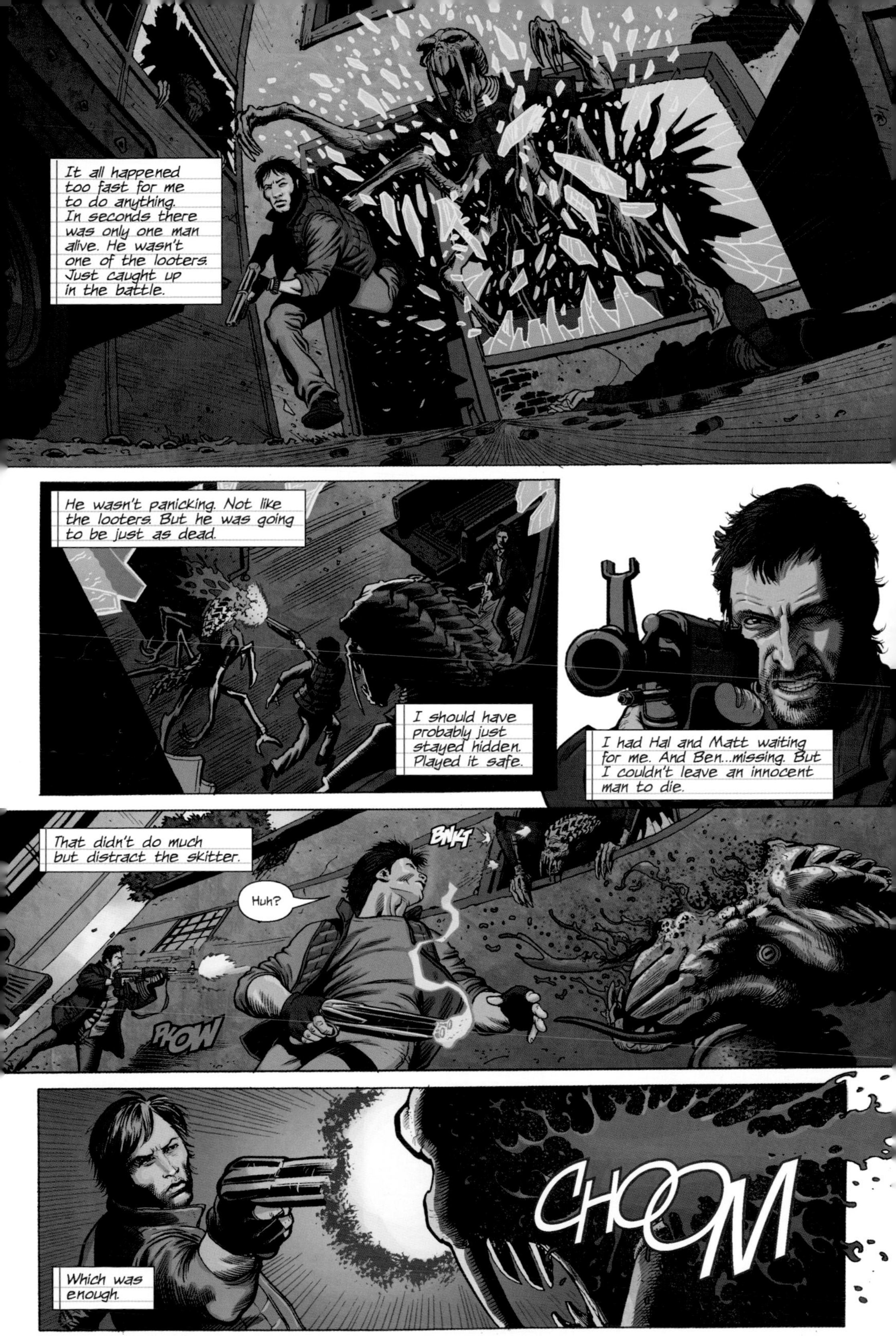
It all happened too fast for me to do anything. In seconds there was only one man alive. He wasn't one of the looters. Just caught up in the battle.
He wasn't panicking. Not like the looters. But he was going to be just as dead.
I should have probably just stayed hidden. Played it safe.
I had Hal and Matt waiting for me. And Ben...missing. But I couldn't leave an innocent man to die.
That didn't do much but distract the skitter.
BNKT
Huh?
PKOW
Which was enough.
CHOOM

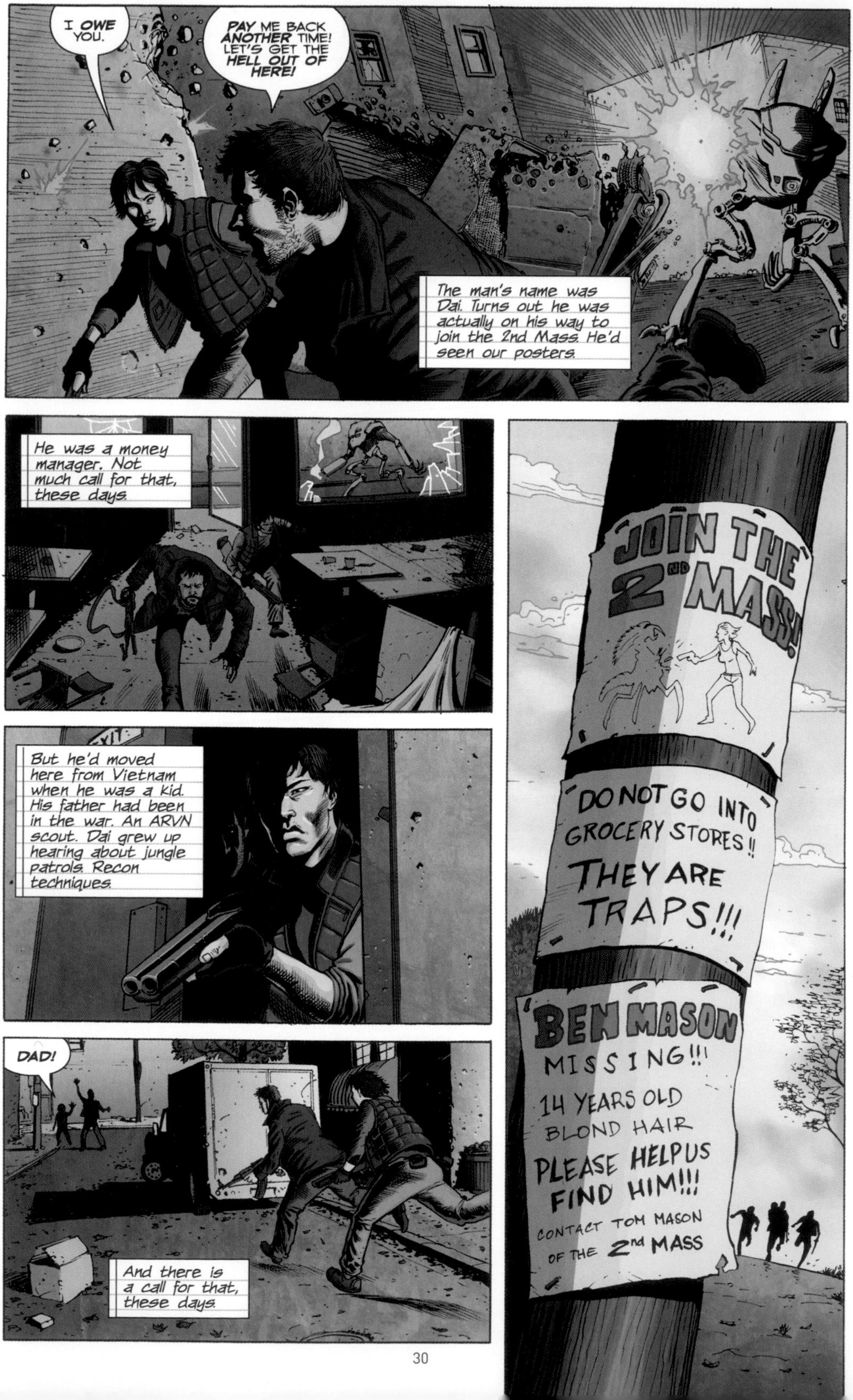
I OWE YOU.
PAY ME BACK ANOTHER TIME! LET'S GET THE HELL OUT OF HERE!
The man's name was Dai. Turns out he was actually on his way to join the 2nd Mass. He'd seen our posters.
He was a money manager. Not much call for that, these days.
But he'd moved here from Vietnam when he was a kid. His father had been in the war. An ARVN scout. Dai grew up hearing about jungle patrols. Recon techniques.
DAD!
And there is a call for that, these days.
JOIN THE 2ND MASS!
DO NOT GO INTO GROCERY STORES!! THEY ARE TRAPS!!!
BEN MASON MISSING!!! 14 YEARS OLD BLOND HAIR PLEASE HELP US FIND HIM!!! CONTACT TOM MASON OF THE 2ND MASS

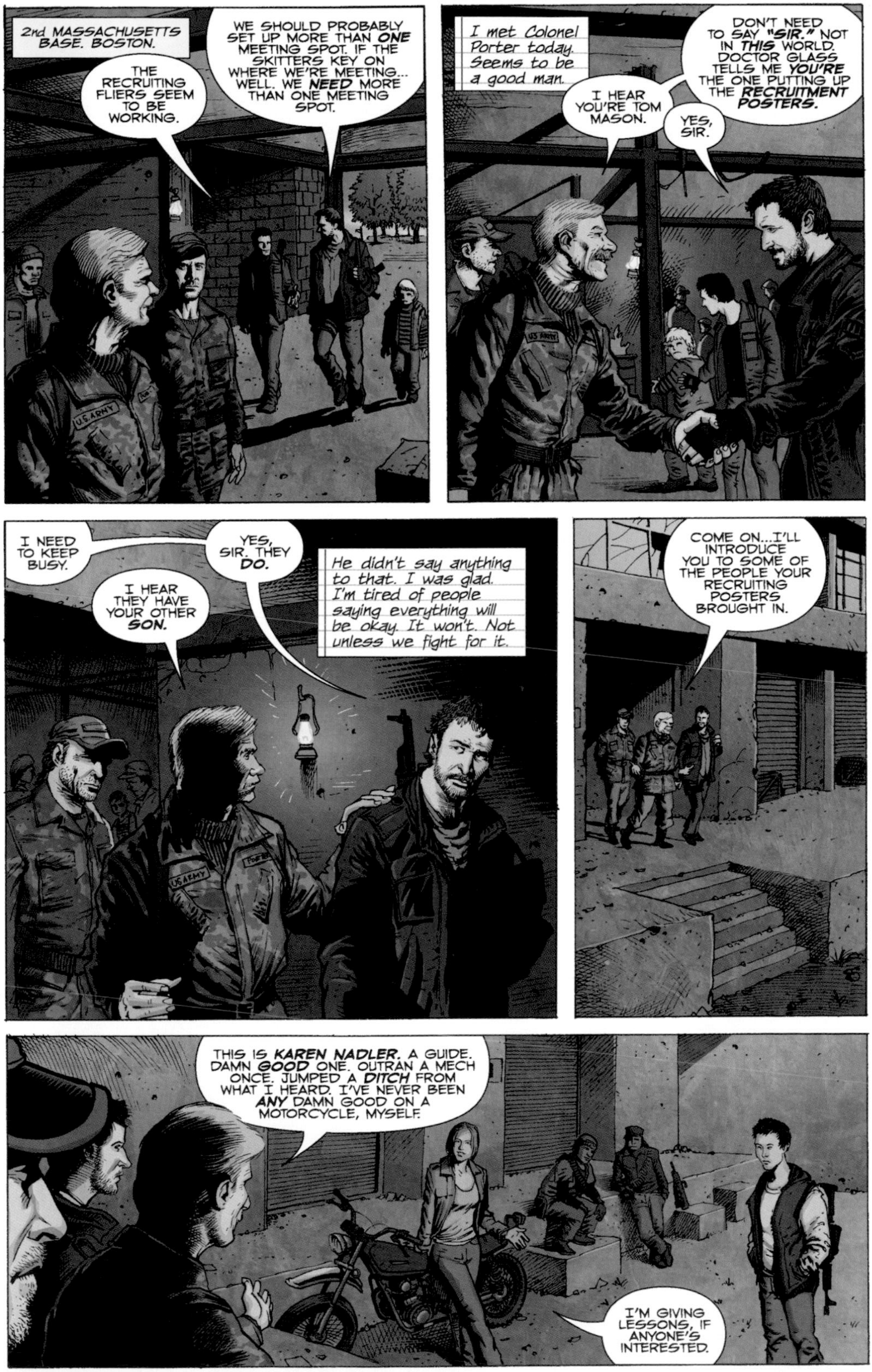
2nd MASSACHUSETTS BASE. BOSTON.
THE RECRUITING FLIERS SEEM TO BE WORKING.
WE SHOULD PROBABLY SET UP MORE THAN ONE MEETING SPOT. IF THE SKITTERS KEY ON WHERE WE'RE MEETING... WELL. WE NEED MORE THAN ONE MEETING SPOT.
I met Colonel Porter today. Seems to be a good man.
I HEAR YOU'RE TOM MASON.
YES, SIR.
DON'T NEED TO SAY "SIR." NOT IN THIS WORLD. DOCTOR GLASS TELLS ME YOU'RE THE ONE PUTTING UP THE RECRUITMENT POSTERS.
I NEED TO KEEP BUSY.
I HEAR THEY HAVE YOUR OTHER SON.
YES, SIR. THEY DO.
He didn't say anything to that. I was glad. I'm tired of people saying everything will be okay. It won't. Not unless we fight for it.
COME ON...I'LL INTRODUCE YOU TO SOME OF THE PEOPLE YOUR RECRUITING POSTERS BROUGHT IN.
THIS IS KAREN NADLER. A GUIDE. DAMN GOOD ONE. OUTRAN A MECH ONCE. JUMPED A DITCH FROM WHAT I HEARD. I'VE NEVER BEEN ANY DAMN GOOD ON A MOTORCYCLE, MYSELF.
I'M GIVING LESSONS, IF ANYONE'S INTERESTED.

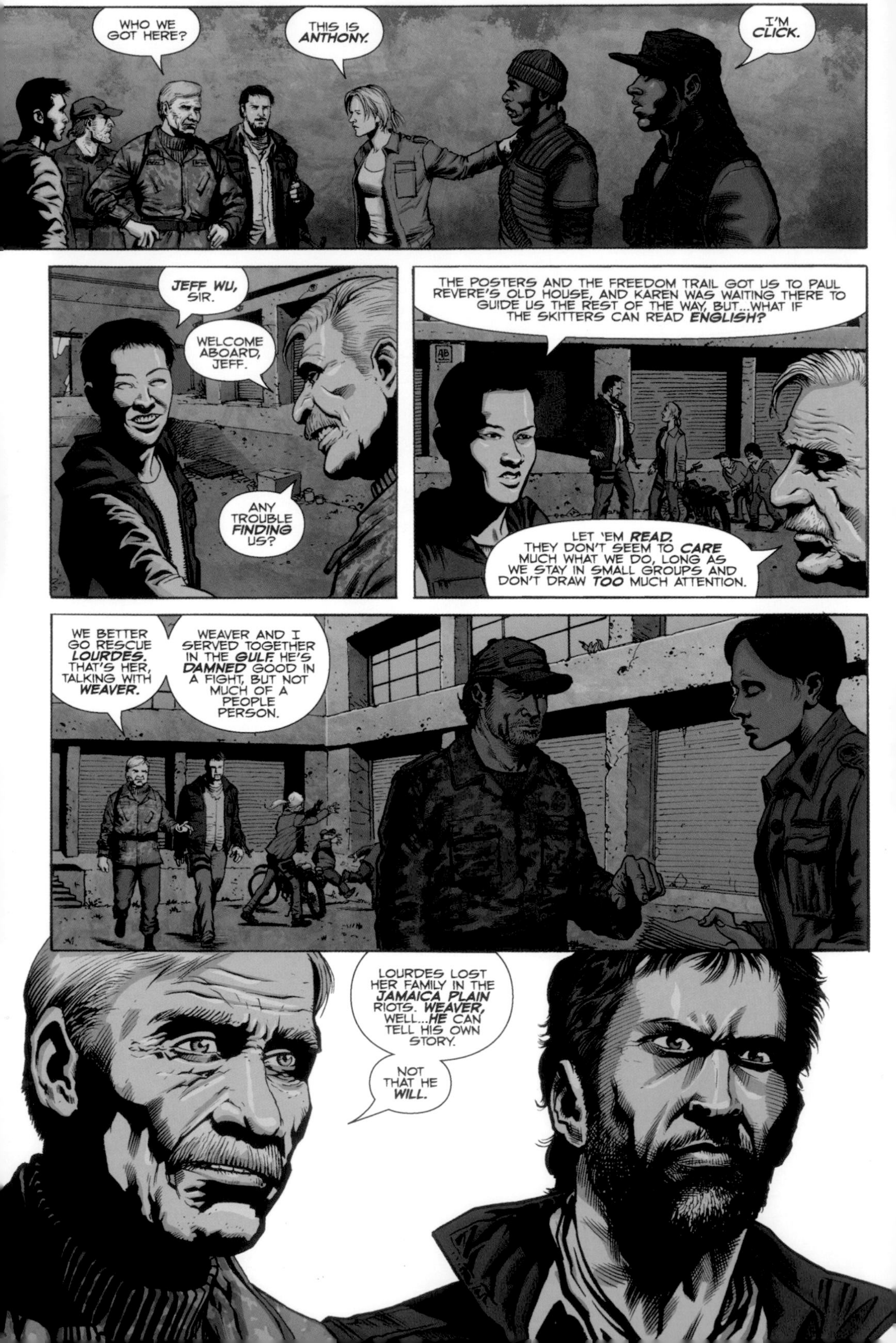
WHO WE GOT HERE?
THIS IS ANTHONY.
I'M CLICK.
JEFF WU, SIR.
WELCOME ABOARD, JEFF.
ANY TROUBLE FINDING US?
THE POSTERS AND THE FREEDOM TRAIL GOT US TO PAUL REVERE'S OLD HOUSE, AND KAREN WAS WAITING THERE TO GUIDE US THE REST OF THE WAY, BUT...WHAT IF THE SKITTERS CAN READ ENGLISH?
LET 'EM READ. THEY DON'T SEEM TO CARE MUCH WHAT WE DO, LONG AS WE STAY IN SMALL GROUPS AND DON'T DRAW TOO MUCH ATTENTION.
WE BETTER GO RESCUE LOURDES. THAT'S HER, TALKING WITH WEAVER.
WEAVER AND I SERVED TOGETHER IN THE GULF. HE'S DAMNED GOOD IN A FIGHT, BUT NOT MUCH OF A PEOPLE PERSON.
LOURDES LOST HER FAMILY IN THE JAMAICA PLAIN RIOTS. WEAVER, WELL...HE CAN TELL HIS OWN STORY.
NOT THAT HE WILL.

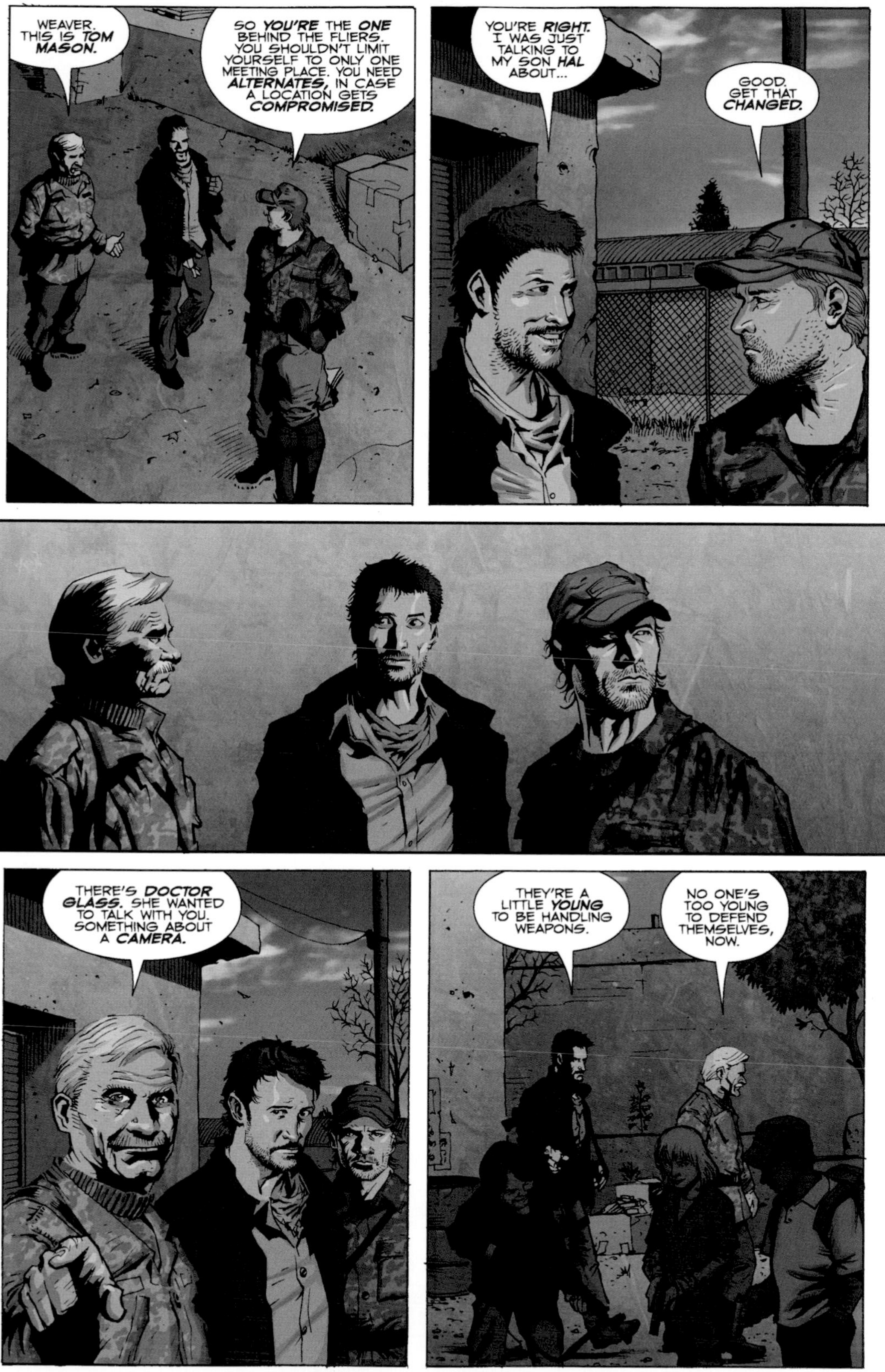
WEAVER. THIS IS TOM MASON.
SO YOU'RE THE ONE BEHIND THE FLIERS. YOU SHOULDN'T LIMIT YOURSELF TO ONLY ONE MEETING PLACE. YOU NEED ALTERNATES, IN CASE A LOCATION GETS COMPROMISED.
YOU'RE RIGHT. I WAS JUST TALKING TO MY SON HAL ABOUT...
GOOD. GET THAT CHANGED.
THERE'S DOCTOR GLASS. SHE WANTED TO TALK WITH YOU. SOMETHING ABOUT A CAMERA.
THEY'RE A LITTLE YOUNG TO BE HANDLING WEAPONS.
NO ONE'S TOO YOUNG TO DEFEND THEMSELVES, NOW.

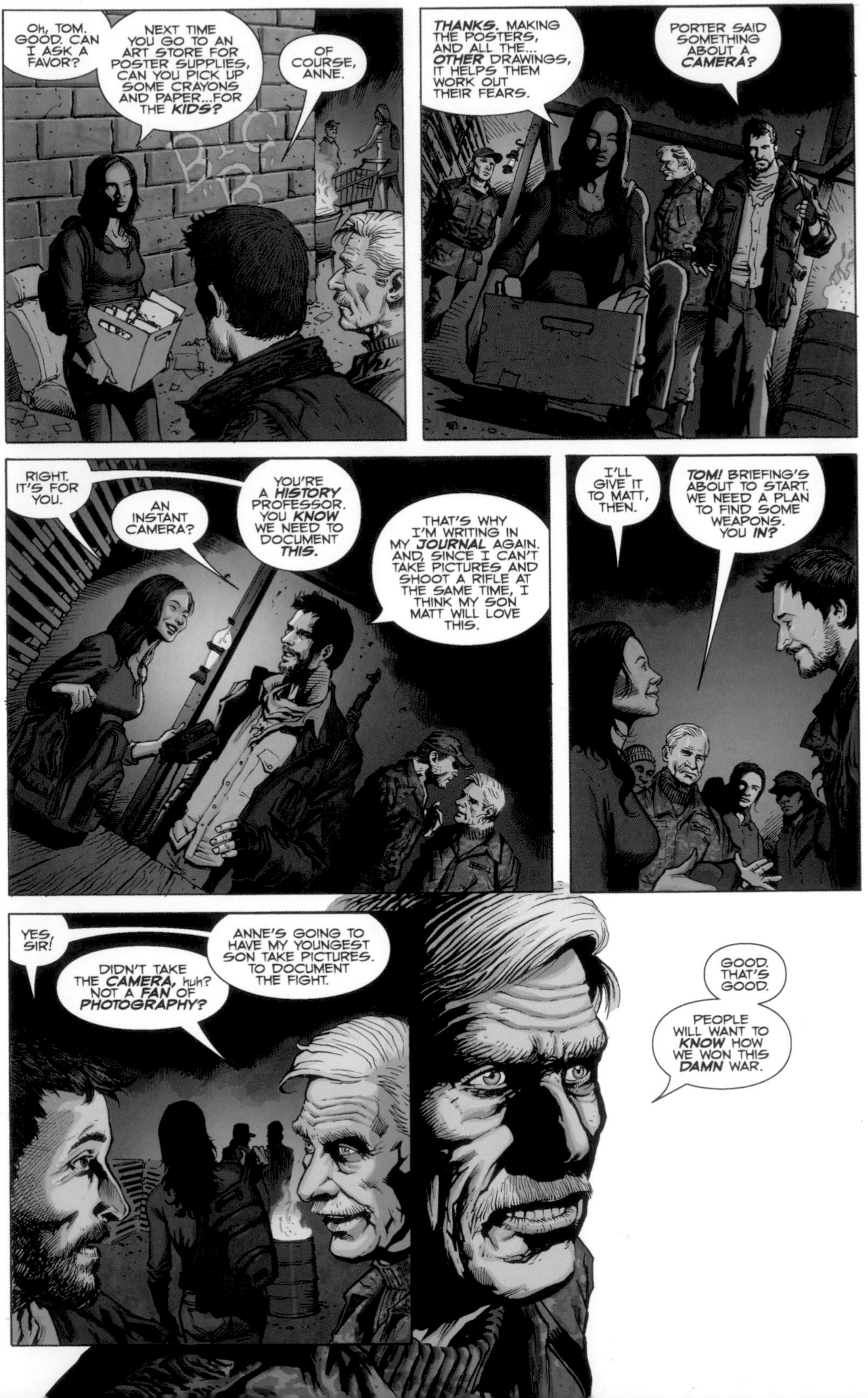
Oh, TOM. GOOD. CAN I ASK A FAVOR?
NEXT TIME YOU GO TO AN ART STORE FOR POSTER SUPPLIES, CAN YOU PICK UP SOME CRAYONS AND PAPER...FOR THE KIDS?
OF COURSE, ANNE.
THANKS. MAKING THE POSTERS, AND ALL THE... OTHER DRAWINGS, IT HELPS THEM WORK OUT THEIR FEARS.
PORTER SAID SOMETHING ABOUT A CAMERA?
RIGHT. IT'S FOR YOU.
AN INSTANT CAMERA?
YOU'RE A HISTORY PROFESSOR. YOU KNOW WE NEED TO DOCUMENT THIS.
THAT'S WHY I'M WRITING IN MY JOURNAL AGAIN. AND, SINCE I CAN'T TAKE PICTURES AND SHOOT A RIFLE AT THE SAME TIME, I THINK MY SON MATT WILL LOVE THIS.
I'LL GIVE IT TO MATT, THEN.
TOM! BRIEFING'S ABOUT TO START. WE NEED A PLAN TO FIND SOME WEAPONS. YOU IN?
YES, SIR!
DIDN'T TAKE THE CAMERA, huh? NOT A FAN OF PHOTOGRAPHY?
ANNE'S GOING TO HAVE MY YOUNGEST SON TAKE PICTURES. TO DOCUMENT THE FIGHT.
GOOD. THAT'S GOOD.
PEOPLE WILL WANT TO KNOW HOW WE WON THIS DAMN WAR.

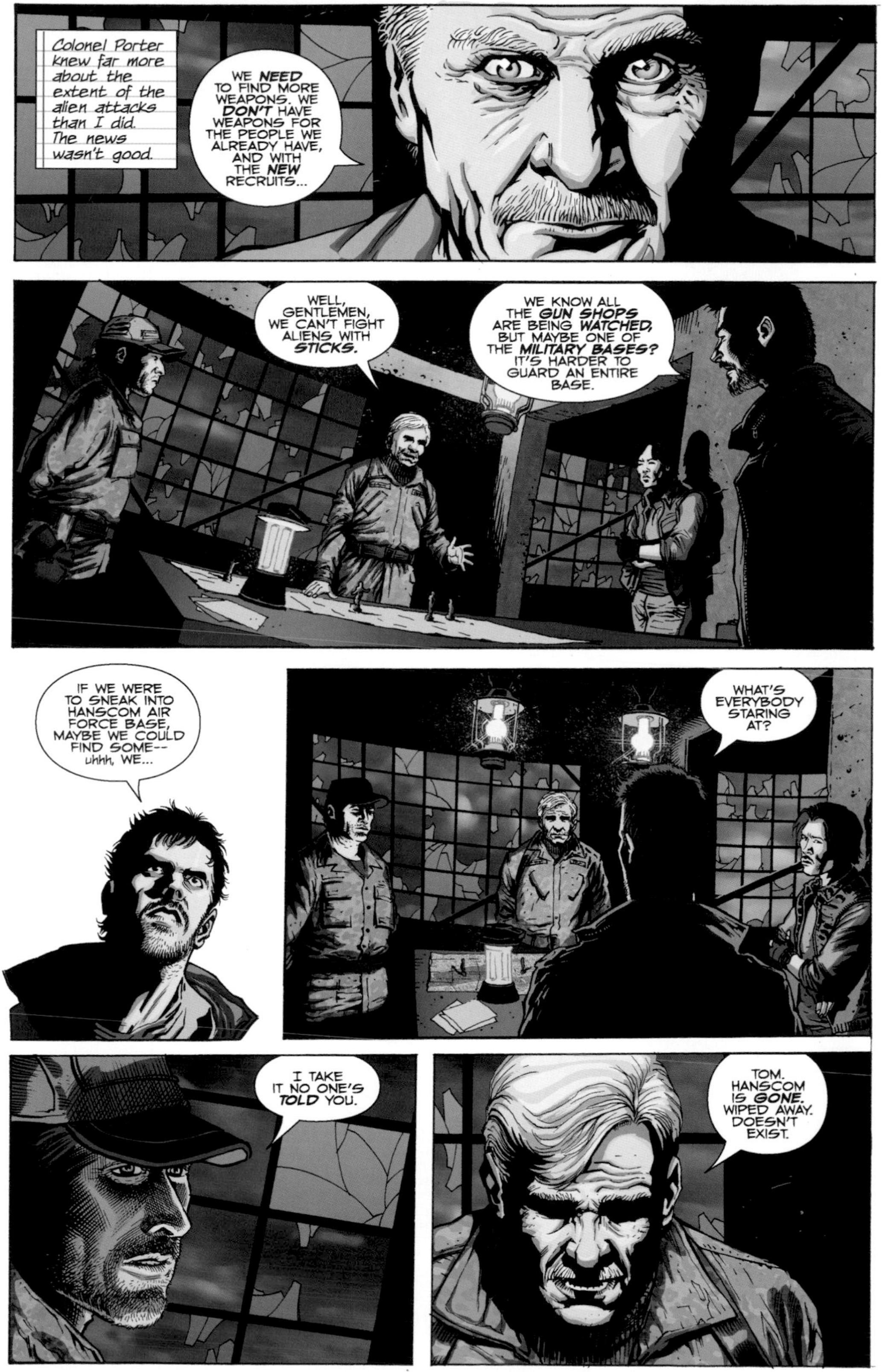
Colonel Porter knew far more about the extent of the alien attacks than I did. The news wasn't good.
WE NEED TO FIND MORE WEAPONS. WE DON'T HAVE WEAPONS FOR THE PEOPLE WE ALREADY HAVE, AND WITH THE NEW RECRUITS...
WELL, GENTLEMEN, WE CAN'T FIGHT ALIENS WITH STICKS.
WE KNOW ALL THE GUN SHOPS ARE BEING WATCHED, BUT MAYBE ONE OF THE MILITARY BASES? IT'S HARDER TO GUARD AN ENTIRE BASE.
IF WE WERE TO SNEAK INTO HANSCOM AIR FORCE BASE, MAYBE WE COULD FIND SOME-- uhhh, WE...
WHAT'S EVERYBODY STARING AT?
I TAKE IT NO ONE'S TOLD YOU.
TOM. HANSCOM IS GONE. WIPED AWAY. DOESN'T EXIST.

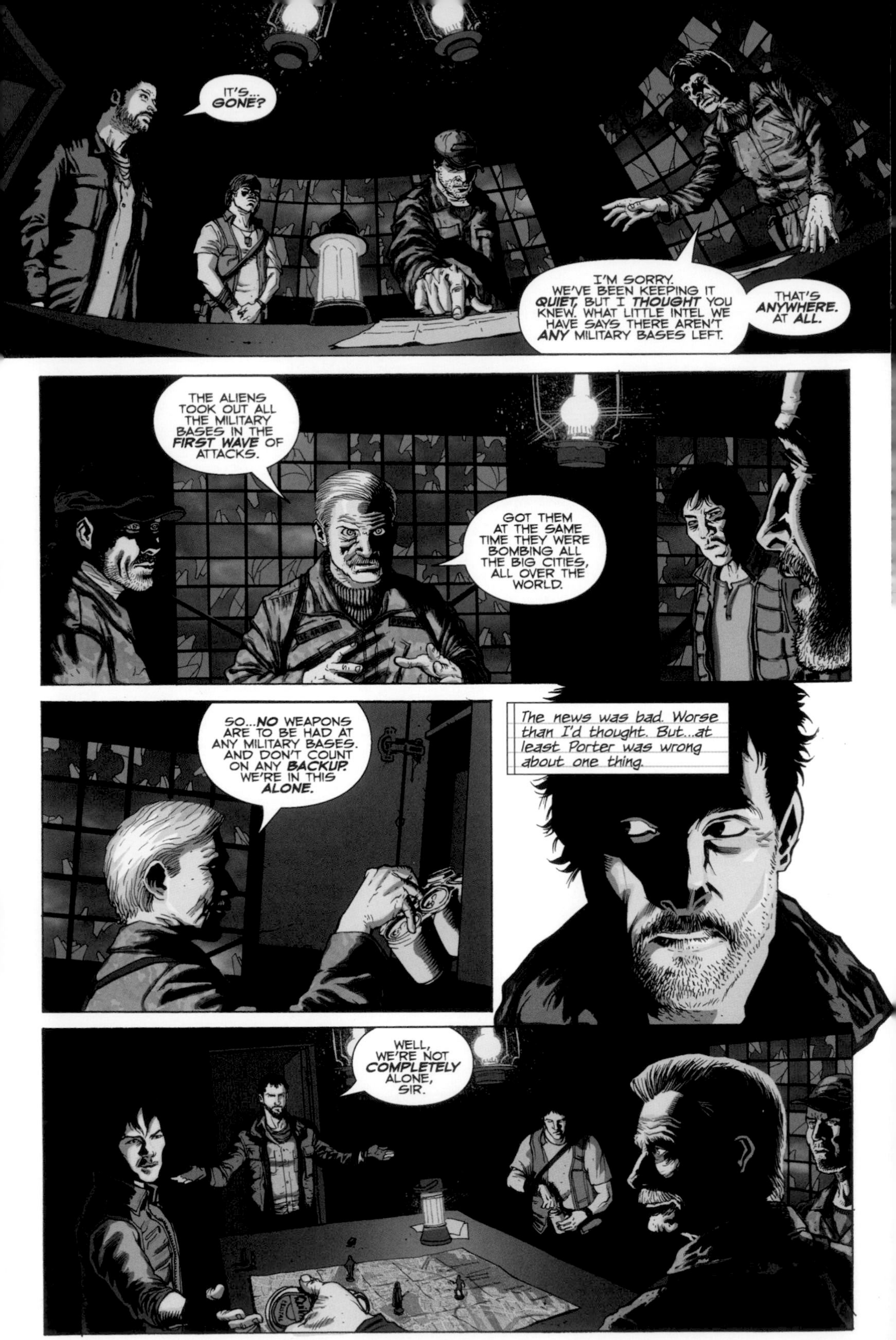
IT'S... GONE?
I'M SORRY. WE'VE BEEN KEEPING IT QUIET, BUT I THOUGHT YOU KNEW. WHAT LITTLE INTEL WE HAVE SAYS THERE AREN'T ANY MILITARY BASES LEFT.
THAT'S ANYWHERE. AT ALL.
THE ALIENS TOOK OUT ALL THE MILITARY BASES IN THE FIRST WAVE OF ATTACKS.
GOT THEM AT THE SAME TIME THEY WERE BOMBING ALL THE BIG CITIES, ALL OVER THE WORLD.
SO...NO WEAPONS ARE TO BE HAD AT ANY MILITARY BASES. AND DON'T COUNT ON ANY BACKUP. WE'RE IN THIS ALONE.
The news was bad. Worse than I'd thought. But...at least Porter was wrong about one thing.
WELL, WE'RE NOT COMPLETELY ALONE, SIR.

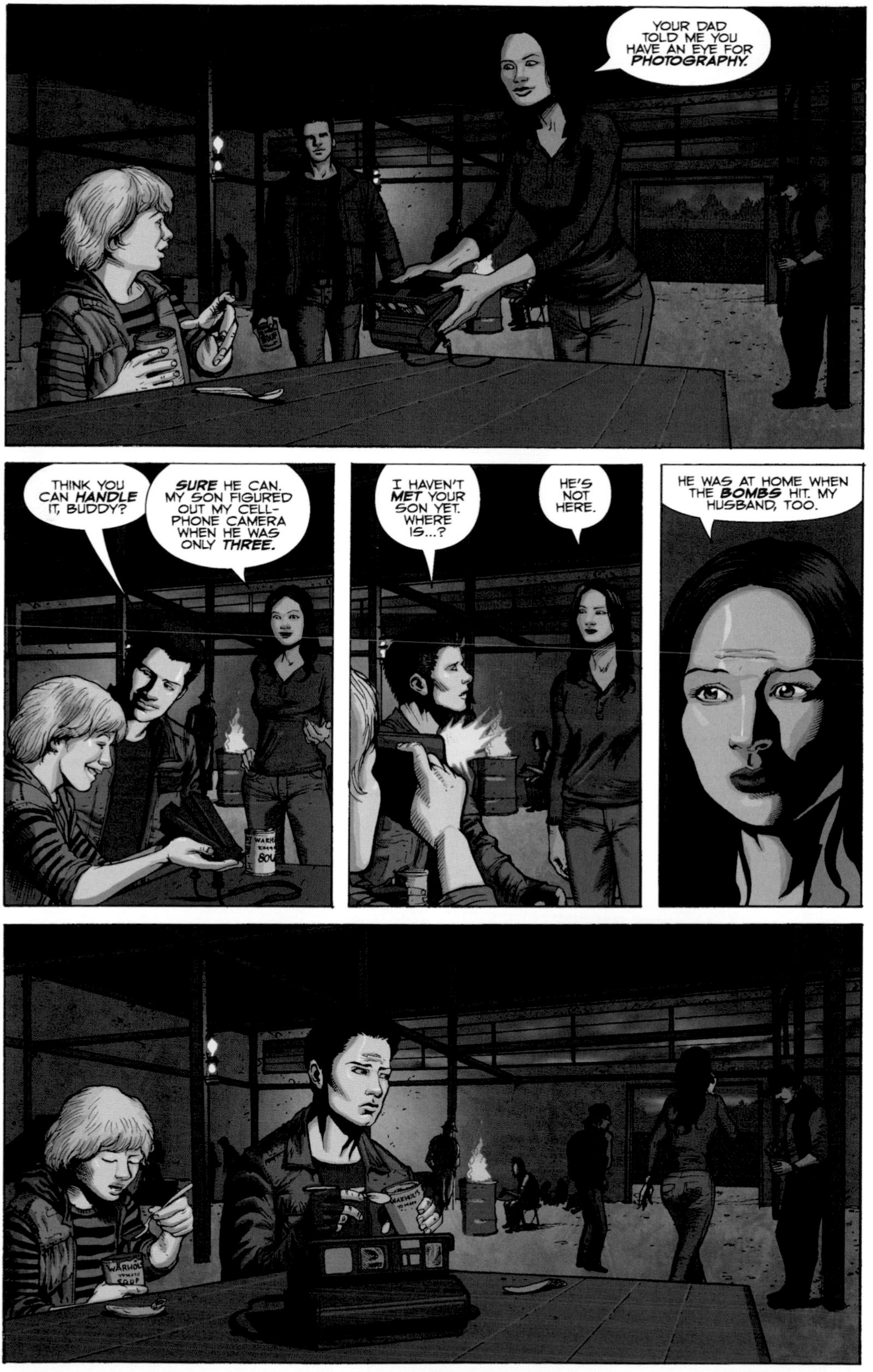
YOUR DAD TOLD ME YOU HAVE AN EYE FOR PHOTOGRAPHY.
THINK YOU CAN HANDLE IT, BUDDY?
SURE HE CAN. MY SON FIGURED OUT MY CELL-PHONE CAMERA WHEN HE WAS ONLY THREE.
I HAVEN'T MET YOUR SON YET. WHERE IS...?
HE'S NOT HERE.
HE WAS AT HOME WHEN THE BOMBS HIT. MY HUSBAND, TOO.

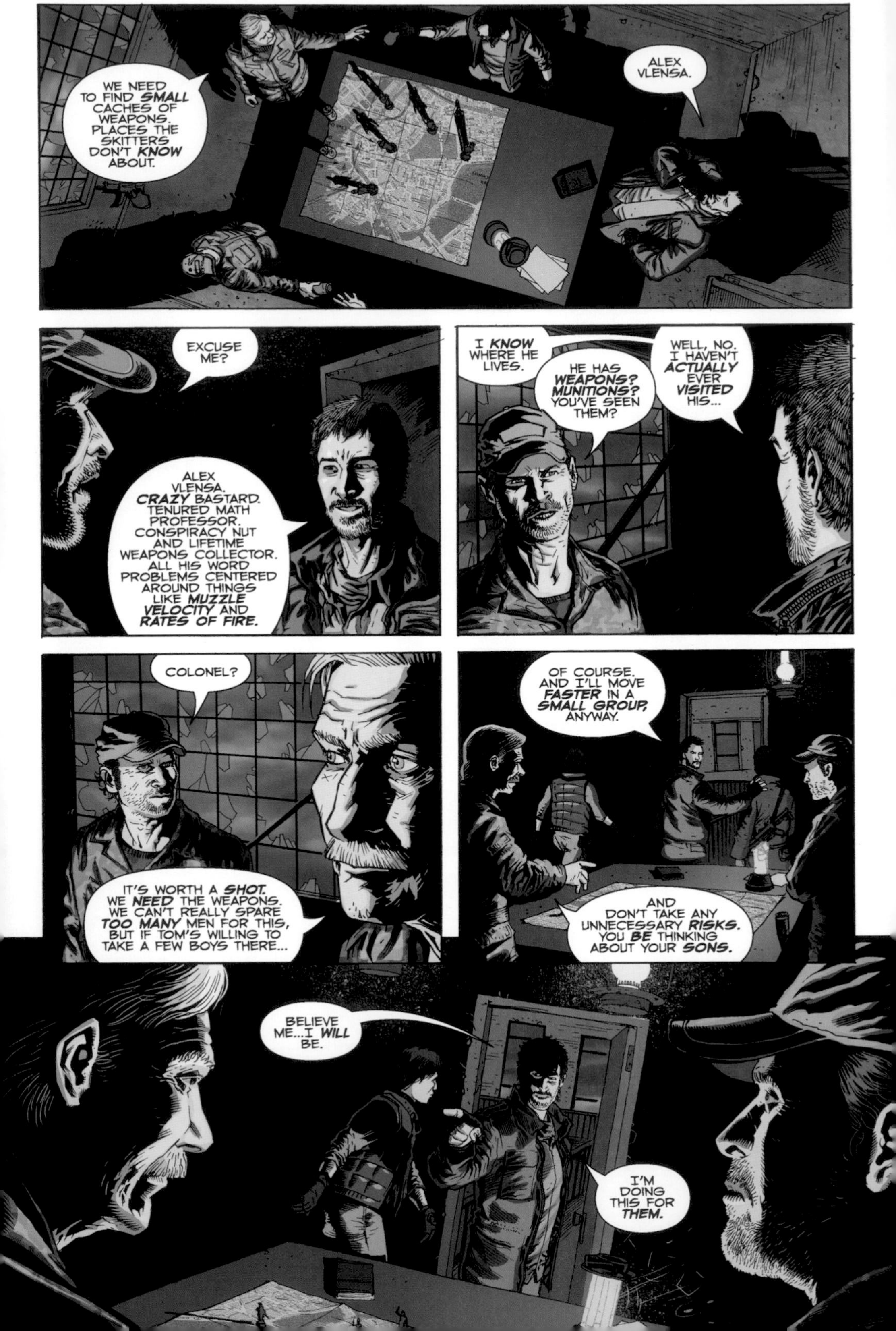
WE NEED TO FIND SMALL CACHES OF WEAPONS. PLACES THE SKITTERS DON'T KNOW ABOUT.
ALEX VLENSA.
EXCUSE ME?
ALEX VLENSA. CRAZY BASTARD. TENURED MATH PROFESSOR. CONSPIRACY NUT AND LIFETIME WEAPONS COLLECTOR. ALL HIS WORD PROBLEMS CENTERED AROUND THINGS LIKE MUZZLE VELOCITY AND RATES OF FIRE.
I KNOW WHERE HE LIVES.
HE HAS WEAPONS? MUNITIONS? YOU'VE SEEN THEM?
WELL, NO. I HAVEN'T ACTUALLY EVER VISITED HIS...
COLONEL?
IT'S WORTH A SHOT. WE NEED THE WEAPONS. WE CAN'T REALLY SPARE TOO MANY MEN FOR THIS, BUT IF TOM'S WILLING TO TAKE A FEW BOYS THERE...
OF COURSE. AND I'LL MOVE FASTER IN A SMALL GROUP, ANYWAY.
AND DON'T TAKE ANY UNNECESSARY RISKS. YOU BE THINKING ABOUT YOUR SONS.
BELIEVE ME...I WILL BE.
I'M DOING THIS FOR THEM.

CHAPTER THREE

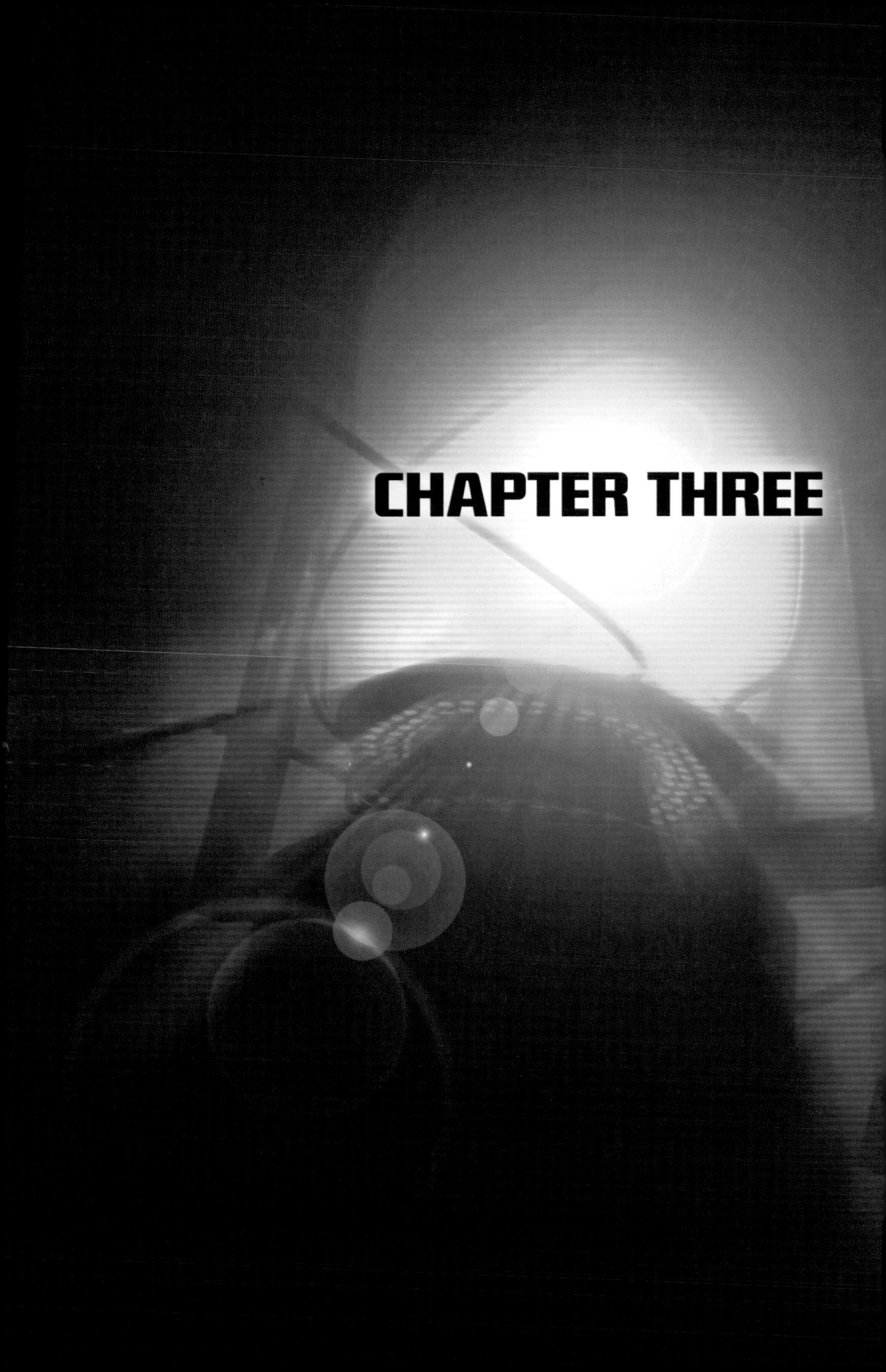

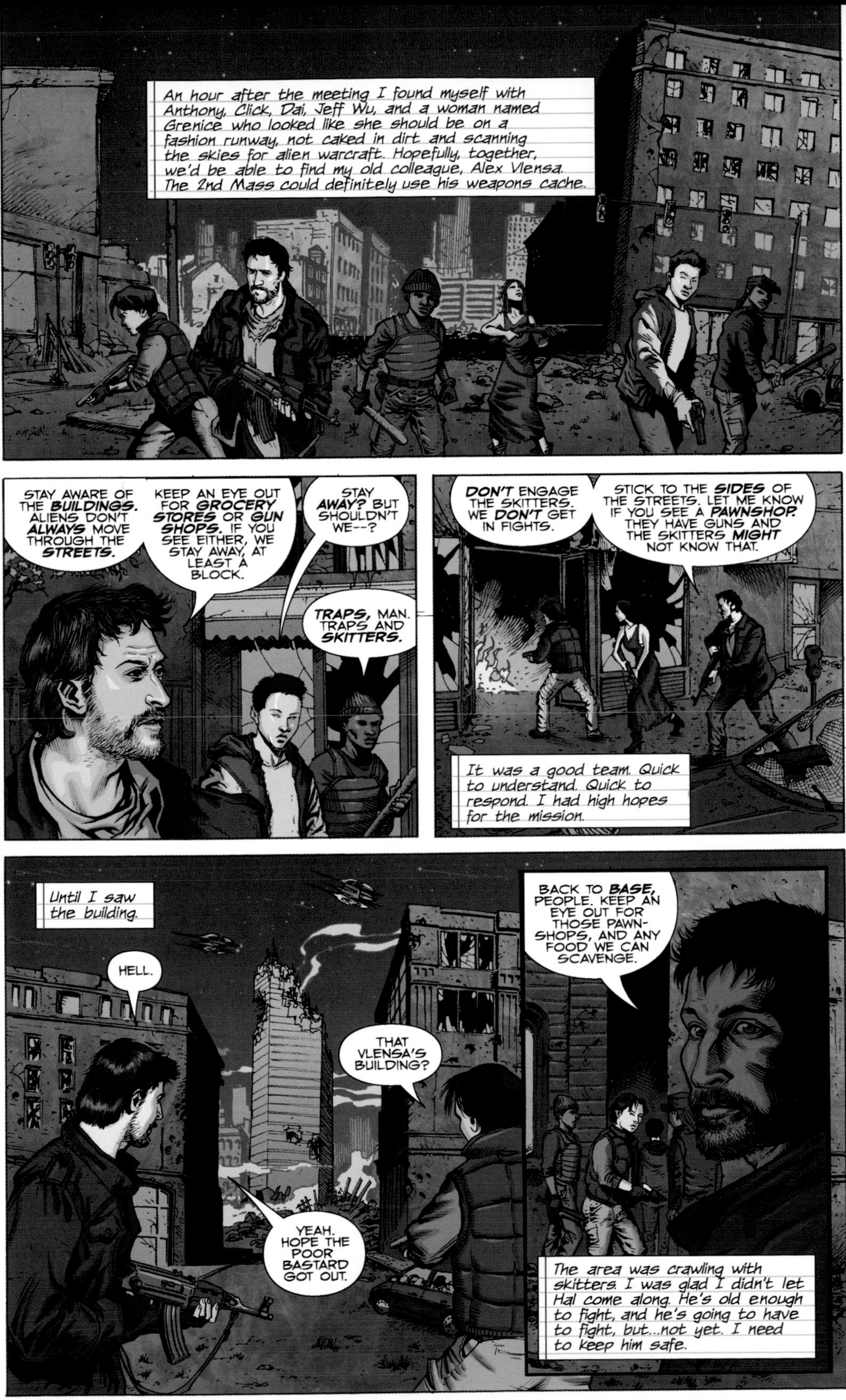

An hour after the meeting I found myself with Anthony, Click, Dai, Jeff Wu, and a woman named Grenice who looked like she should be on a fashion runway, not caked in dirt and scanning the skies for alien warcraft. Hopefully, together, we'd be able to find my old colleague, Alex Vlensa. The 2nd Mass could definitely use his weapons cache.
STAY AWARE OF THE BUILDINGS. ALIENS DON'T ALWAYS MOVE THROUGH THE STREETS.
KEEP AN EYE OUT FOR GROCERY STORES OR GUN SHOPS. IF YOU SEE EITHER, WE STAY AWAY, AT LEAST A BLOCK.
STAY AWAY? BUT SHOULDN'T WE--?
TRAPS, MAN. TRAPS AND SKITTERS.
DON'T ENGAGE THE SKITTERS. WE DON'T GET IN FIGHTS.
STICK TO THE SIDES OF THE STREETS. LET ME KNOW IF YOU SEE A PAWNSHOP. THEY HAVE GUNS AND THE SKITTERS MIGHT NOT KNOW THAT.
It was a good team. Quick to understand. Quick to respond. I had high hopes for the mission.
Until I saw the building.
HELL.
THAT VLENSA'S BUILDING?
YEAH. HOPE THE POOR BASTARD GOT OUT.
BACK TO BASE, PEOPLE. KEEP AN EYE OUT FOR THOSE PAWN-SHOPS, AND ANY FOOD WE CAN SCAVENGE.
The area was crawling with skitters. I was glad I didn't let Hal come along. He's old enough to fight, and he's going to have to fight, but...not yet. I need to keep him safe.

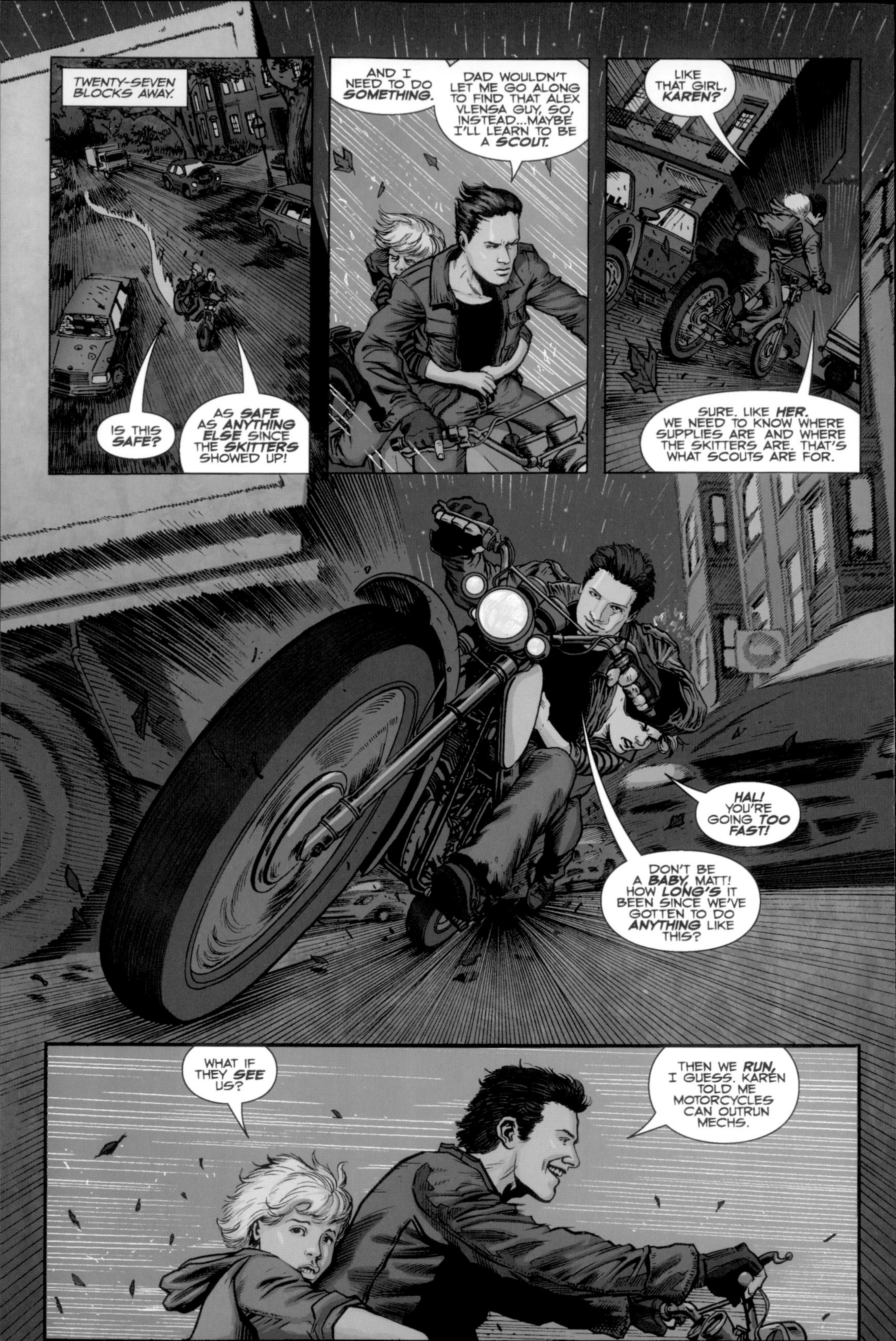
TWENTY-SEVEN BLOCKS AWAY.
IS THIS SAFE?
AS SAFE AS ANYTHING ELSE SINCE THE SKITTERS SHOWED UP!
AND I NEED TO DO SOMETHING.
DAD WOULDN'T LET ME GO ALONG TO FIND THAT ALEX VLENSA GUY, SO, INSTEAD...MAYBE I'LL LEARN TO BE A SCOUT.
LIKE THAT GIRL, KAREN?
SURE. LIKE HER. WE NEED TO KNOW WHERE SUPPLIES ARE AND WHERE THE SKITTERS ARE. THAT'S WHAT SCOUTS ARE FOR.
HAL! YOU'RE GOING TOO FAST!
DON'T BE A BABY, MATT! HOW LONG'S IT BEEN SINCE WE'VE GOTTEN TO DO ANYTHING LIKE THIS?
WHAT IF THEY SEE US?
THEN WE RUN, I GUESS. KAREN TOLD ME MOTORCYCLES CAN OUTRUN MECHS.

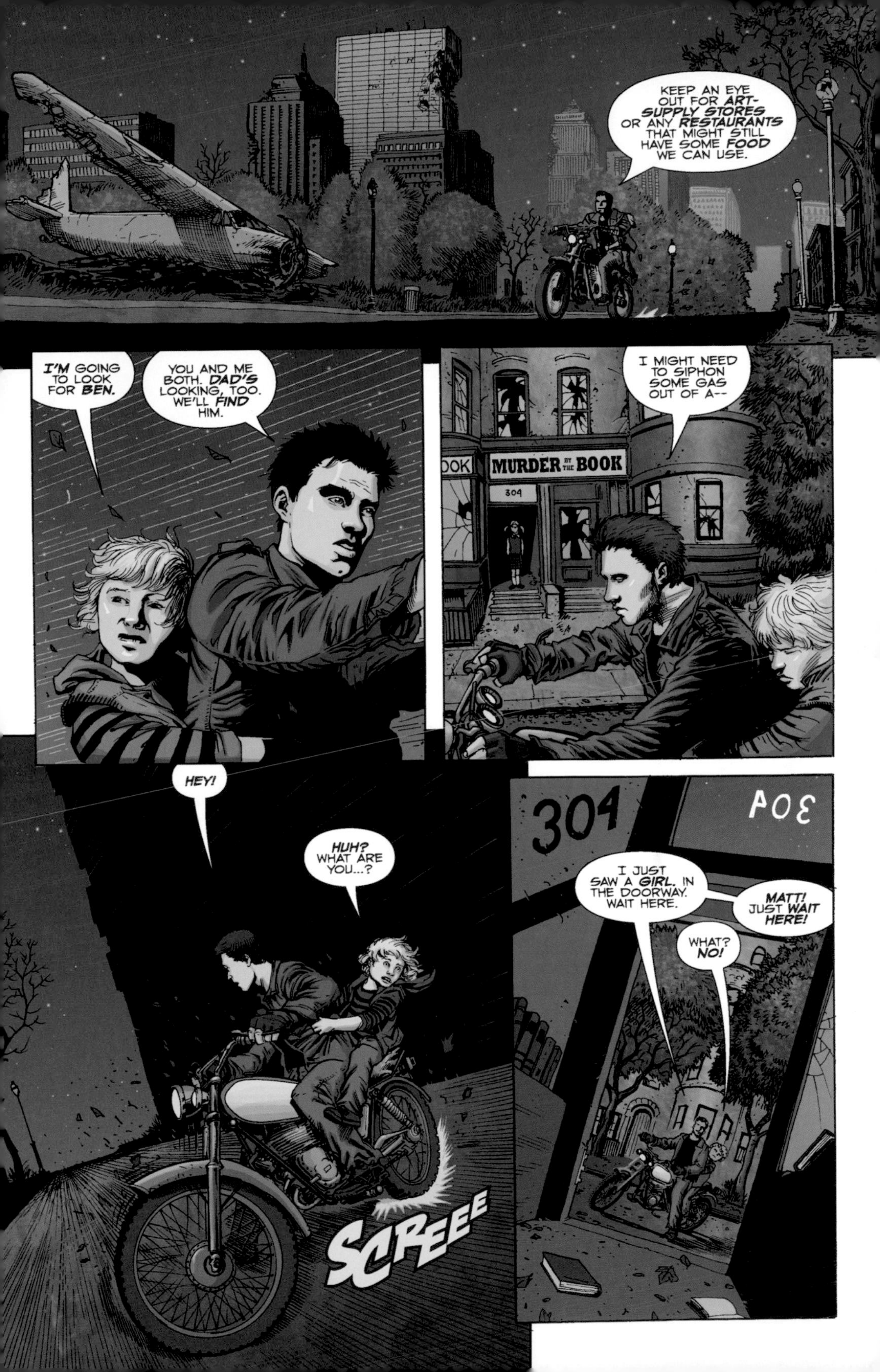

KEEP AN EYE OUT FOR ART-SUPPLY STORES OR ANY RESTAURANTS THAT MIGHT STILL HAVE SOME FOOD WE CAN USE.
I'M GOING TO LOOK FOR BEN.
YOU AND ME BOTH. DAD'S LOOKING, TOO. WE'LL FIND HIM.
I MIGHT NEED TO SIPHON SOME GAS OUT OF A--
MURDER BY THE BOOK
304
HEY!
HUH? WHAT ARE YOU...?
SCREEE
304
I JUST SAW A GIRL. IN THE DOORWAY. WAIT HERE.
MATT! JUST WAIT HERE!
WHAT? NO!

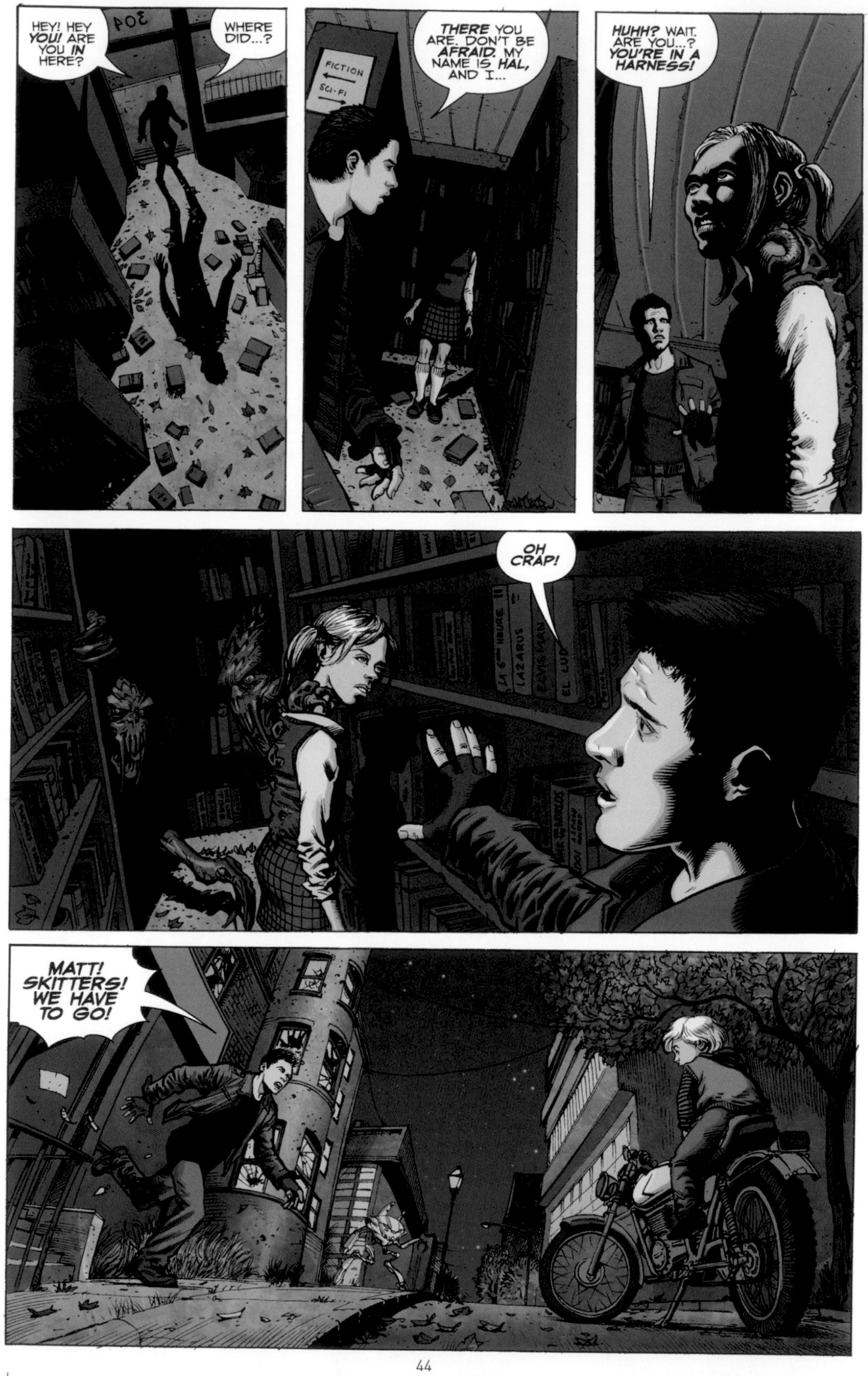
HEY! HEY YOU! ARE YOU IN HERE?
WHERE DID...?
FICTION
SCI-FI
THERE YOU ARE. DON'T BE AFRAID. MY NAME IS HAL, AND I...
HUHH? WAIT. ARE YOU...? YOU'RE IN A HARNESS!
OH CRAP!
MATT! SKITTERS! WE HAVE TO GO!

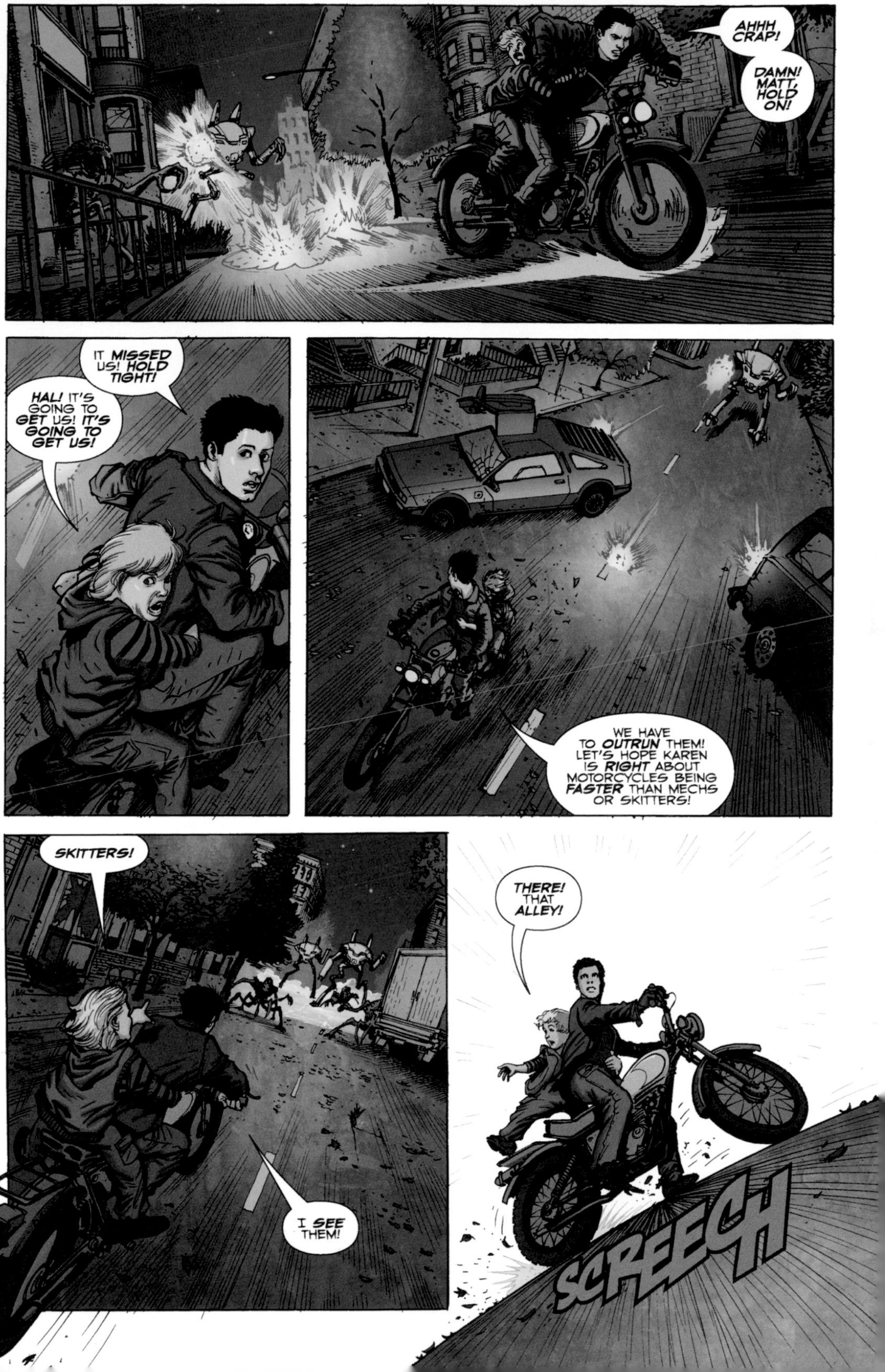
AHHH CRAP!
DAMN! MATT, HOLD ON!
IT MISSED US! HOLD TIGHT!
HAL! IT'S GOING TO GET US! IT'S GOING TO GET US!
WE HAVE TO OUTRUN THEM! LET'S HOPE KAREN IS RIGHT ABOUT MOTORCYCLES BEING FASTER THAN MECHS OR SKITTERS!
SKITTERS!
I SEE THEM!
THERE! THAT ALLEY!
SCREECH

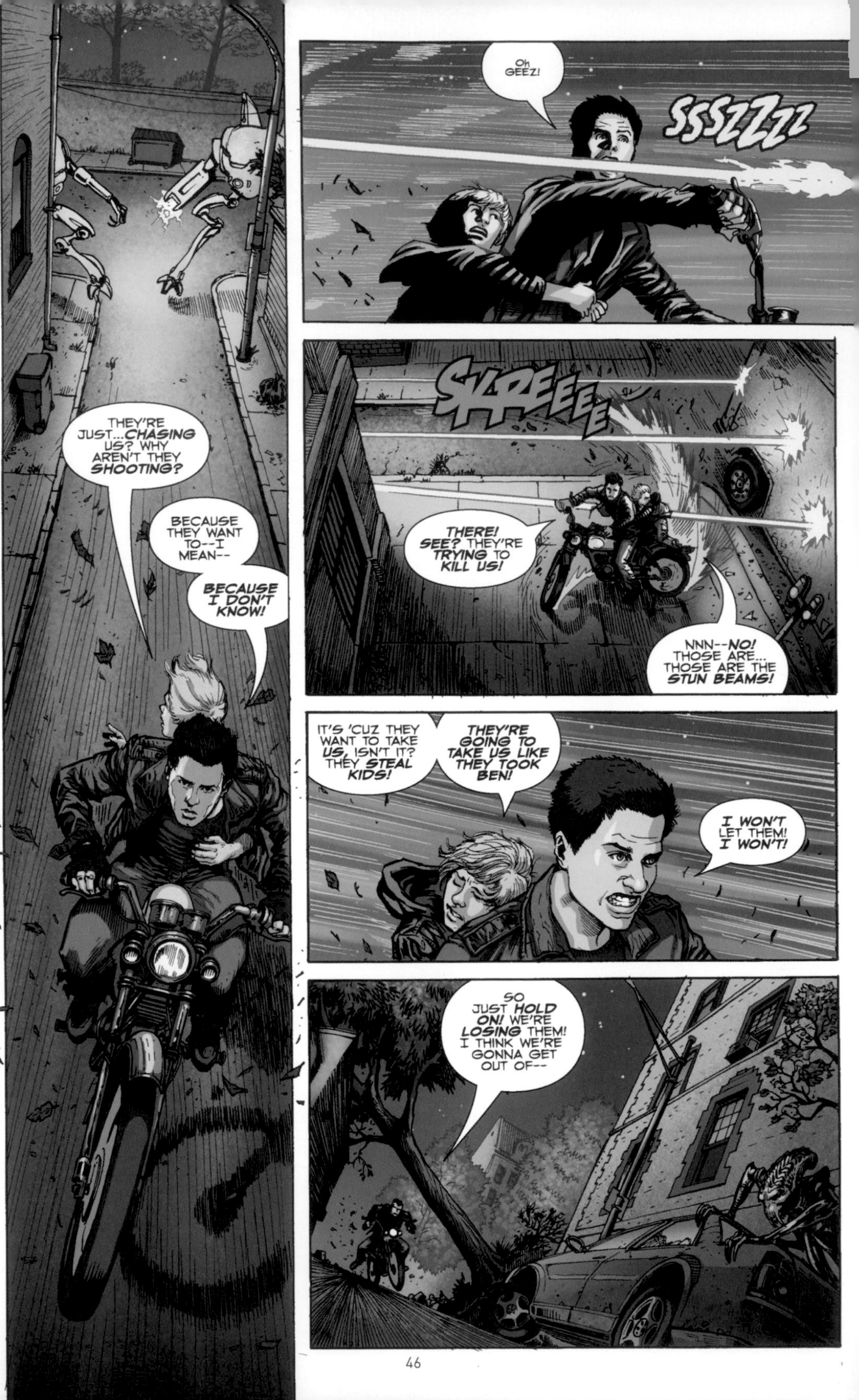
THEY'RE JUST...CHASING US? WHY AREN'T THEY SHOOTING?
BECAUSE THEY WANT TO--I MEAN--
BECAUSE I DON'T KNOW!
Oh GEEZ!
SSSZZZZZ
SKREEEEE
THERE! SEE? THEY'RE TRYING TO KILL US!
NNN--NO! THOSE ARE... THOSE ARE THE STUN BEAMS!
IT'S 'CUZ THEY WANT TO TAKE US, ISN'T IT? THEY STEAL KIDS!
THEY'RE GOING TO TAKE US LIKE THEY TOOK BEN!
I WON'T LET THEM! I WON'T!
SO JUST HOLD ON! WE'RE LOSING THEM! I THINK WE'RE GONNA GET OUT OF--

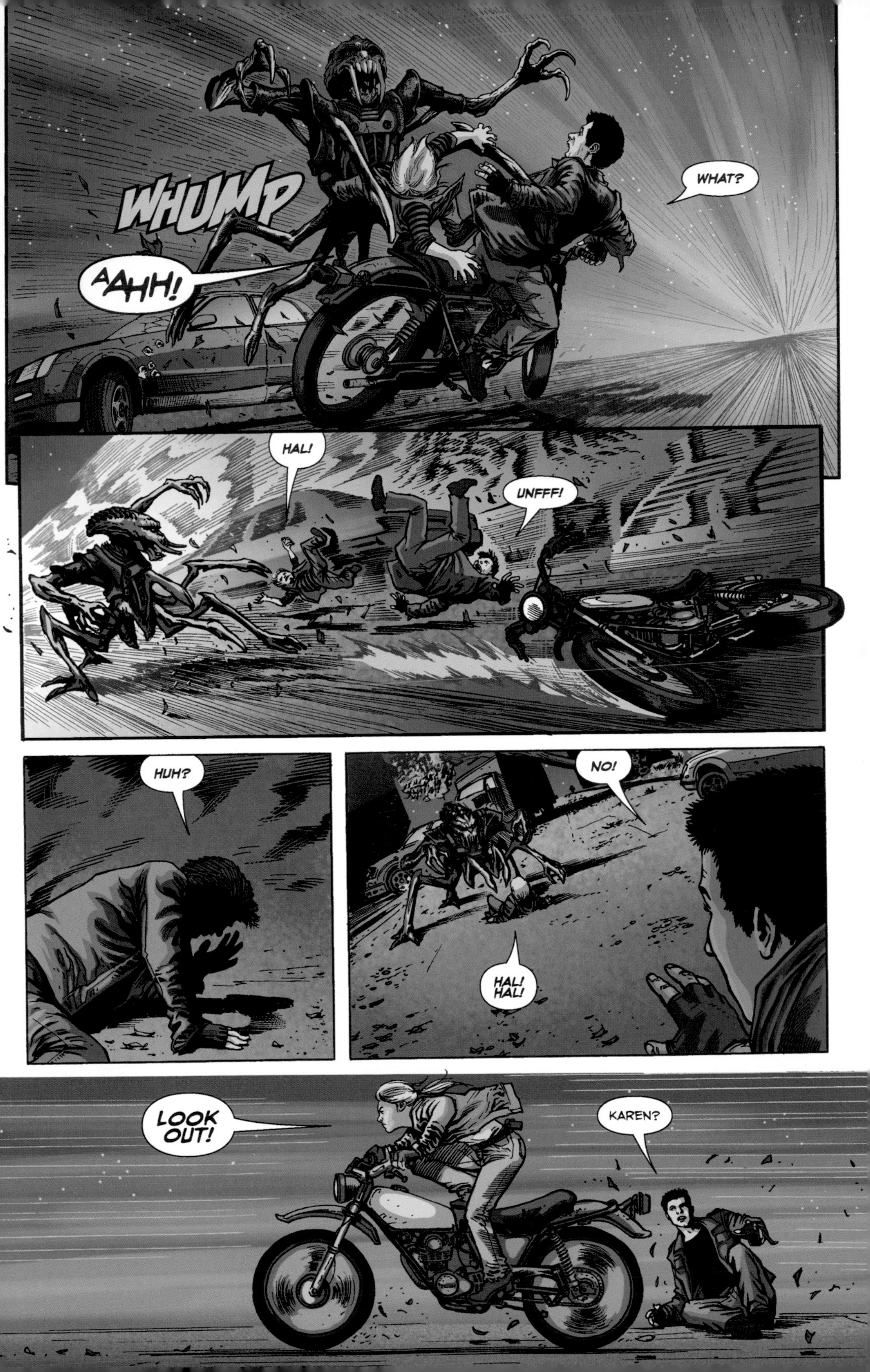
WHUMP
AAHH!
WHAT?
HAL!
UNFFF!
HUH?
NO!
HAL! HAL!
LOOK OUT!
KAREN?

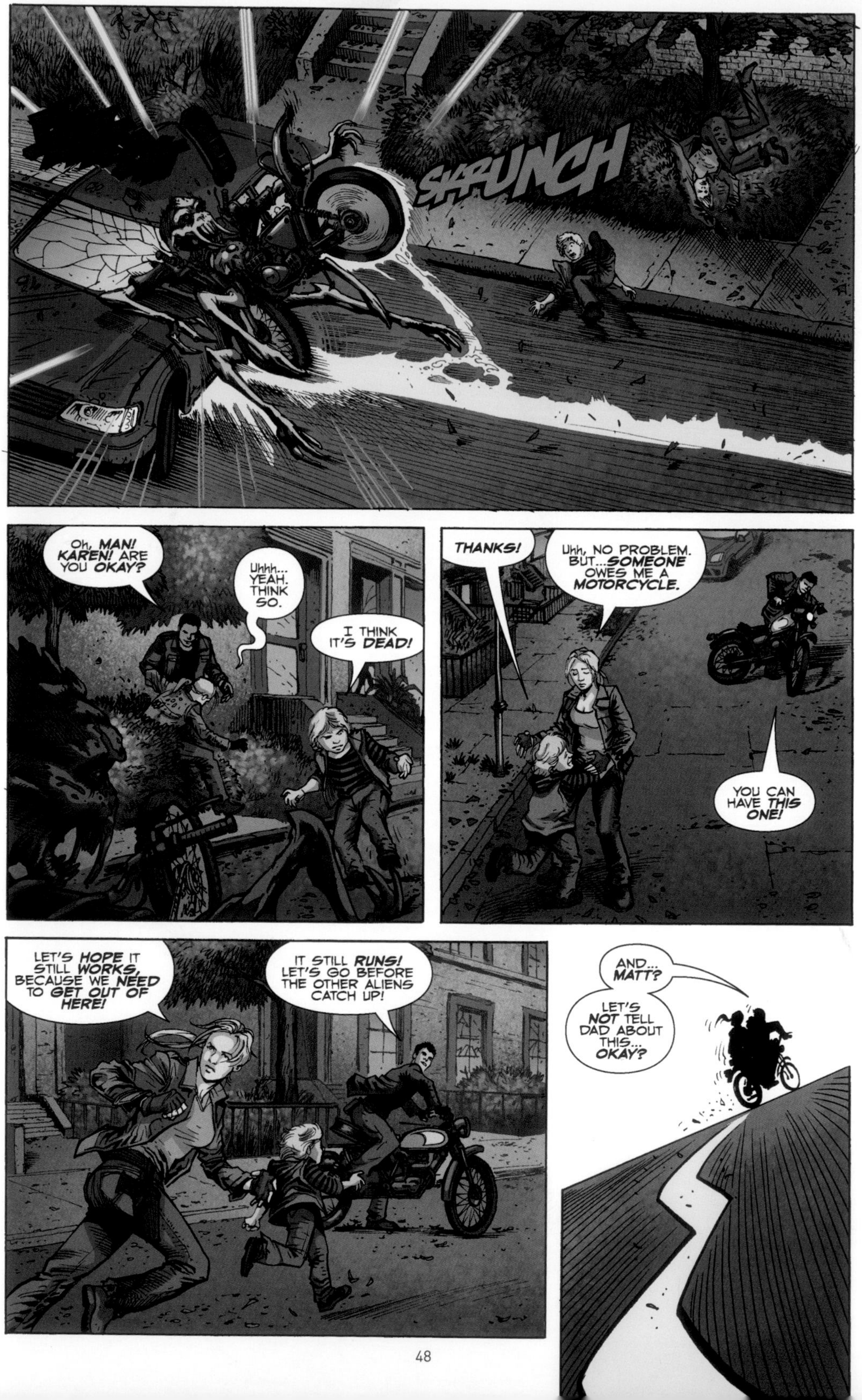
SKRUNCH
Oh, MAN! KAREN! ARE YOU OKAY?
Uhhh... YEAH. THINK SO.
I THINK IT'S DEAD!
THANKS!
Uhh, NO PROBLEM. BUT...SOMEONE OWES ME A MOTORCYCLE.
YOU CAN HAVE THIS ONE!
LET'S HOPE IT STILL WORKS, BECAUSE WE NEED TO GET OUT OF HERE!
IT STILL RUNS! LET'S GO BEFORE THE OTHER ALIENS CATCH UP!
AND... MATT?
LET'S NOT TELL DAD ABOUT THIS... OKAY?

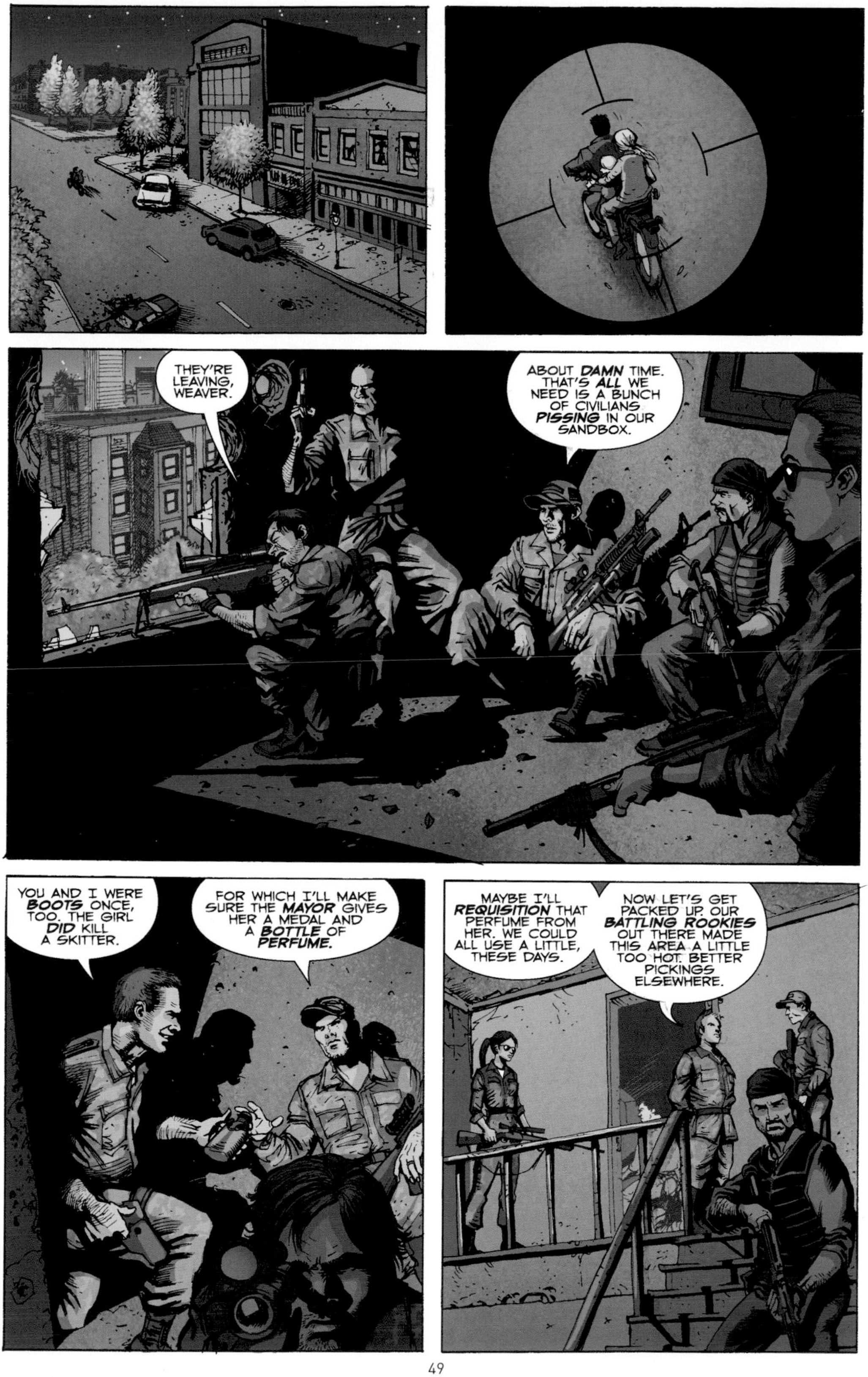
THEY'RE LEAVING, WEAVER.
ABOUT DAMN TIME. THAT'S ALL WE NEED IS A BUNCH OF CIVILIANS PISSING IN OUR SANDBOX.
YOU AND I WERE BOOTS ONCE, TOO. THE GIRL DID KILL A SKITTER.
FOR WHICH I'LL MAKE SURE THE MAYOR GIVES HER A MEDAL AND A BOTTLE OF PERFUME.
MAYBE I'LL REQUISITION THAT PERFUME FROM HER. WE COULD ALL USE A LITTLE, THESE DAYS.
NOW LET'S GET PACKED UP. OUR BATTLING ROOKIES OUT THERE MADE THIS AREA A LITTLE TOO HOT. BETTER PICKINGS ELSEWHERE.

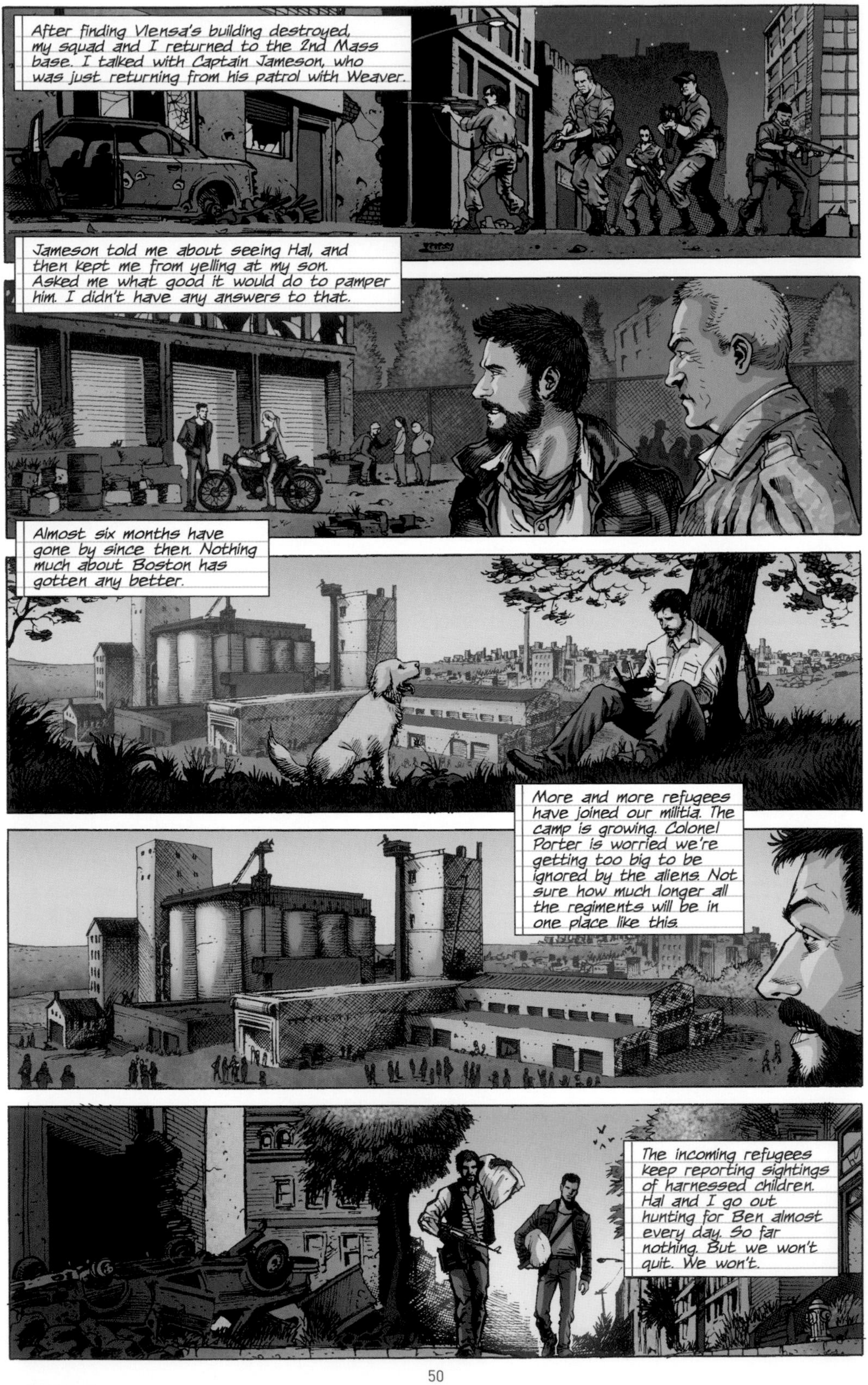
After finding Vlensa's building destroyed, my squad and I returned to the 2nd Mass base. I talked with Captain Jameson, who was just returning from his patrol with Weaver.
Jameson told me about seeing Hal, and then kept me from yelling at my son. Asked me what good it would do to pamper him. I didn't have any answers to that.
Almost six months have gone by since then. Nothing much about Boston has gotten any better.
More and more refugees have joined our militia. The camp is growing. Colonel Porter is worried we're getting too big to be ignored by the aliens. Not sure how much longer all the regiments will be in one place like this.
The incoming refugees keep reporting sightings of harnessed children. Hal and I go out hunting for Ben almost every day. So far nothing. But we won't quit. We won't.

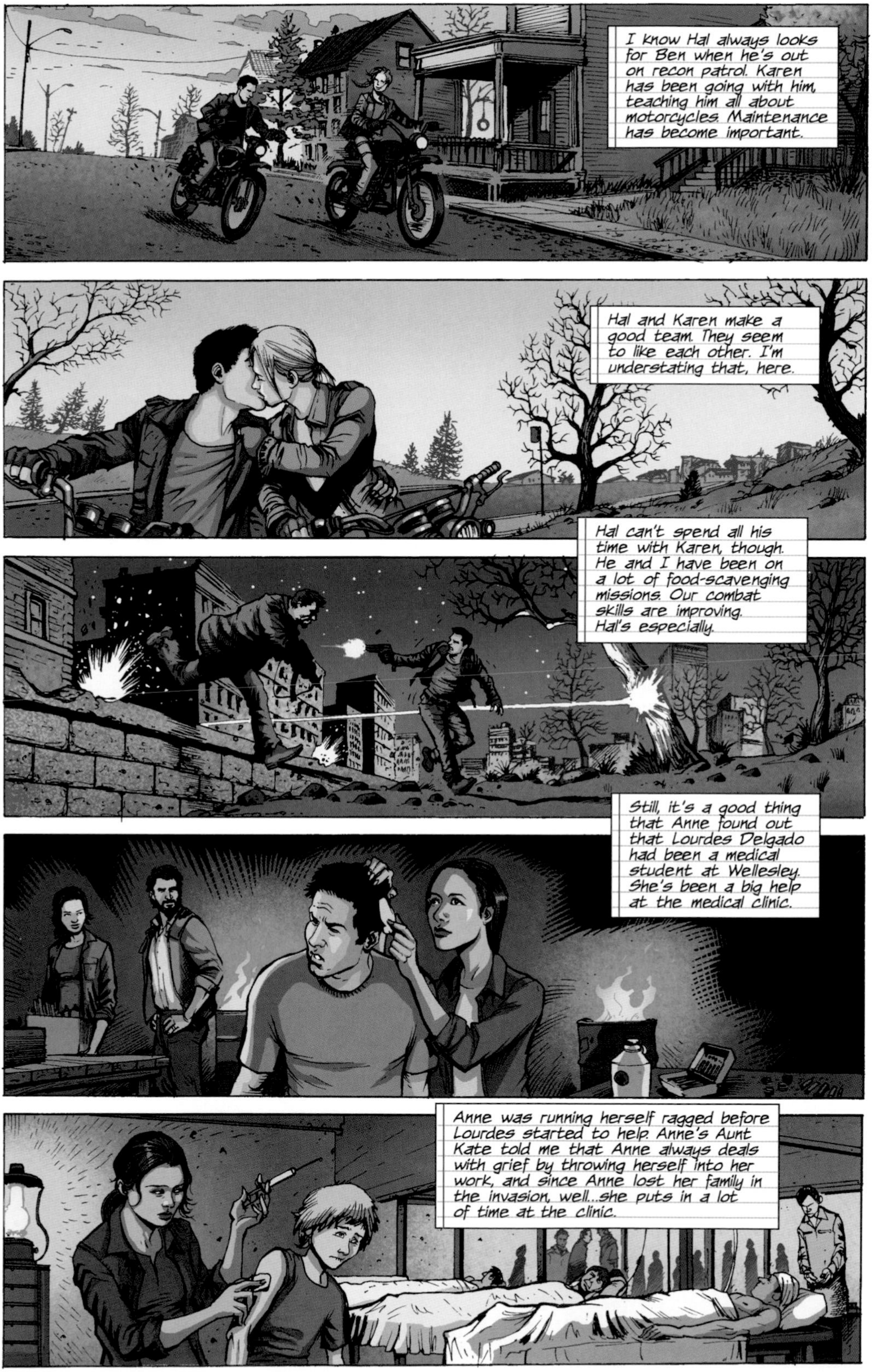
I know Hal always looks for Ben when he's out on recon patrol. Karen has been going with him, teaching him all about motorcycles. Maintenance has become important.
Hal and Karen make a good team. They seem to like each other. I'm understating that, here.
Hal can't spend all his time with Karen, though. He and I have been on a lot of food-scavenging missions. Our combat skills are improving. Hal's especially.
Still, it's a good thing that Anne found out that Lourdes Delgado had been a medical student at Wellesley. She's been a big help at the medical clinic.
Anne was running herself ragged before Lourdes started to help. Anne's Aunt Kate told me that Anne always deals with grief by throwing herself into her work, and since Anne lost her family in the invasion, well...she puts in a lot of time at the clinic.

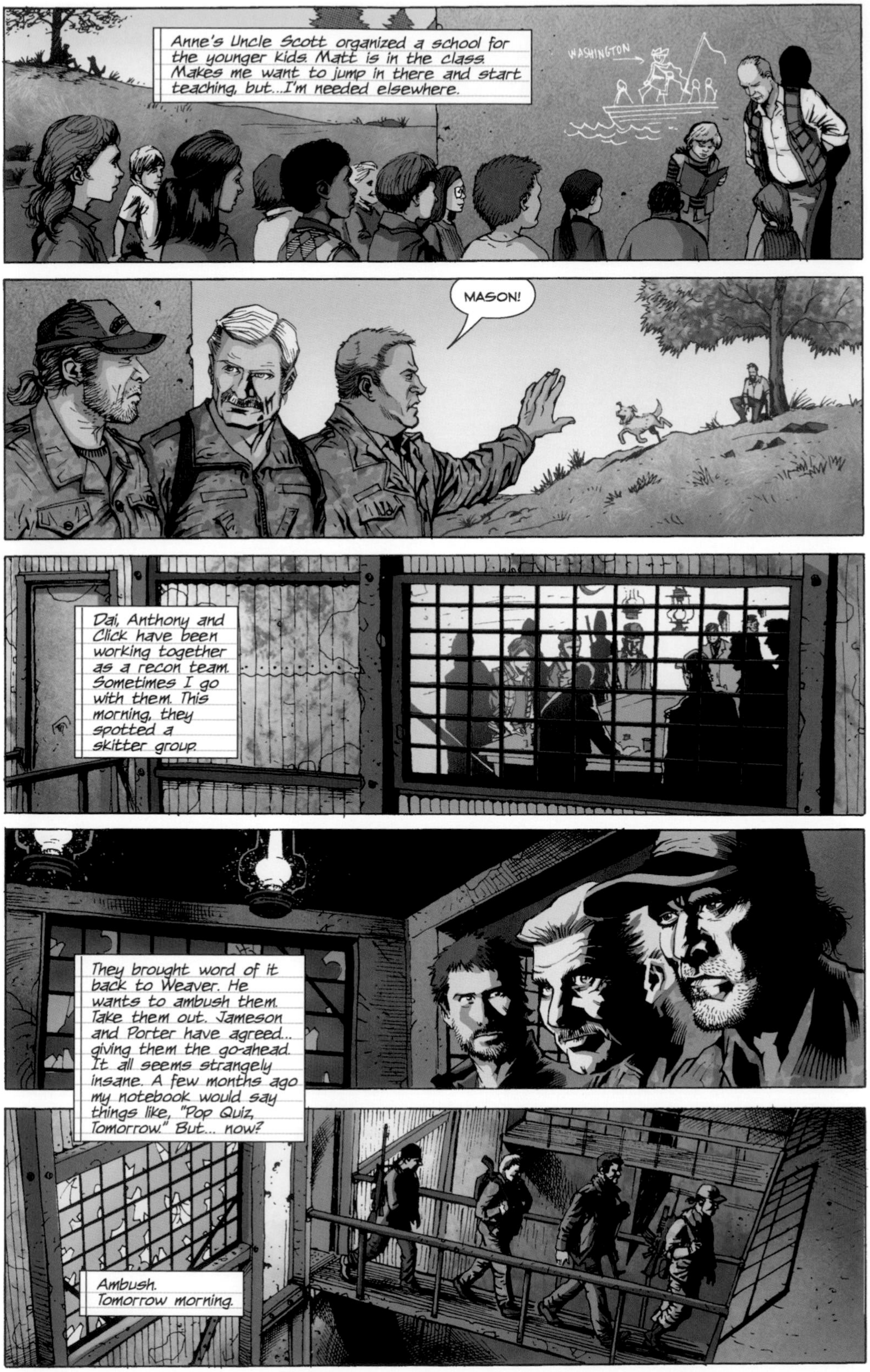
Anne's Uncle Scott organized a school for the younger kids. Matt is in the class. Makes me want to jump in there and start teaching, but...I'm needed elsewhere.
WASHINGTON
MASON!
Dai, Anthony and Click have been working together as a recon team. Sometimes I go with them. This morning, they spotted a skitter group.
They brought word of it back to Weaver. He wants to ambush them. Take them out. Jameson and Porter have agreed... giving them the go-ahead. It all seems strangely insane. A few months ago my notebook would say things like, "Pop Quiz, Tomorrow." But... now?
Ambush. Tomorrow morning.

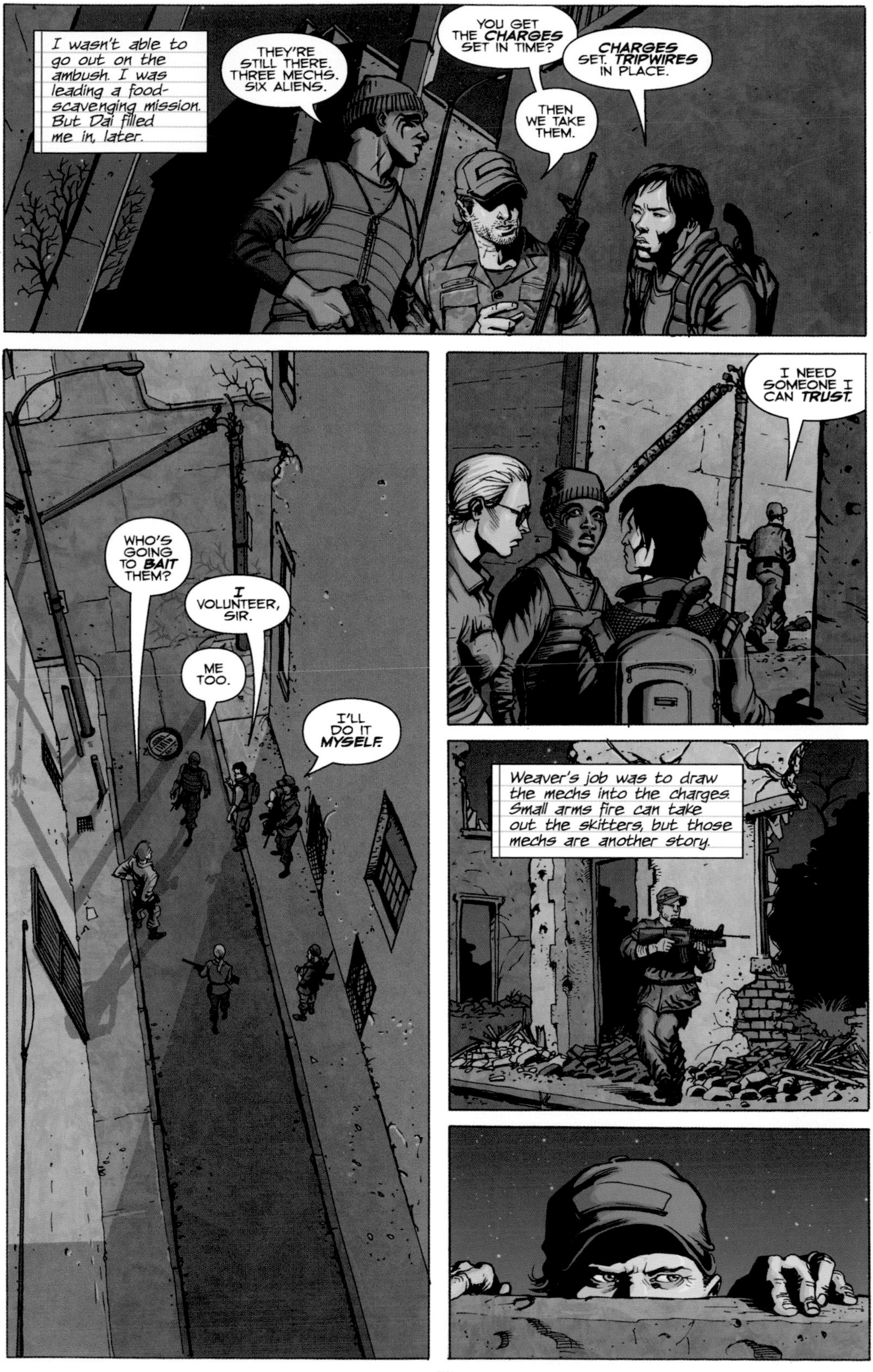
I wasn't able to go out on the ambush. I was leading a food-scavenging mission. But Dai filled me in, later.
THEY'RE STILL THERE. THREE MECHS. SIX ALIENS.
YOU GET THE CHARGES SET IN TIME?
CHARGES SET. TRIPWIRES IN PLACE.
THEN WE TAKE THEM.
WHO'S GOING TO BAIT THEM?
I VOLUNTEER, SIR.
ME TOO.
I'LL DO IT MYSELF.
I NEED SOMEONE I CAN TRUST.
Weaver's job was to draw the mechs into the charges. Small arms fire can take out the skitters, but those mechs are another story.

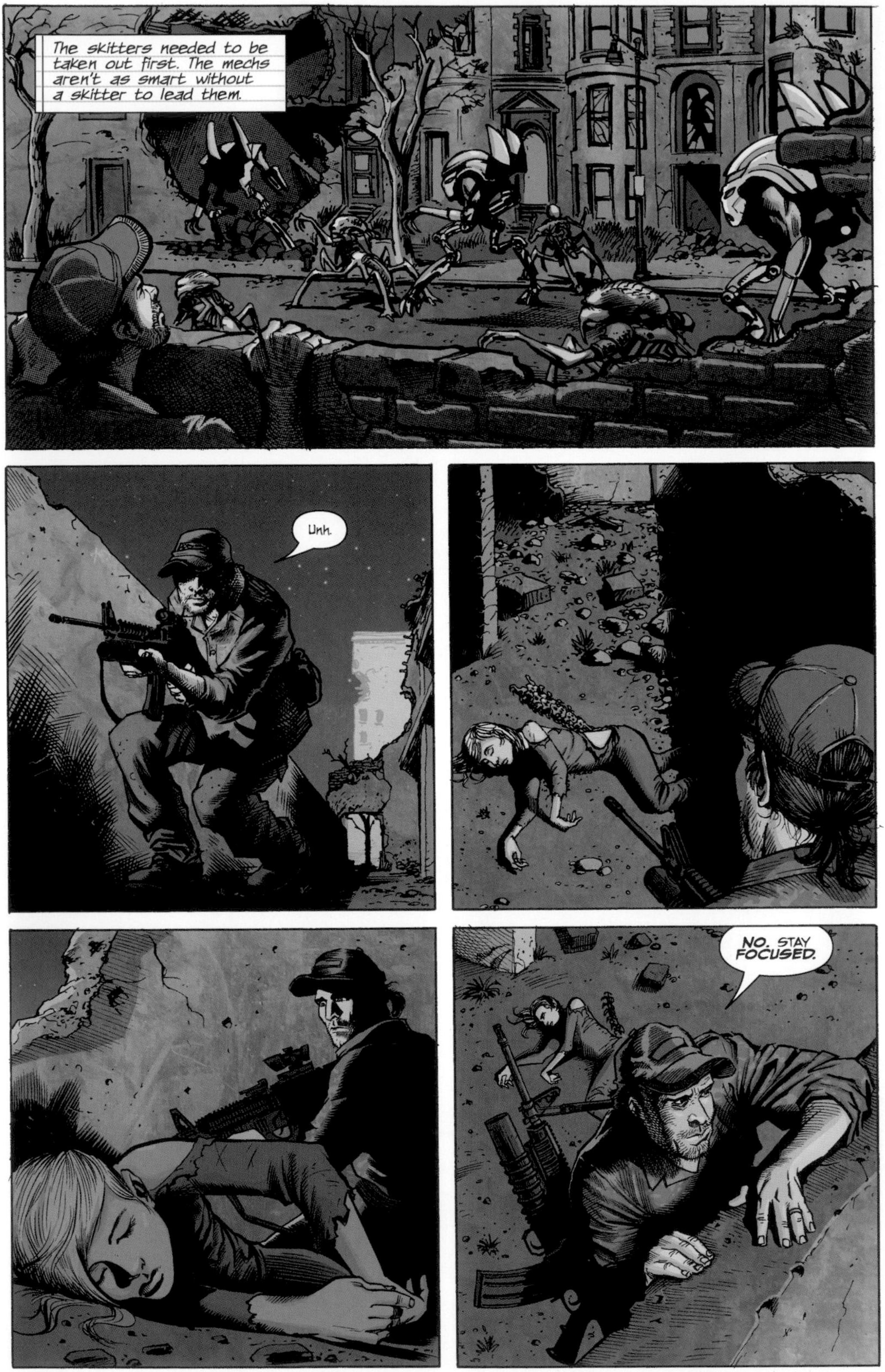
The skitters needed to be taken out first. The mechs aren't as smart without a skitter to lead them.
Unh.
NO. STAY FOCUSED.

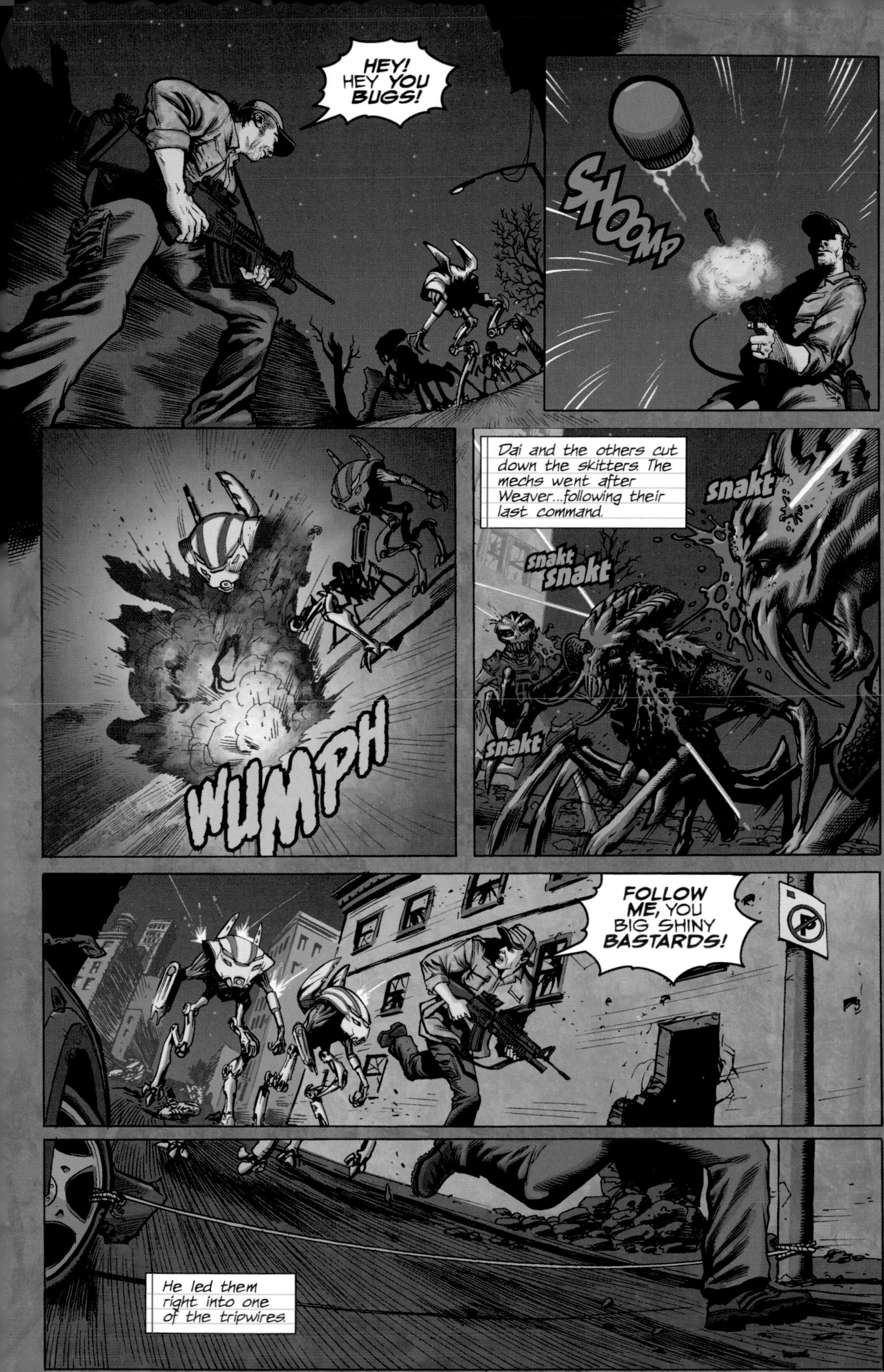
HEY! HEY YOU BUGS!
SHOOMP
WUMPH
Dai and the others cut down the skitters. The mechs went after Weaver...following their last command.
snakt
snakt snakt
snakt
FOLLOW ME, YOU BIG SHINY BASTARDS!
He led them right into one of the tripwires.

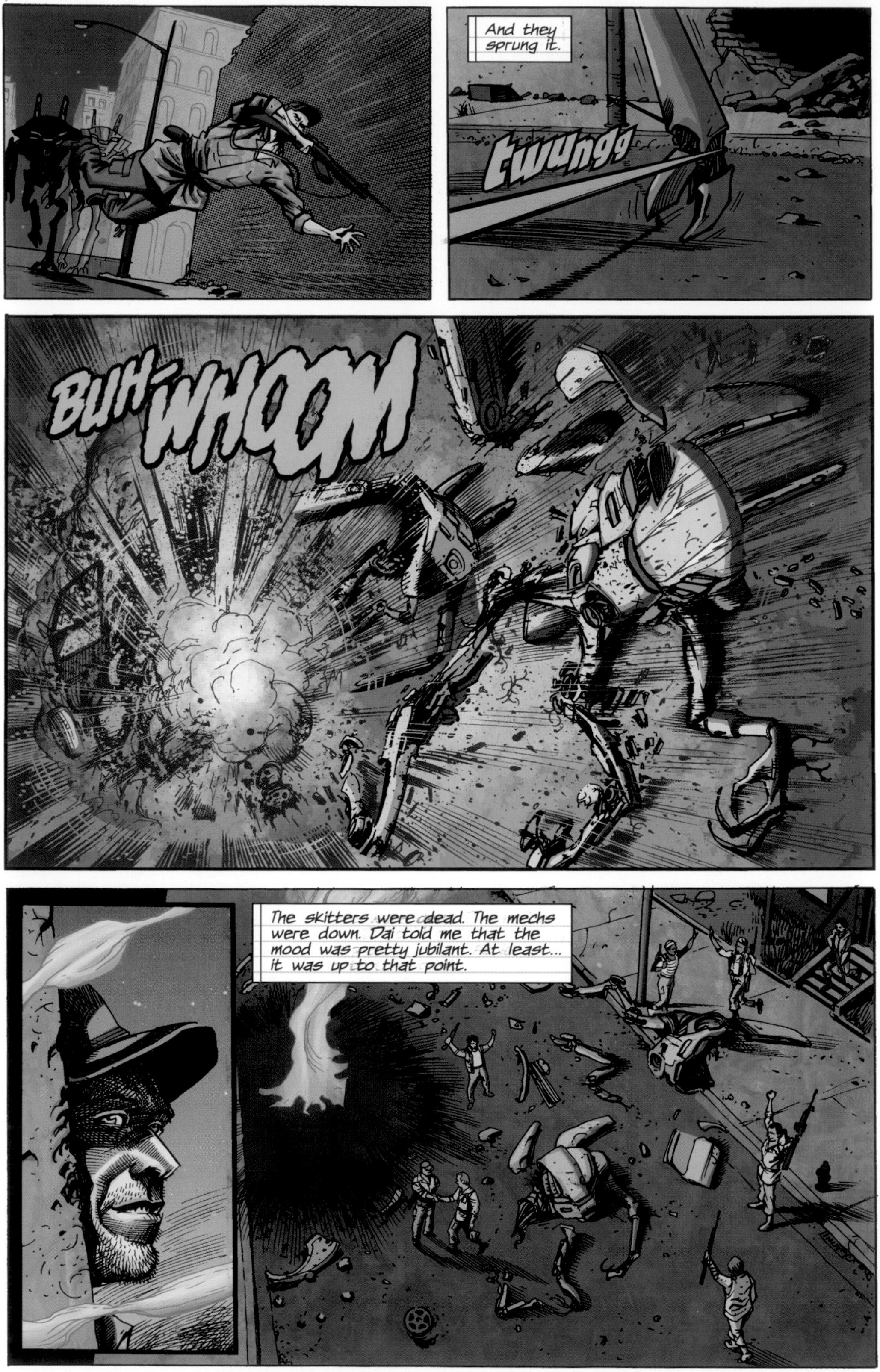

And they sprung it.
twungg
BUH-WHOOM
The skitters were dead. The mechs were down. Dai told me that the mood was pretty jubilant. At least... it was up to that point.

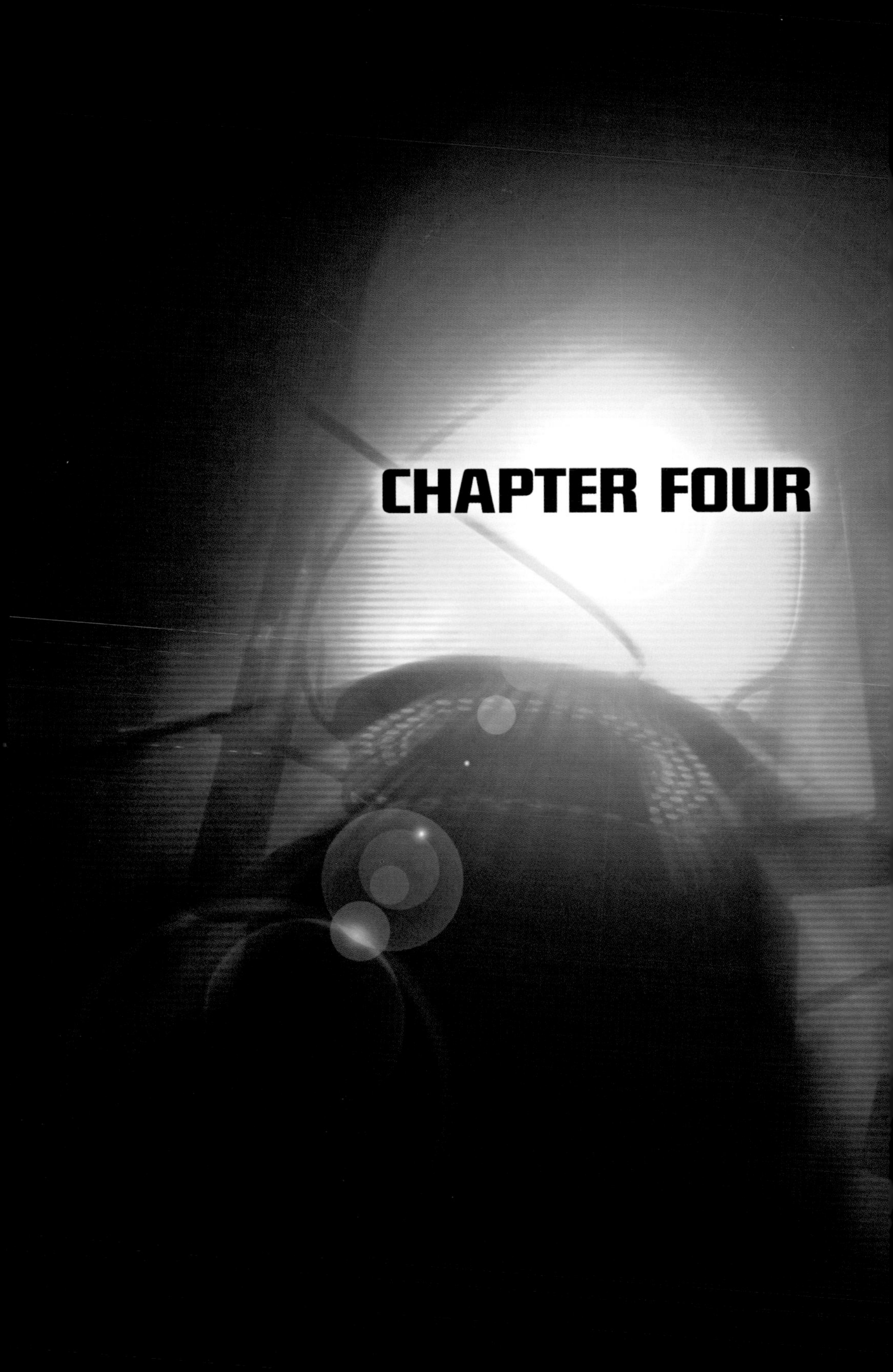

CHAPTER FOUR

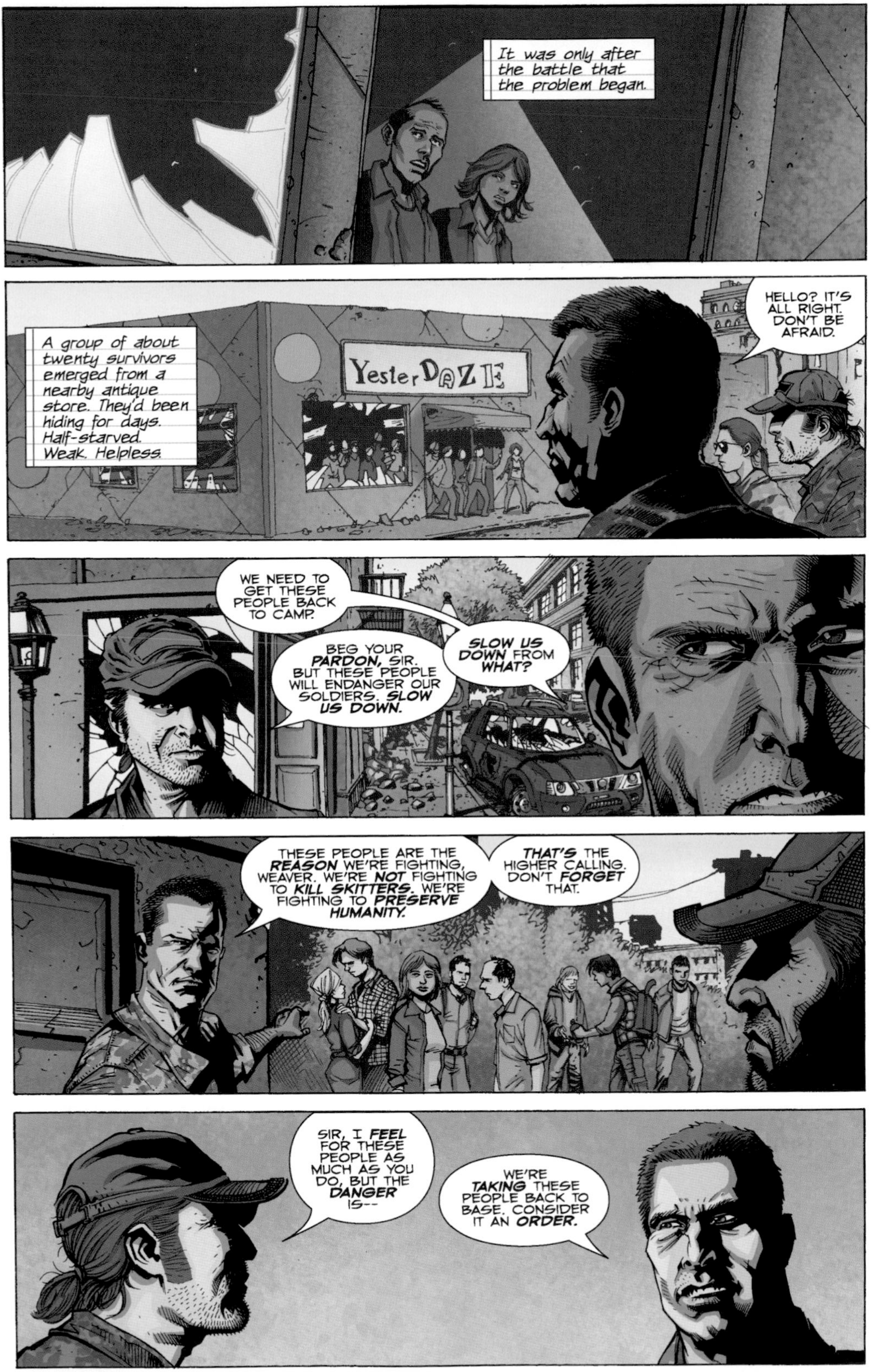
It was only after the battle that the problem began.
A group of about twenty survivors emerged from a nearby antique store. They'd been hiding for days. Half-starved. Weak. Helpless.
Yester DAZE
HELLO? IT'S ALL RIGHT. DON'T BE AFRAID.
WE NEED TO GET THESE PEOPLE BACK TO CAMP.
BEG YOUR PARDON, SIR. BUT THESE PEOPLE WILL ENDANGER OUR SOLDIERS. SLOW US DOWN.
SLOW US DOWN FROM WHAT?
THESE PEOPLE ARE THE REASON WE'RE FIGHTING, WEAVER. WE'RE NOT FIGHTING TO KILL SKITTERS. WE'RE FIGHTING TO PRESERVE HUMANITY.
THAT'S THE HIGHER CALLING. DON'T FORGET THAT.
SIR, I FEEL FOR THESE PEOPLE AS MUCH AS YOU DO, BUT THE DANGER IS--
WE'RE TAKING THESE PEOPLE BACK TO BASE. CONSIDER IT AN ORDER.

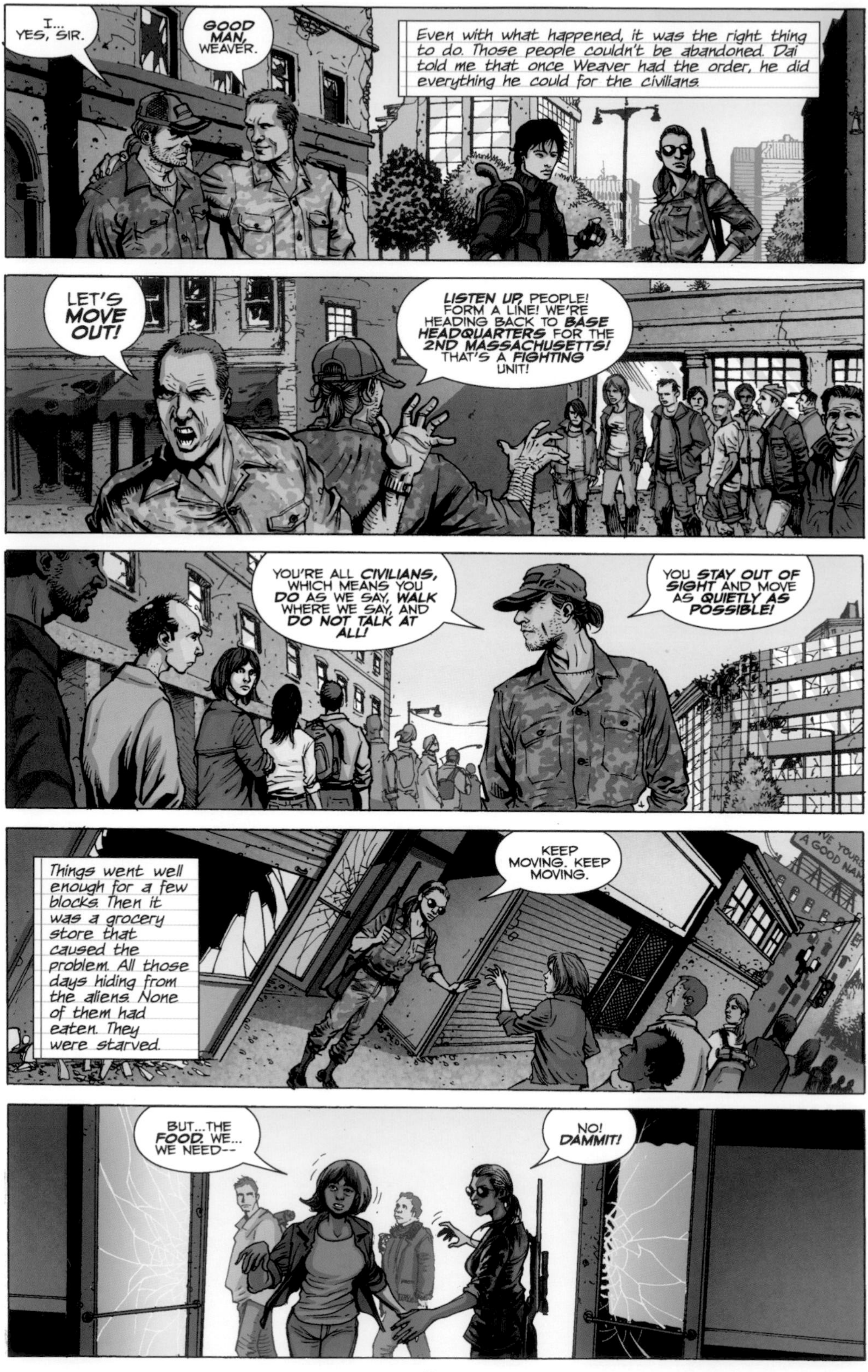

I... YES, SIR.
GOOD MAN, WEAVER.
Even with what happened, it was the right thing to do. Those people couldn't be abandoned. Dai told me that once Weaver had the order, he did everything he could for the civilians.
LET'S MOVE OUT!
LISTEN UP, PEOPLE! FORM A LINE! WE'RE HEADING BACK TO BASE HEADQUARTERS FOR THE 2ND MASSACHUSETTS! THAT'S A FIGHTING UNIT!
YOU'RE ALL CIVILIANS, WHICH MEANS YOU DO AS WE SAY, WALK WHERE WE SAY, AND DO NOT TALK AT ALL!
YOU STAY OUT OF SIGHT AND MOVE AS QUIETLY AS POSSIBLE!
Things went well enough for a few blocks. Then it was a grocery store that caused the problem. All those days hiding from the aliens. None of them had eaten. They were starved.
KEEP MOVING. KEEP MOVING.
BUT...THE FOOD. WE... WE NEED--
NO! DAMMIT!

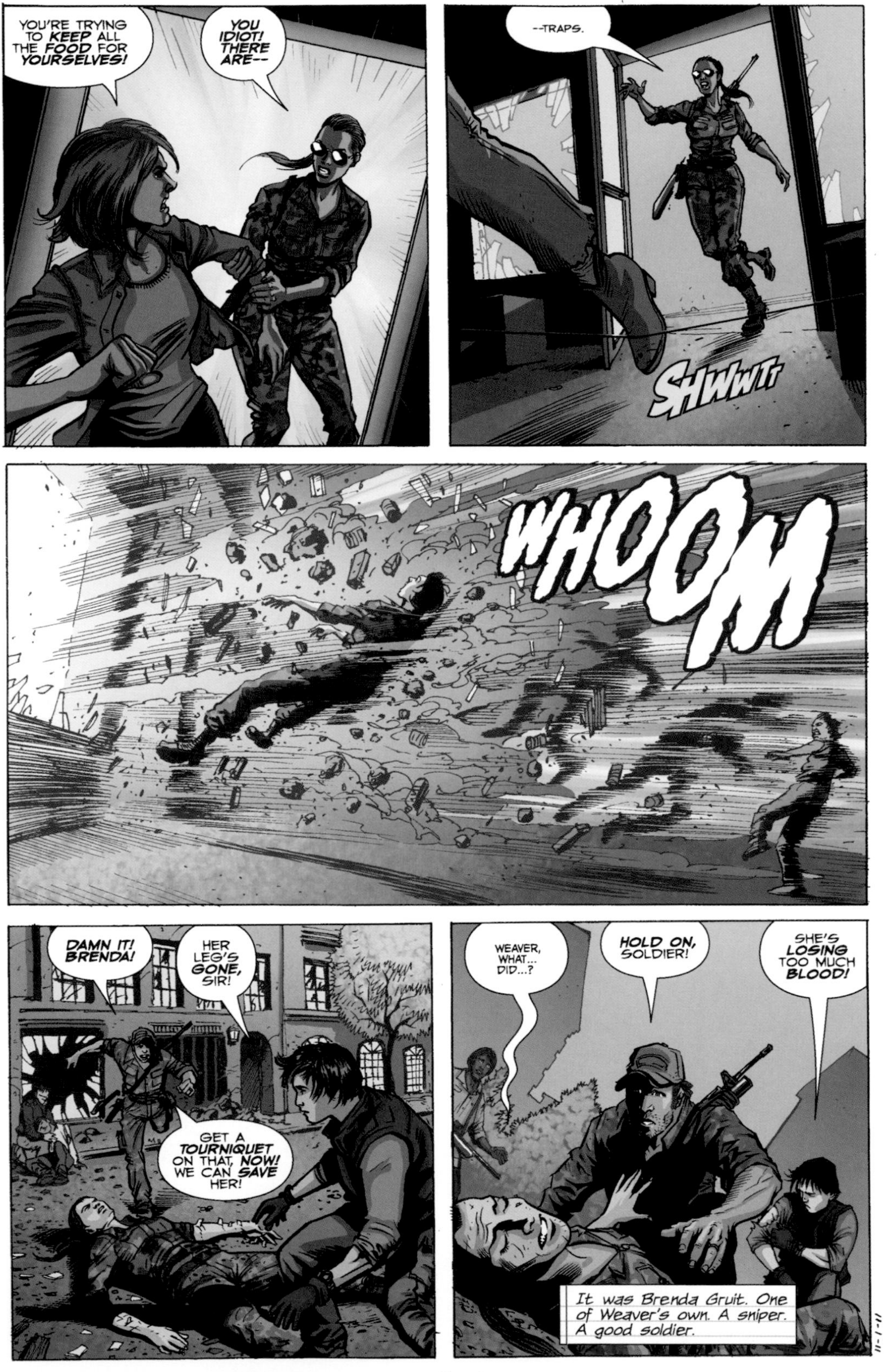
YOU'RE TRYING TO KEEP ALL THE FOOD FOR YOURSELVES!
YOU IDIOT! THERE ARE--
--TRAPS.
SHWWTT
WHOOM
DAMN IT! BRENDA!
HER LEG'S GONE, SIR!
GET A TOURNIQUET ON THAT, NOW! WE CAN SAVE HER!
WEAVER, WHAT... DID...?
HOLD ON, SOLDIER!
SHE'S LOSING TOO MUCH BLOOD!
It was Brenda Gruit. One of Weaver's own. A sniper. A good soldier.

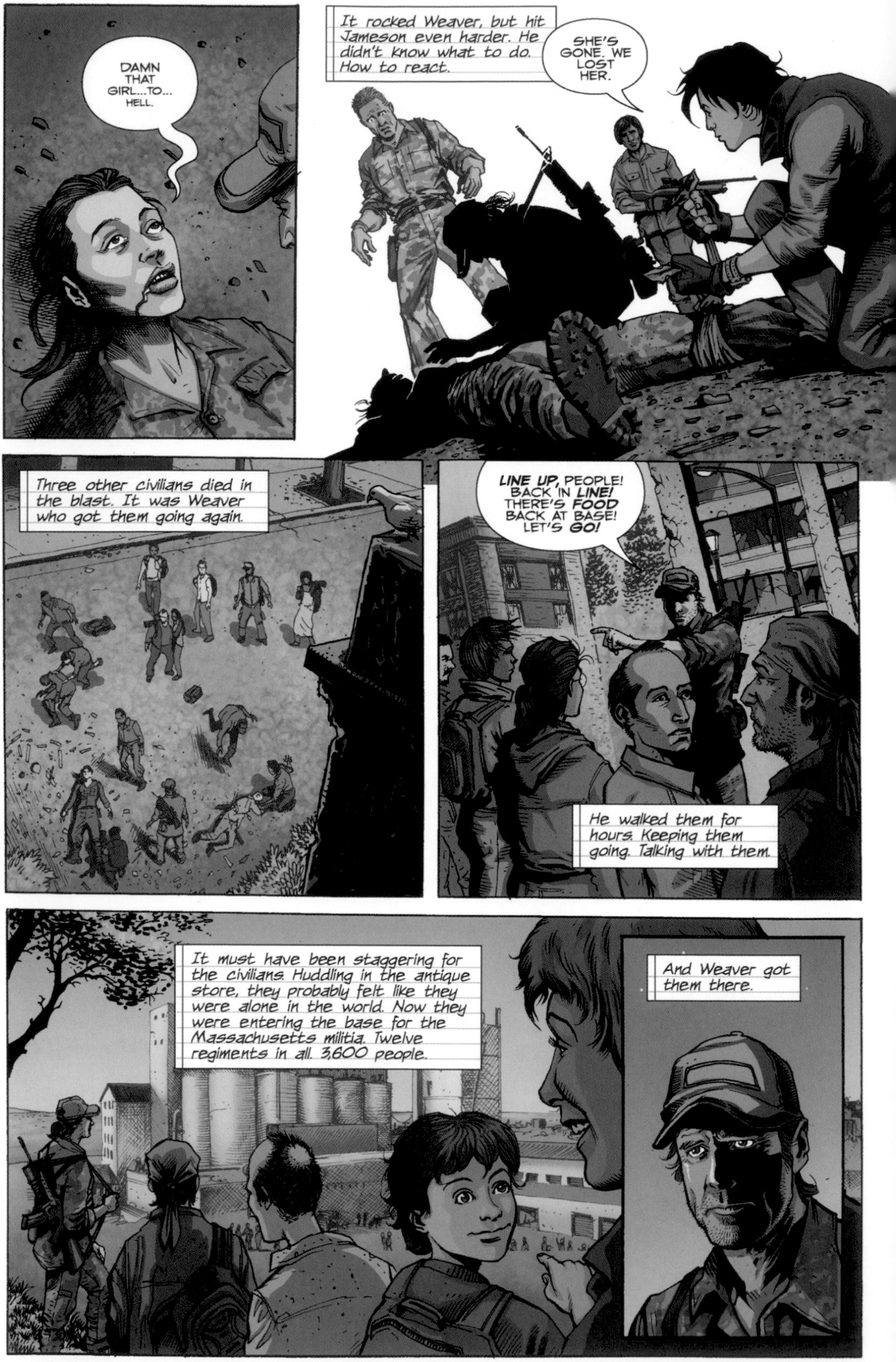
DAMN THAT GIRL...TO... HELL.
It rocked Weaver, but hit Jameson even harder. He didn't know what to do. How to react.
SHE'S GONE. WE LOST HER.
Three other civilians died in the blast. It was Weaver who got them going again.
LINE UP, PEOPLE! BACK IN LINE! THERE'S FOOD BACK AT BASE! LET'S GO!
He walked them for hours. Keeping them going. Talking with them.
It must have been staggering for the civilians. Huddling in the antique store, they probably felt like they were alone in the world. Now they were entering the base for the Massachusetts militia. Twelve regiments in all. 3,600 people.
And Weaver got them there.

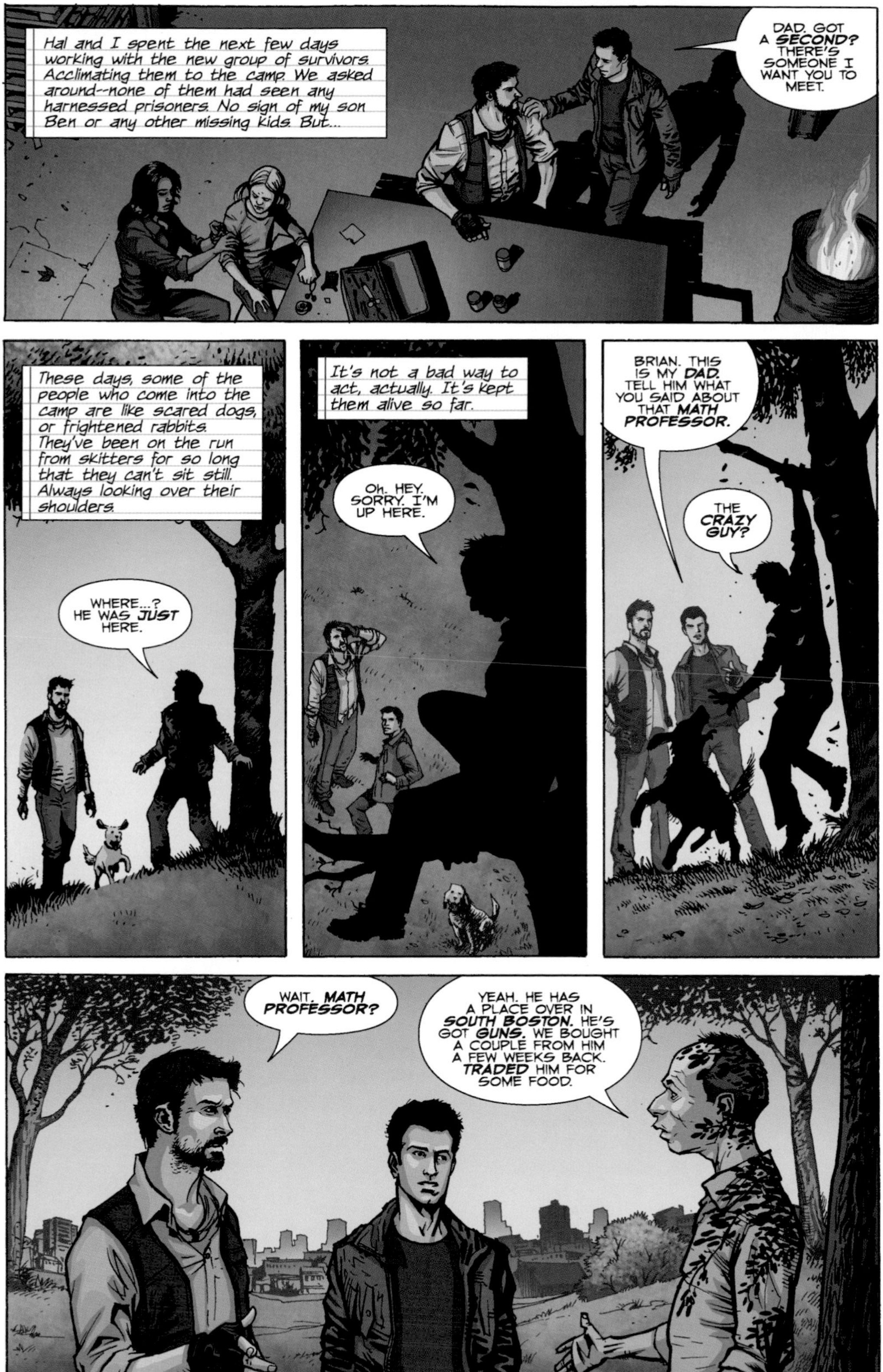

Hal and I spent the next few days working with the new group of survivors. Acclimating them to the camp. We asked around--none of them had seen any harnessed prisoners. No sign of my son Ben or any other missing kids. But...
DAD. GOT A SECOND? THERE'S SOMEONE I WANT YOU TO MEET.
These days, some of the people who come into the camp are like scared dogs, or frightened rabbits. They've been on the run from skitters for so long that they can't sit still. Always looking over their shoulders.
WHERE...? HE WAS JUST HERE.
It's not a bad way to act, actually. It's kept them alive so far.
Oh. HEY. SORRY. I'M UP HERE.
BRIAN. THIS IS MY DAD. TELL HIM WHAT YOU SAID ABOUT THAT MATH PROFESSOR.
THE CRAZY GUY?
WAIT. MATH PROFESSOR?
YEAH. HE HAS A PLACE OVER IN SOUTH BOSTON. HE'S GOT GUNS. WE BOUGHT A COUPLE FROM HIM A FEW WEEKS BACK. TRADED HIM FOR SOME FOOD.

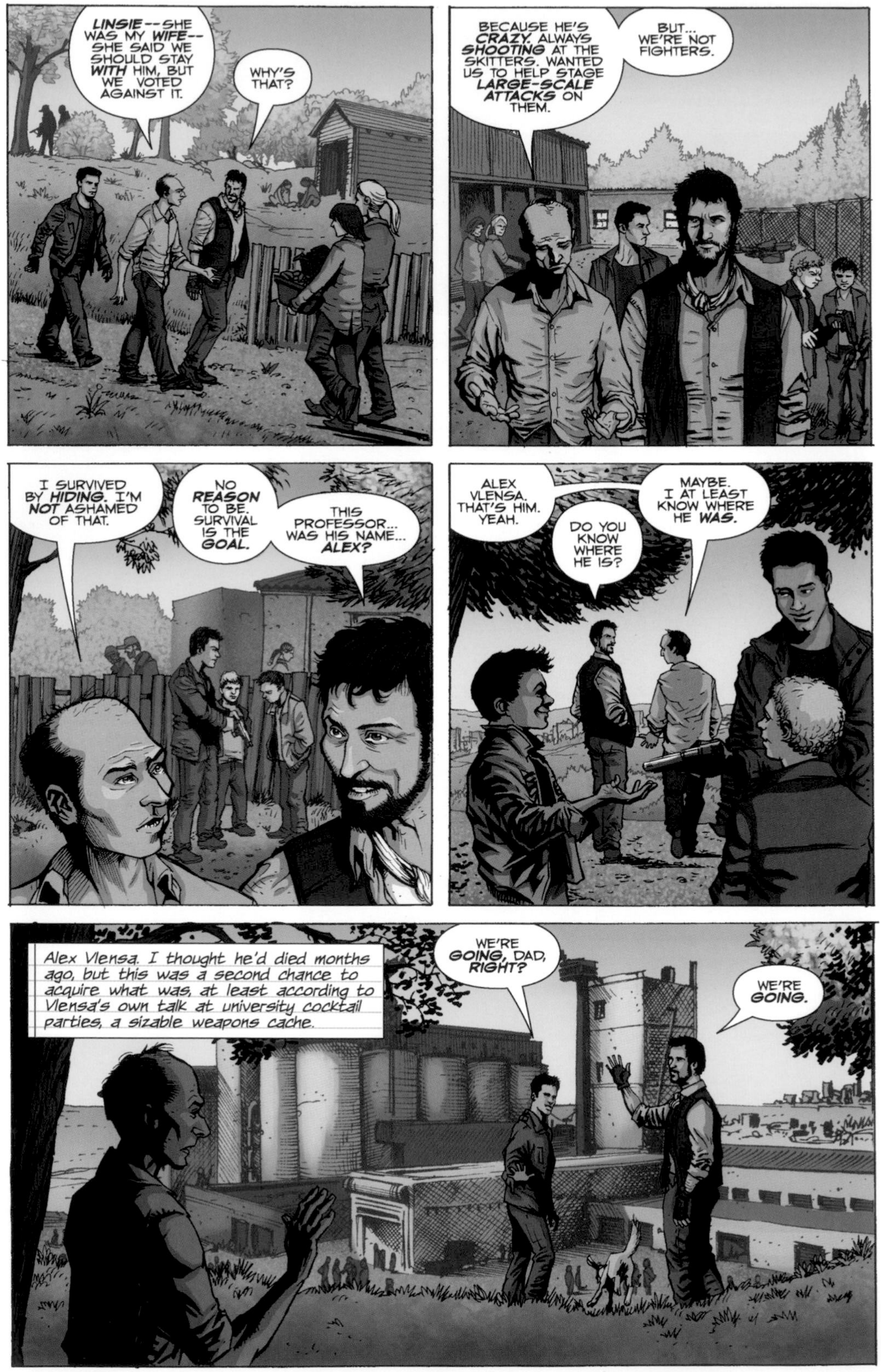
LINSIE--SHE WAS MY WIFE--SHE SAID WE SHOULD STAY WITH HIM, BUT WE VOTED AGAINST IT.
WHY'S THAT?
BECAUSE HE'S CRAZY. ALWAYS SHOOTING AT THE SKITTERS. WANTED US TO HELP STAGE LARGE-SCALE ATTACKS ON THEM.
BUT... WE'RE NOT FIGHTERS.
I SURVIVED BY HIDING. I'M NOT ASHAMED OF THAT.
NO REASON TO BE. SURVIVAL IS THE GOAL.
THIS PROFESSOR... WAS HIS NAME... ALEX?
ALEX VLENSA. THAT'S HIM. YEAH.
DO YOU KNOW WHERE HE IS?
MAYBE. I AT LEAST KNOW WHERE HE WAS.
Alex Vlensa. I thought he'd died months ago, but this was a second chance to acquire what was, at least according to Vlensa's own talk at university cocktail parties, a sizable weapons cache.
WE'RE GOING, DAD, RIGHT?
WE'RE GOING.

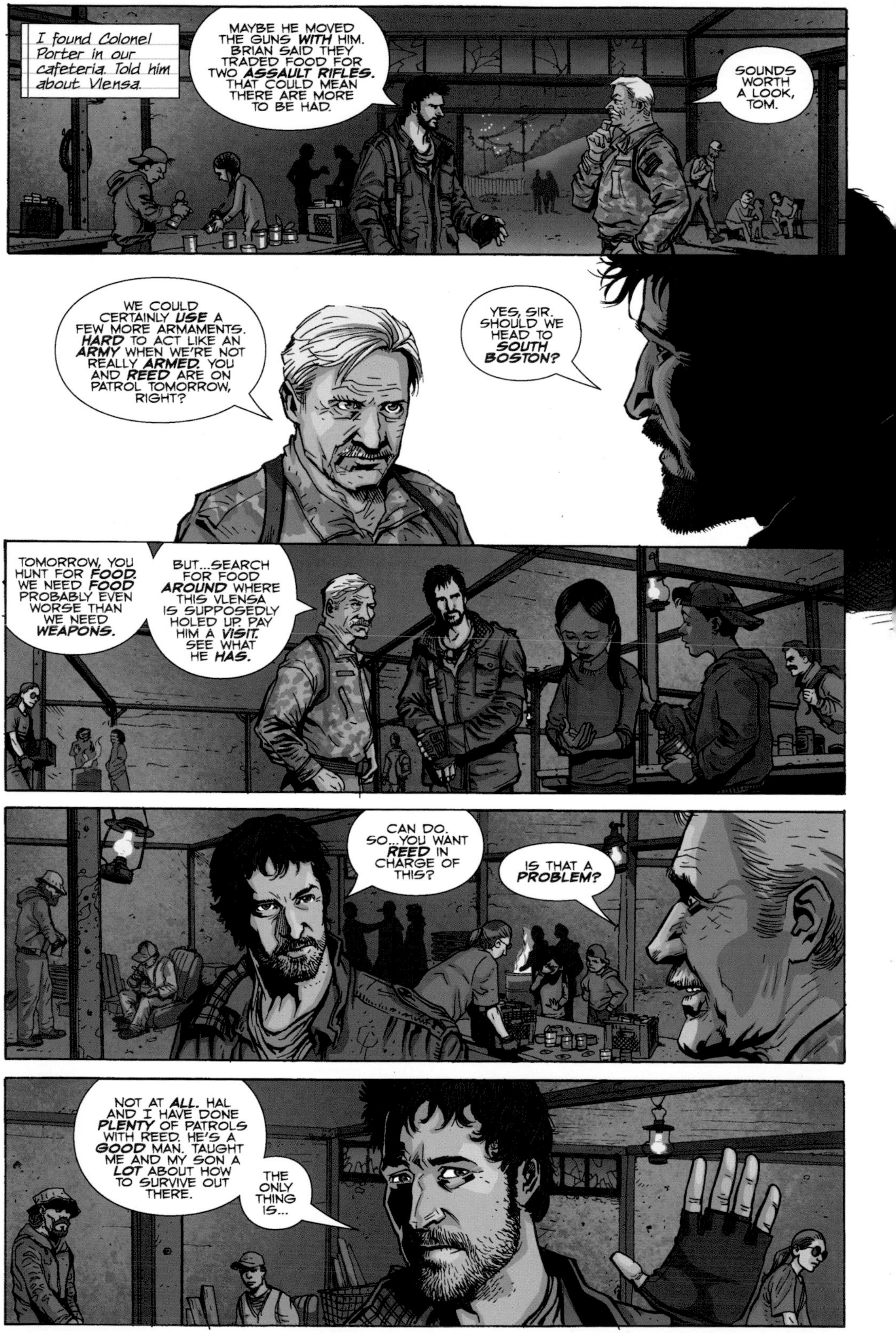
I found Colonel Porter in our cafeteria. Told him about Vlensa.
MAYBE HE MOVED THE GUNS WITH HIM. BRIAN SAID THEY TRADED FOOD FOR TWO ASSAULT RIFLES. THAT COULD MEAN THERE ARE MORE TO BE HAD.
SOUNDS WORTH A LOOK, TOM.
WE COULD CERTAINLY USE A FEW MORE ARMAMENTS. HARD TO ACT LIKE AN ARMY WHEN WE'RE NOT REALLY ARMED. YOU AND REED ARE ON PATROL TOMORROW, RIGHT?
YES, SIR. SHOULD WE HEAD TO SOUTH BOSTON?
TOMORROW, YOU HUNT FOR FOOD. WE NEED FOOD PROBABLY EVEN WORSE THAN WE NEED WEAPONS.
BUT...SEARCH FOR FOOD AROUND WHERE THIS VLENSA IS SUPPOSEDLY HOLED UP. PAY HIM A VISIT. SEE WHAT HE HAS.
CAN DO. SO...YOU WANT REED IN CHARGE OF THIS?
IS THAT A PROBLEM?
NOT AT ALL. HAL AND I HAVE DONE PLENTY OF PATROLS WITH REED. HE'S A GOOD MAN. TAUGHT ME AND MY SON A LOT ABOUT HOW TO SURVIVE OUT THERE.
THE ONLY THING IS...

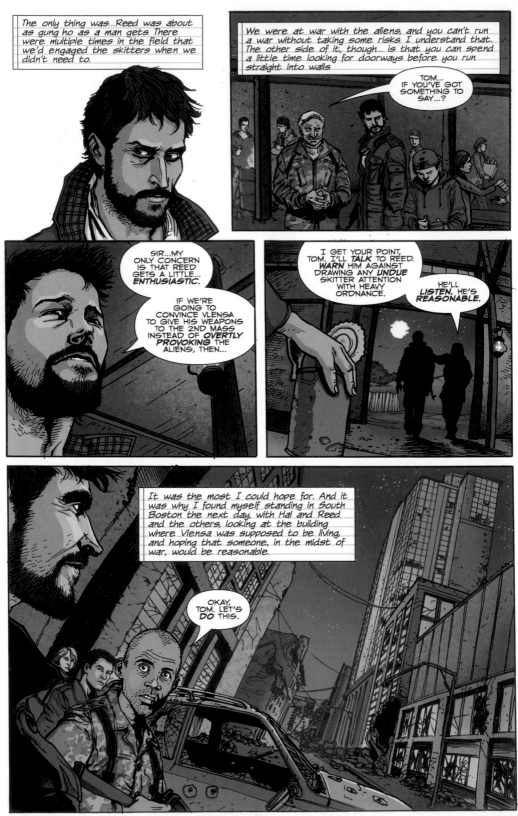

The only thing was...Reed was about as gung ho as a man gets. There were multiple times in the field that we'd engaged the skitters when we didn't need to.

We were at war with the aliens, and you can't run a war without taking some risks. I understand that. The other side of it, though... is that you can spend a little time looking for doorways before you run straight into walls.

TOM... IF YOU'VE GOT SOMETHING TO SAY...?

SIR...MY ONLY CONCERN IS THAT REED GETS A LITTLE... ENTHUSIASTIC.

IF WE'RE GOING TO CONVINCE VLENSA TO GIVE HIS WEAPONS TO THE 2ND MASS INSTEAD OF OVERTLY PROVOKING THE ALIENS, THEN...

I GET YOUR POINT, TOM. I'LL TALK TO REED. WARN HIM AGAINST DRAWING ANY UNDUE SKITTER ATTENTION WITH HEAVY ORDNANCE.

HE'LL LISTEN. HE'S REASONABLE.

It was the most I could hope for. And it was why I found myself standing in South Boston the next day, with Hal and Reed and the others, looking at the building where Vlensa was supposed to be living, and hoping that someone, in the midst of war, would be reasonable.

OKAY, TOM. LET'S DO THIS.

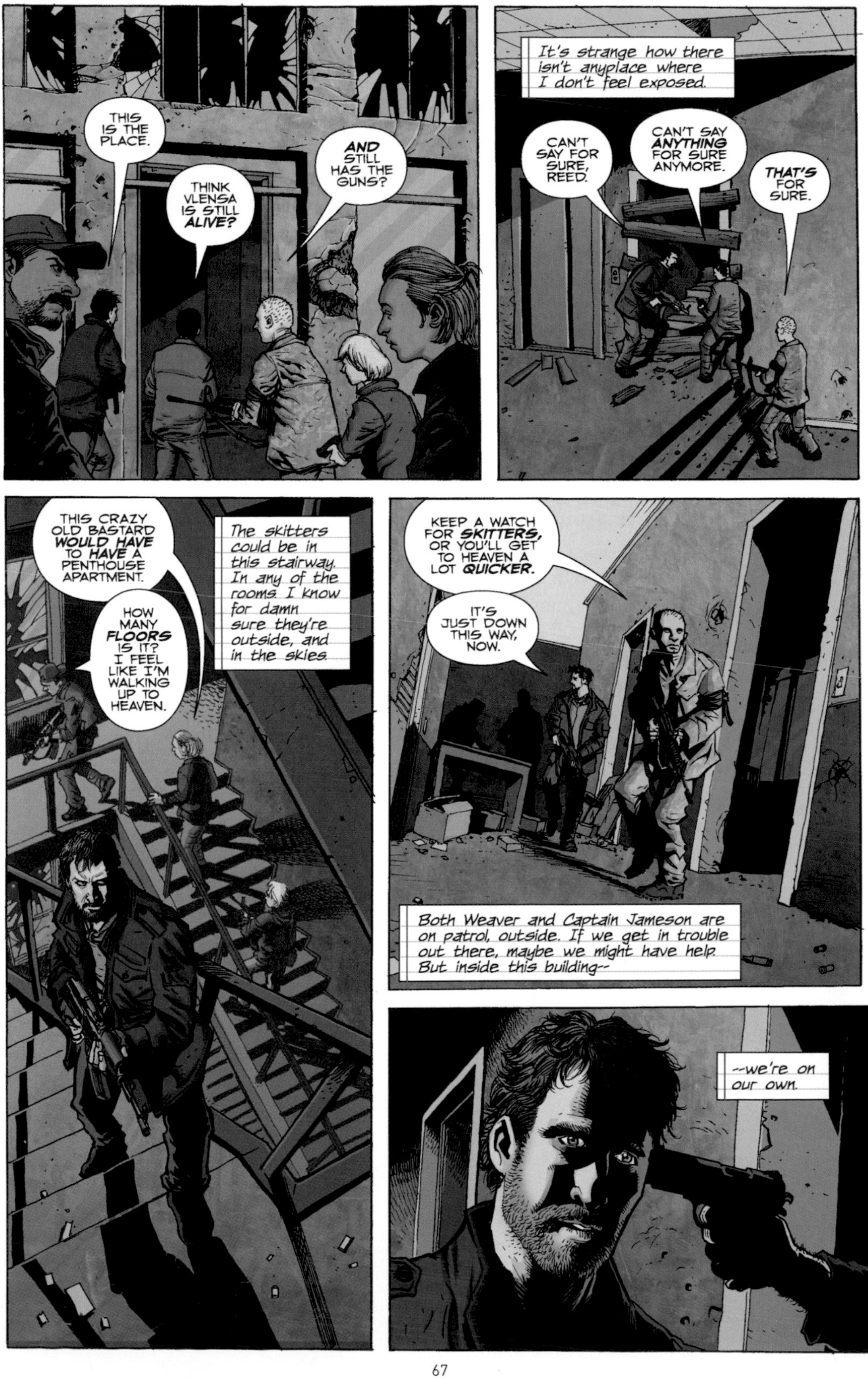
THIS IS THE PLACE.
THINK VLENSA IS STILL ALIVE?
AND STILL HAS THE GUNS?
It's strange how there isn't anyplace where I don't feel exposed.
CAN'T SAY FOR SURE, REED.
CAN'T SAY ANYTHING FOR SURE ANYMORE.
THAT'S FOR SURE.
THIS CRAZY OLD BASTARD WOULD HAVE TO HAVE A PENTHOUSE APARTMENT.
HOW MANY FLOORS IS IT? I FEEL LIKE I'M WALKING UP TO HEAVEN.
The skitters could be in this stairway. In any of the rooms. I know for damn sure they're outside, and in the skies.
KEEP A WATCH FOR SKITTERS, OR YOU'LL GET TO HEAVEN A LOT QUICKER.
IT'S JUST DOWN THIS WAY, NOW.
Both Weaver and Captain Jameson are on patrol, outside. If we get in trouble out there, maybe we might have help. But inside this building--
--we're on our own.

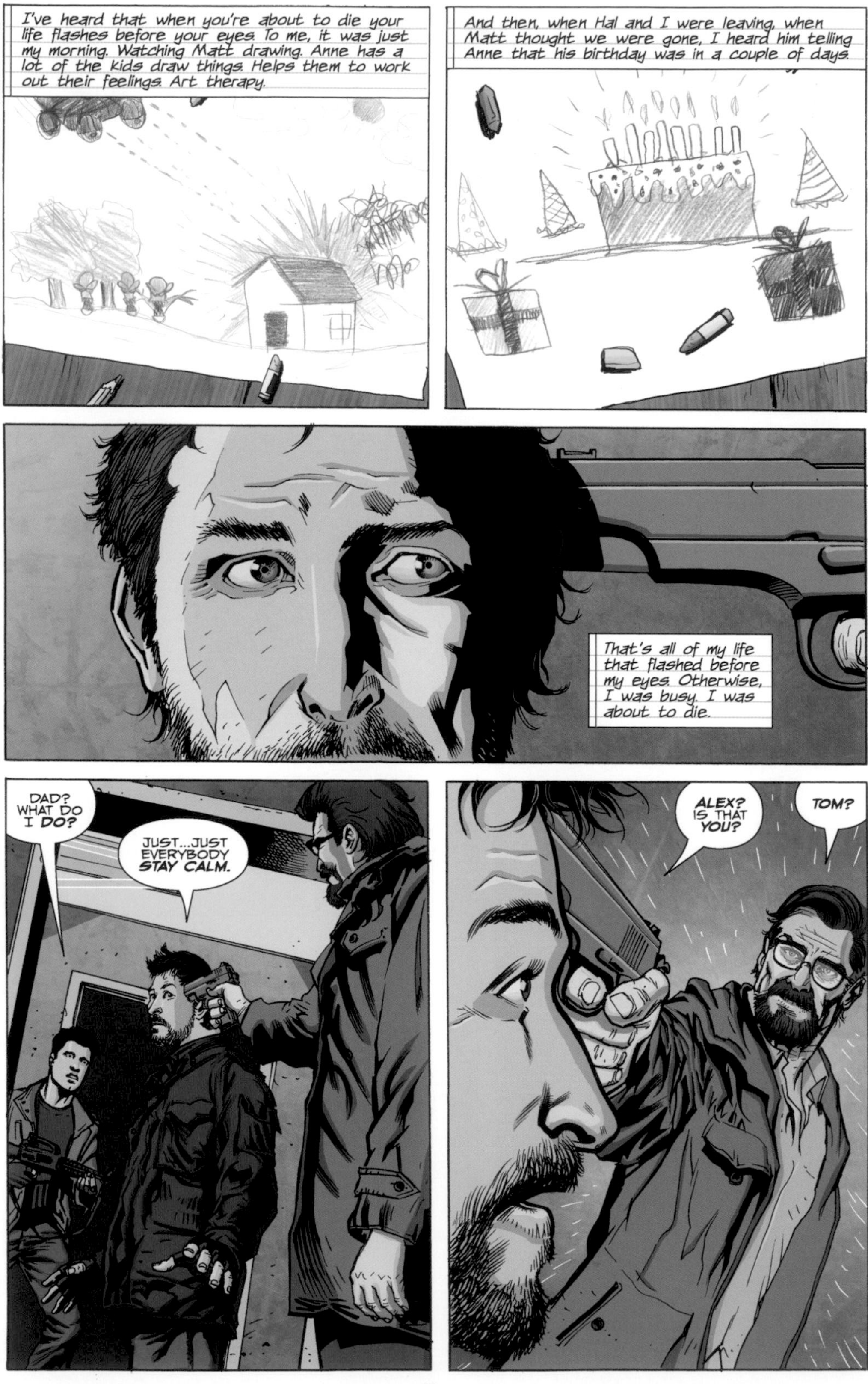
I've heard that when you're about to die your life flashes before your eyes. To me, it was just my morning. Watching Matt drawing. Anne has a lot of the kids draw things. Helps them to work out their feelings. Art therapy.
And then, when Hal and I were leaving, when Matt thought we were gone, I heard him telling Anne that his birthday was in a couple of days.
That's all of my life that flashed before my eyes. Otherwise, I was busy. I was about to die.
DAD? WHAT DO I DO?
JUST...JUST EVERYBODY STAY CALM.
ALEX? IS THAT YOU?
TOM?

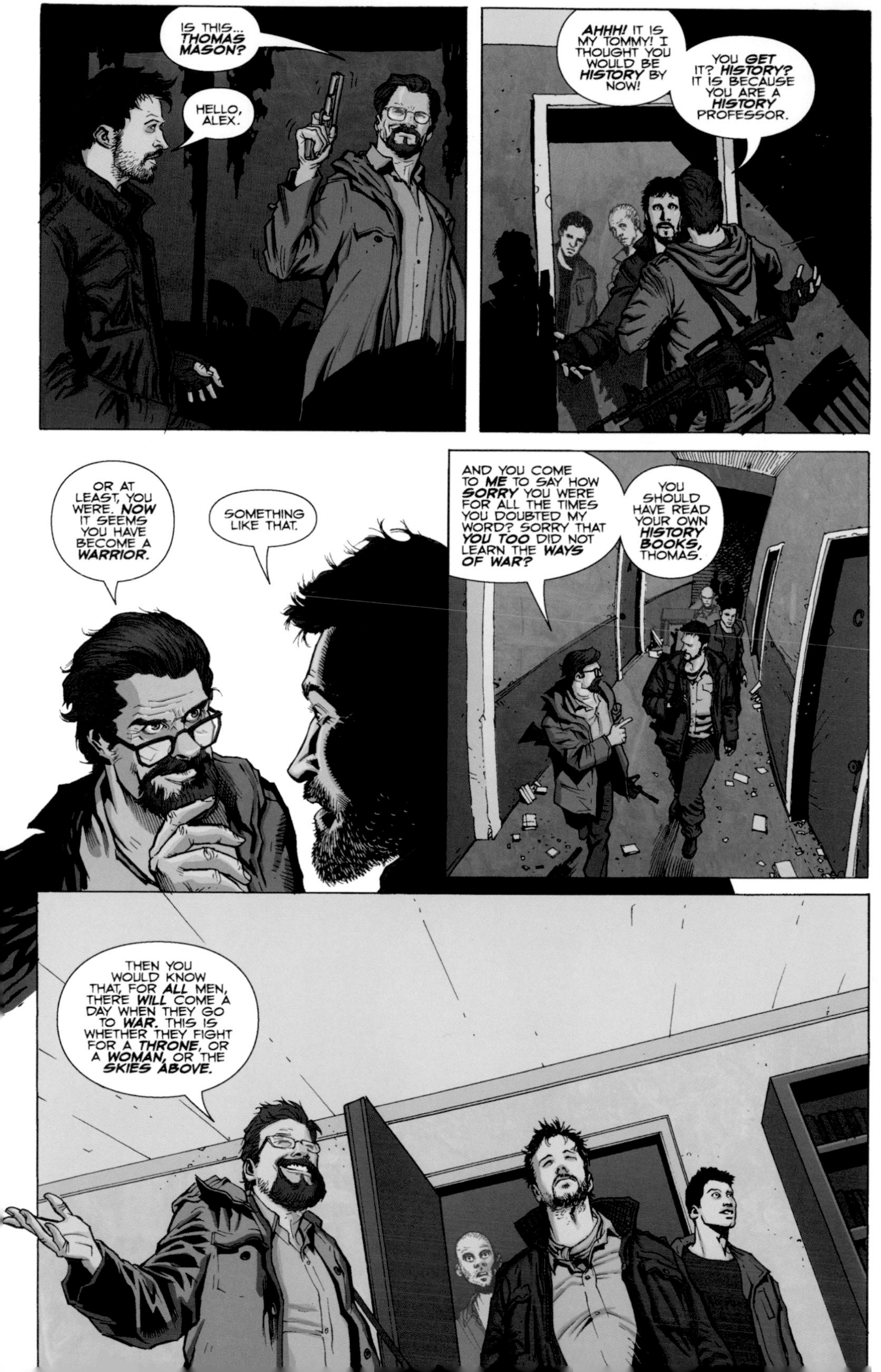

IS THIS... THOMAS MASON?
HELLO, ALEX.
AHHH! IT IS MY TOMMY! I THOUGHT YOU WOULD BE HISTORY BY NOW!
YOU GET IT? HISTORY? IT IS BECAUSE YOU ARE A HISTORY PROFESSOR.
OR AT LEAST, YOU WERE. NOW IT SEEMS YOU HAVE BECOME A WARRIOR.
SOMETHING LIKE THAT.
AND YOU COME TO ME TO SAY HOW SORRY YOU WERE FOR ALL THE TIMES YOU DOUBTED MY WORD? SORRY THAT YOU TOO DID NOT LEARN THE WAYS OF WAR?
YOU SHOULD HAVE READ YOUR OWN HISTORY BOOKS, THOMAS.
THEN YOU WOULD KNOW THAT, FOR ALL MEN, THERE WILL COME A DAY WHEN THEY GO TO WAR. THIS IS WHETHER THEY FIGHT FOR A THRONE, OR A WOMAN, OR THE SKIES ABOVE.

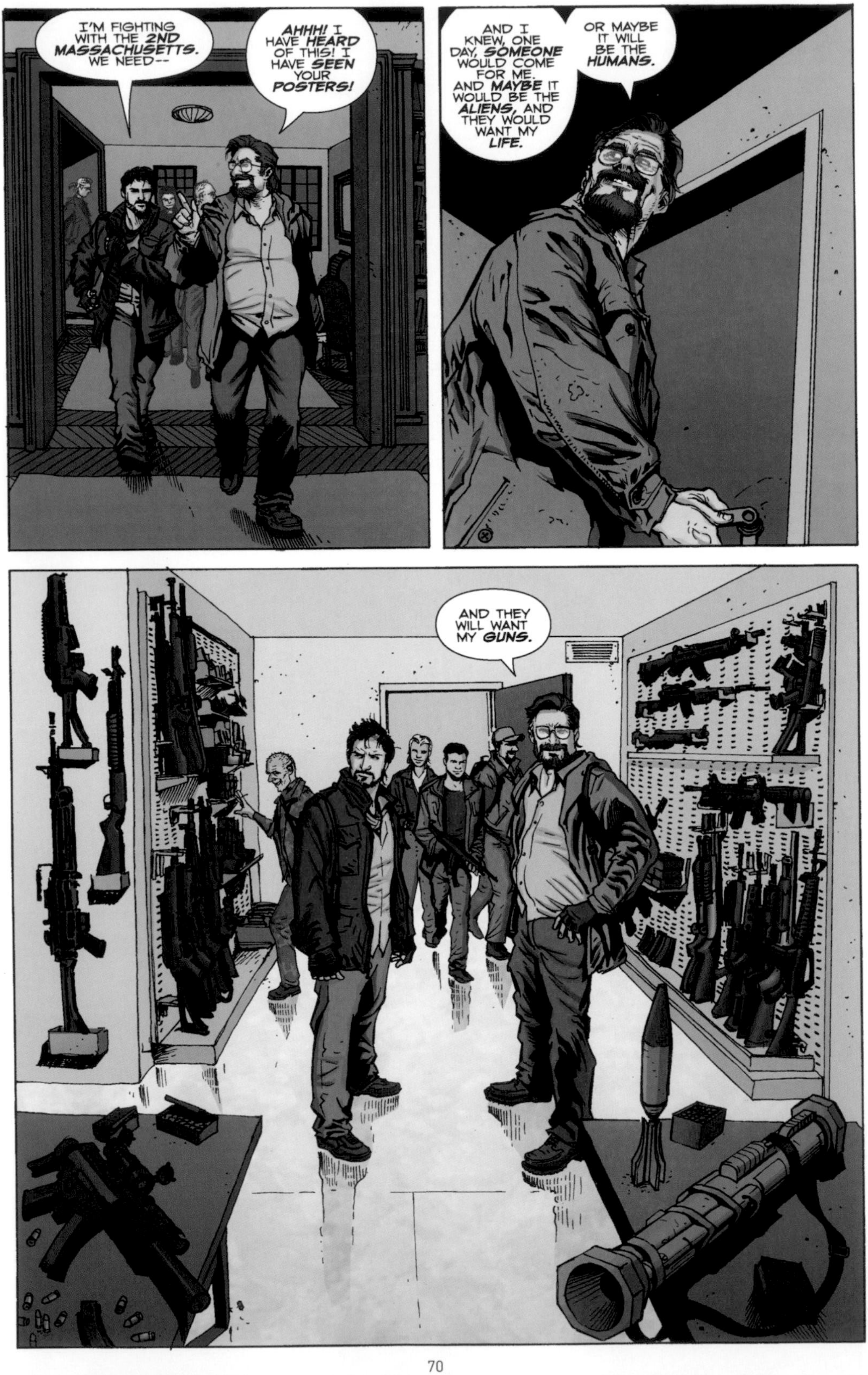

I'M FIGHTING WITH THE 2ND MASSACHUSETTS. WE NEED--
AHHH! I HAVE HEARD OF THIS! I HAVE SEEN YOUR POSTERS!
AND I KNEW, ONE DAY, SOMEONE WOULD COME FOR ME. AND MAYBE IT WOULD BE THE ALIENS, AND THEY WOULD WANT MY LIFE.
OR MAYBE IT WILL BE THE HUMANS.
AND THEY WILL WANT MY GUNS.

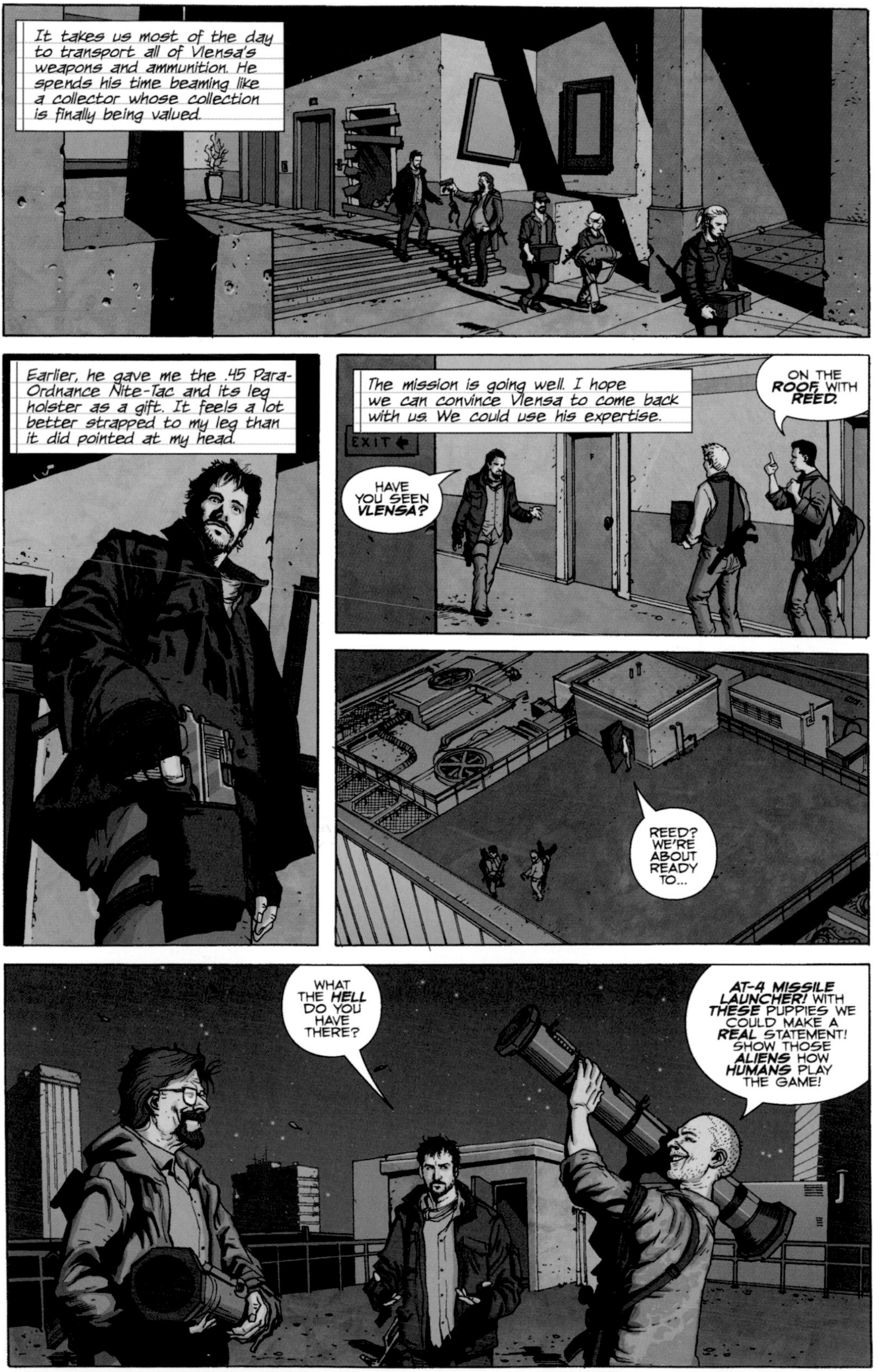

It takes us most of the day to transport all of Vlensa's weapons and ammunition. He spends his time beaming like a collector whose collection is finally being valued.
Earlier, he gave me the .45 Para-Ordnance Nite-Tac and its leg holster as a gift. It feels a lot better strapped to my leg than it did pointed at my head.
The mission is going well. I hope we can convince Vlensa to come back with us. We could use his expertise.
EXIT
HAVE YOU SEEN VLENSA?
ON THE ROOF, WITH REED.
REED? WE'RE ABOUT READY TO...
WHAT THE HELL DO YOU HAVE THERE?
AT-4 MISSILE LAUNCHER! WITH THESE PUPPIES WE COULD MAKE A REAL STATEMENT! SHOW THOSE ALIENS HOW HUMANS PLAY THE GAME!

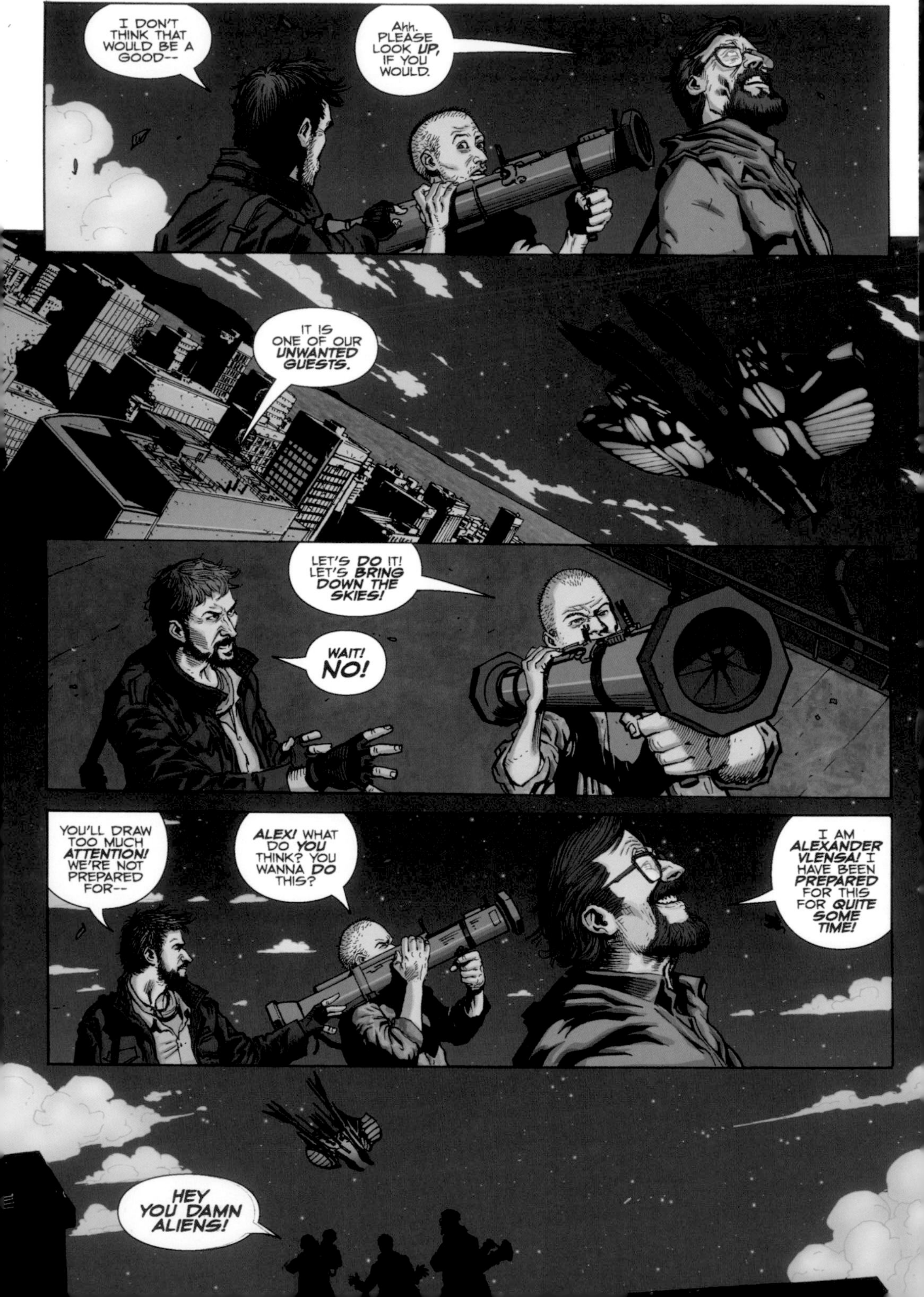
I DON'T THINK THAT WOULD BE A GOOD--
Ahh. PLEASE LOOK UP, IF YOU WOULD.
IT IS ONE OF OUR UNWANTED GUESTS.
LET'S DO IT! LET'S BRING DOWN THE SKIES!
WAIT! NO!
YOU'LL DRAW TOO MUCH ATTENTION! WE'RE NOT PREPARED FOR--
ALEX! WHAT DO YOU THINK? YOU WANNA DO THIS?
I AM ALEXANDER VLENSA! I HAVE BEEN PREPARED FOR THIS FOR QUITE SOME TIME!
HEY YOU DAMN ALIENS!

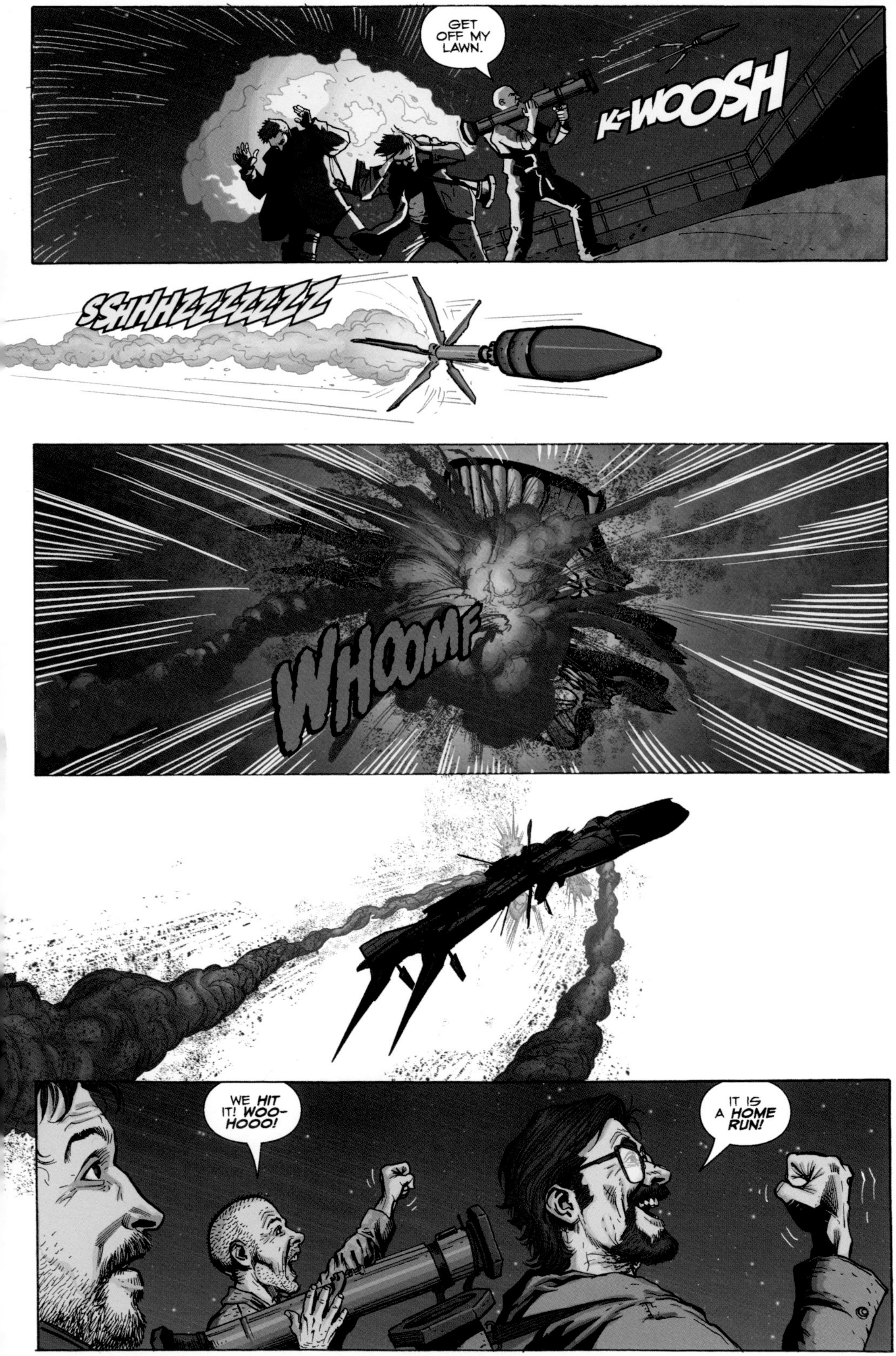
GET OFF MY LAWN.
K-WOOSH
SSHHZZZZZZZ
WHOOMF
WE HIT IT! WOO-HOOO!
IT IS A HOME RUN!

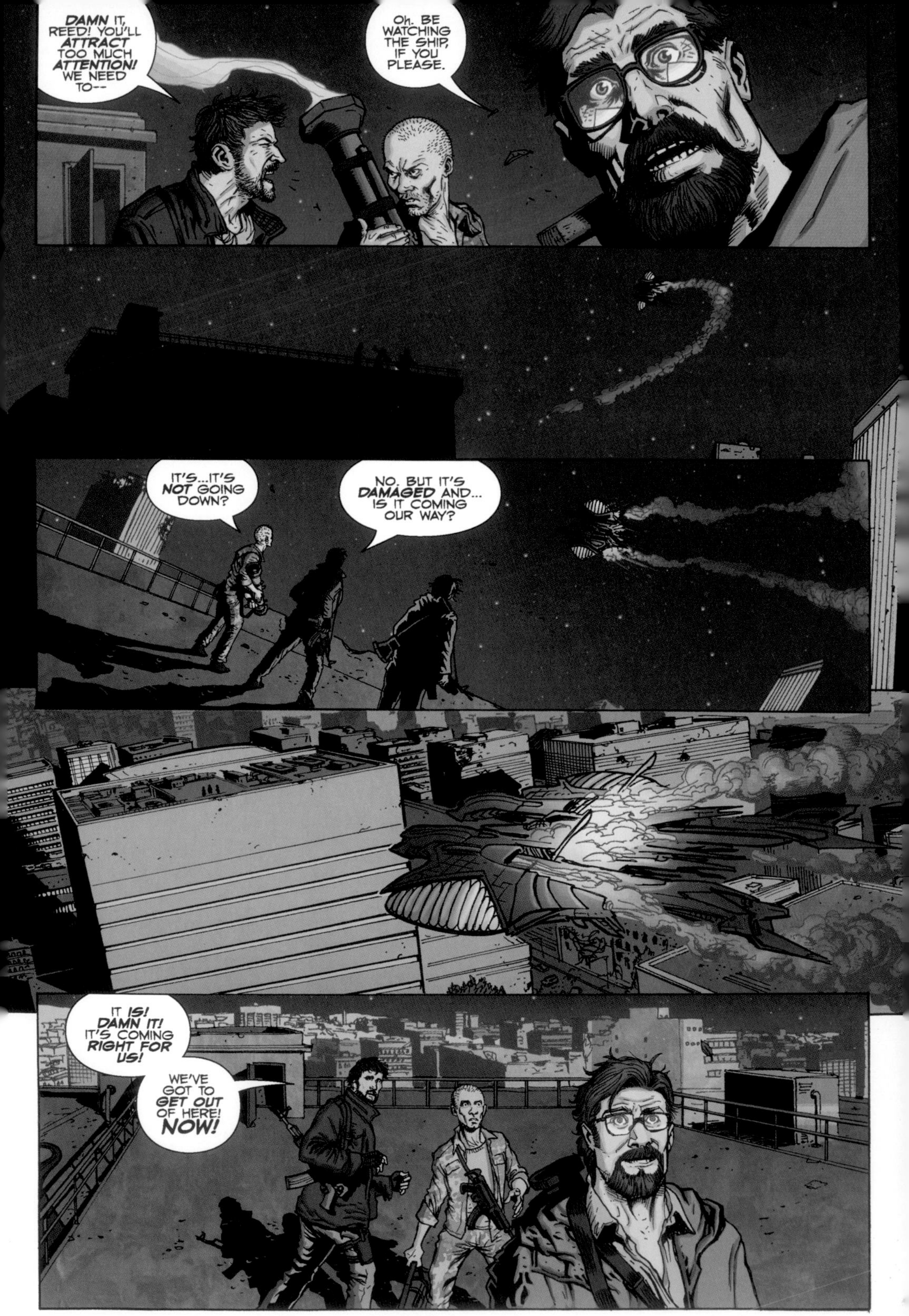
DAMN IT, REED! YOU'LL ATTRACT TOO MUCH ATTENTION! WE NEED TO--
Oh. BE WATCHING THE SHIP, IF YOU PLEASE.
IT'S...IT'S NOT GOING DOWN?
NO. BUT IT'S DAMAGED AND... IS IT COMING OUR WAY?
IT IS! DAMN IT! IT'S COMING RIGHT FOR US!
WE'VE GOT TO GET OUT OF HERE! NOW!

CHAPTER FIVE

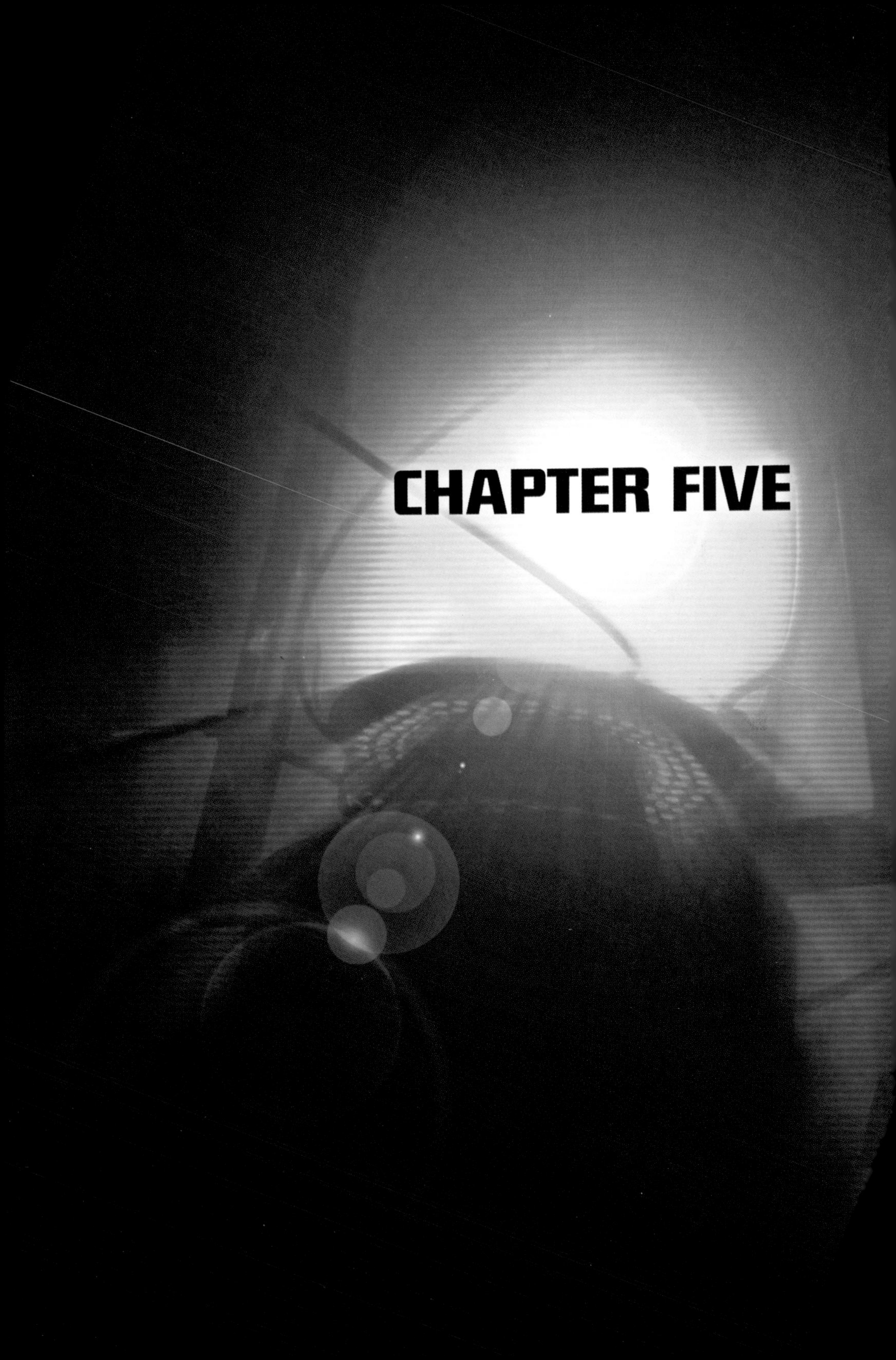

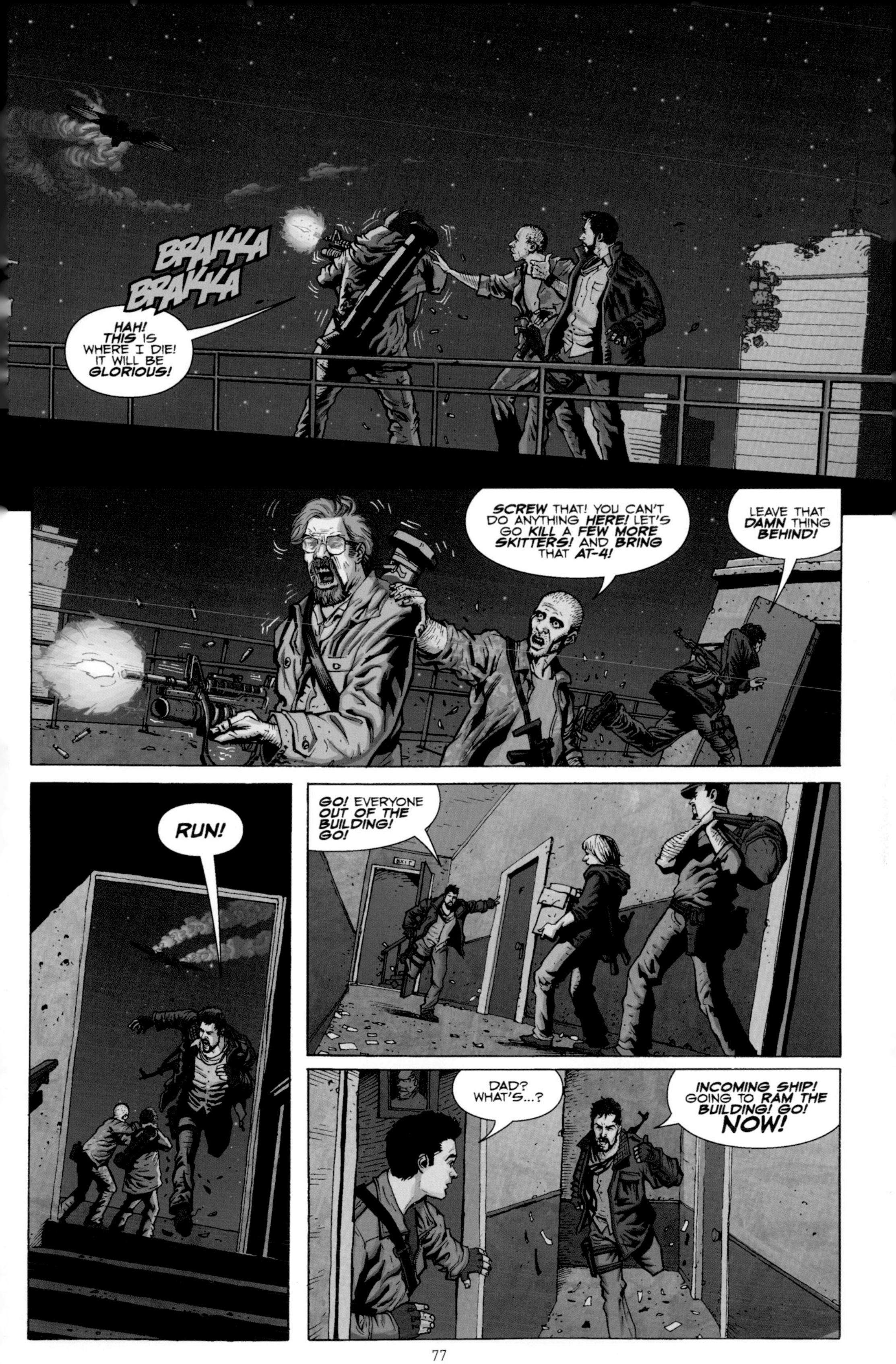
BRAKKA BRAKKA
HAH! THIS IS WHERE I DIE! IT WILL BE GLORIOUS!
SCREW THAT! YOU CAN'T DO ANYTHING HERE! LET'S GO KILL A FEW MORE SKITTERS! AND BRING THAT AT-4!
LEAVE THAT DAMN THING BEHIND!
RUN!
GO! EVERYONE OUT OF THE BUILDING! GO!
DAD? WHAT'S...?
INCOMING SHIP! GOING TO RAM THE BUILDING! GO! NOW!

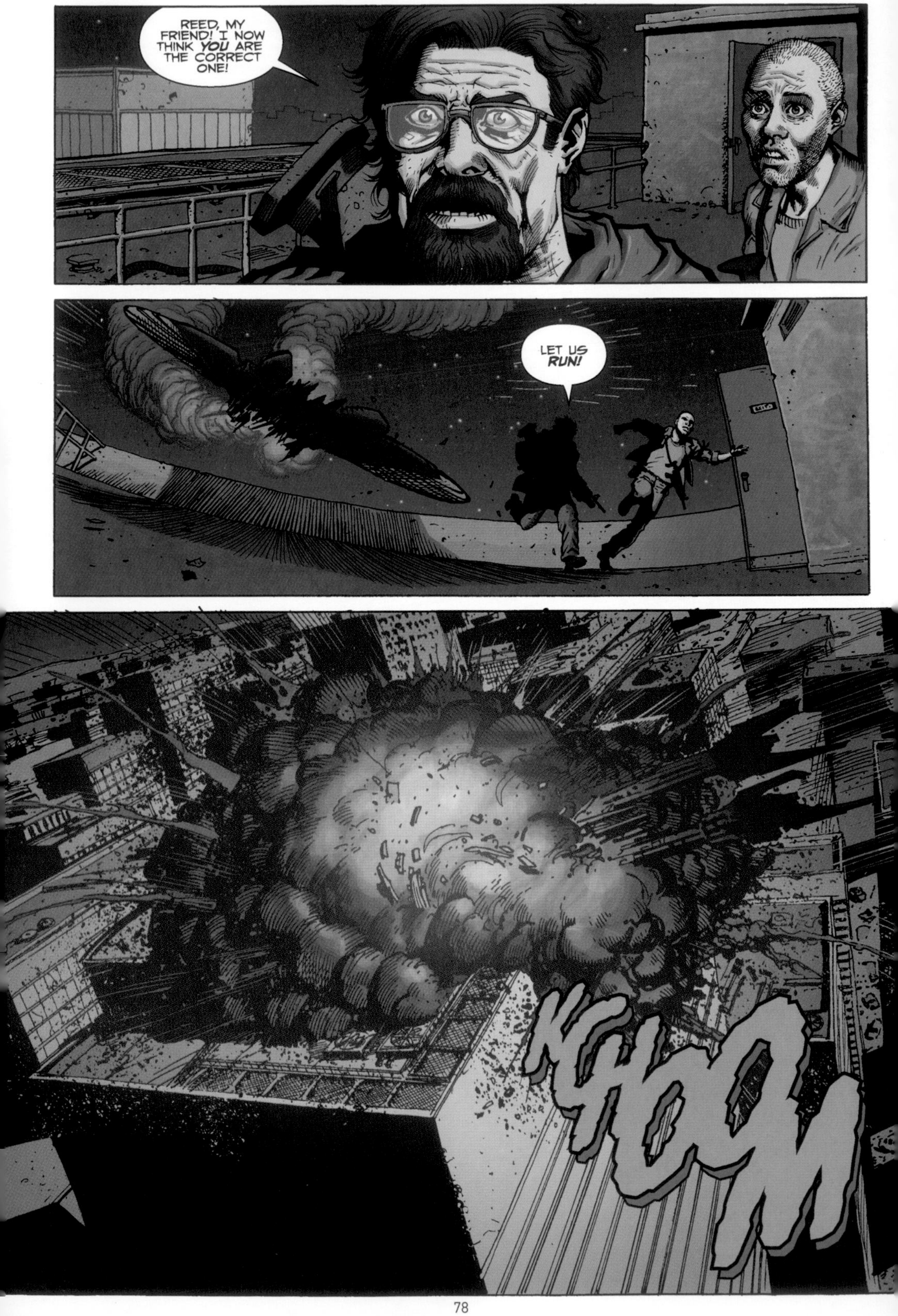
REED, MY FRIEND! I NOW THINK YOU ARE THE CORRECT ONE!
LET US RUN!
KOOM

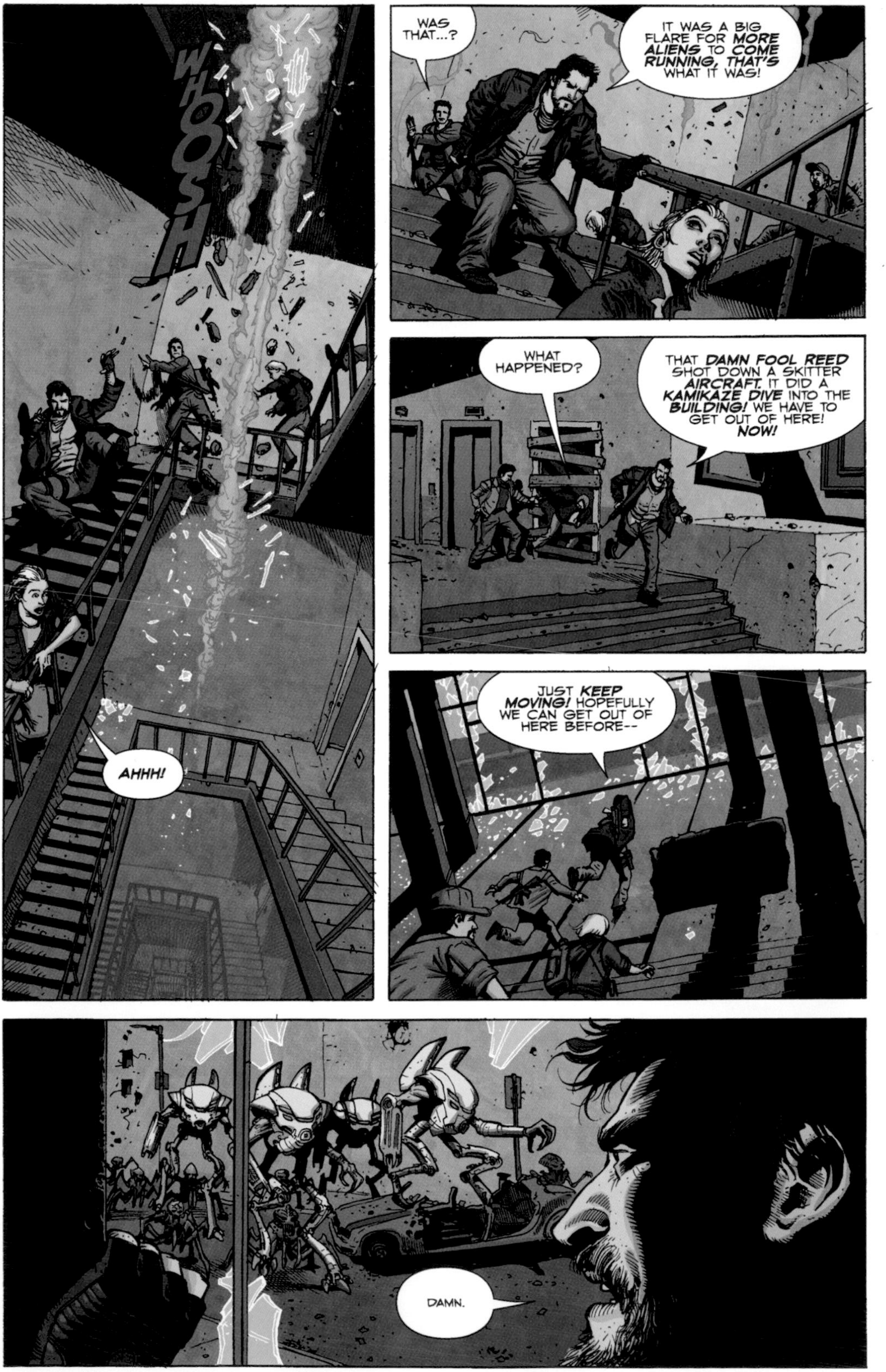
WHOOSH
AHHH!
WAS THAT...?
IT WAS A BIG FLARE FOR MORE ALIENS TO COME RUNNING, THAT'S WHAT IT WAS!
WHAT HAPPENED?
THAT DAMN FOOL REED SHOT DOWN A SKITTER AIRCRAFT. IT DID A KAMIKAZE DIVE INTO THE BUILDING! WE HAVE TO GET OUT OF HERE! NOW!
JUST KEEP MOVING! HOPEFULLY WE CAN GET OUT OF HERE BEFORE--
DAMN.

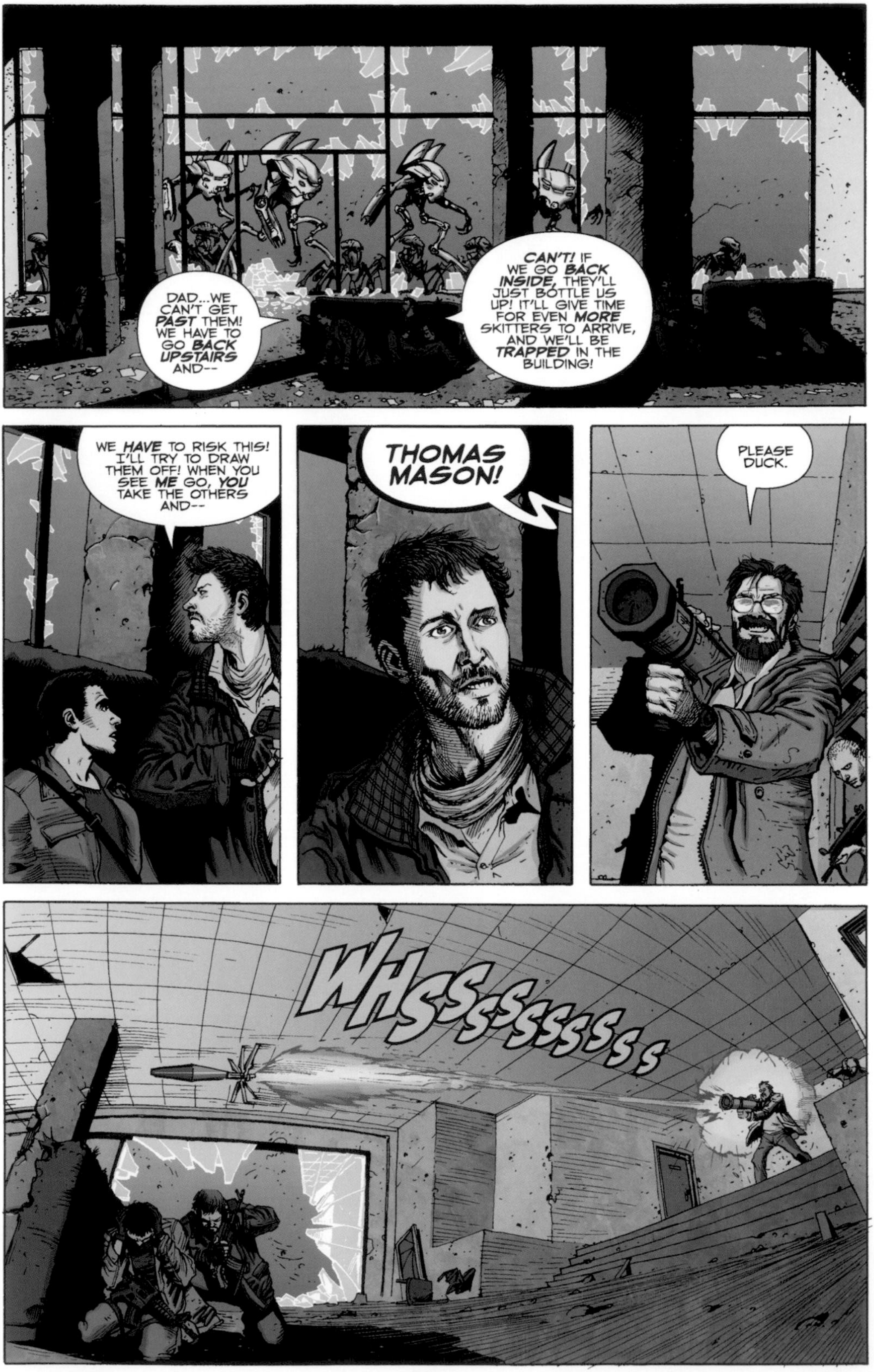
DAD...WE CAN'T GET PAST THEM! WE HAVE TO GO BACK UPSTAIRS AND--
CAN'T! IF WE GO BACK INSIDE, THEY'LL JUST BOTTLE US UP! IT'LL GIVE TIME FOR EVEN MORE SKITTERS TO ARRIVE, AND WE'LL BE TRAPPED IN THE BUILDING!
WE HAVE TO RISK THIS! I'LL TRY TO DRAW THEM OFF! WHEN YOU SEE ME GO, YOU TAKE THE OTHERS AND--
THOMAS MASON!
PLEASE DUCK.
WHSSSSSSSSSS

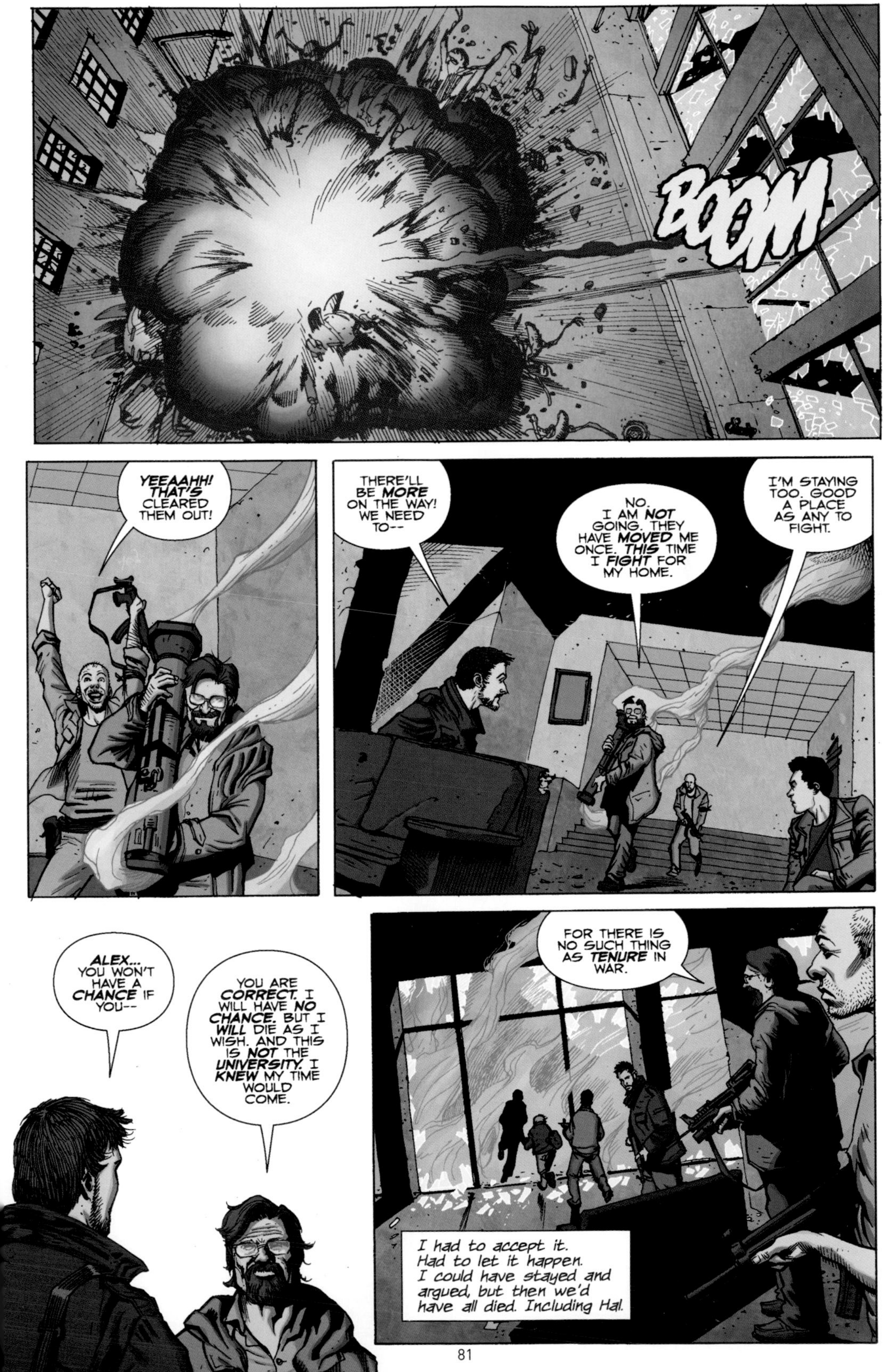
BOOM
YEEAAHH! THAT'S CLEARED THEM OUT!
THERE'LL BE MORE ON THE WAY! WE NEED TO--
NO. I AM NOT GOING. THEY HAVE MOVED ME ONCE. THIS TIME I FIGHT FOR MY HOME.
I'M STAYING TOO. GOOD A PLACE AS ANY TO FIGHT.
ALEX... YOU WON'T HAVE A CHANCE IF YOU--
YOU ARE CORRECT. I WILL HAVE NO CHANCE. BUT I WILL DIE AS I WISH. AND THIS IS NOT THE UNIVERSITY. I KNEW MY TIME WOULD COME.
FOR THERE IS NO SUCH THING AS TENURE IN WAR.
I had to accept it. Had to let it happen. I could have stayed and argued, but then we'd have all died. Including Hal.

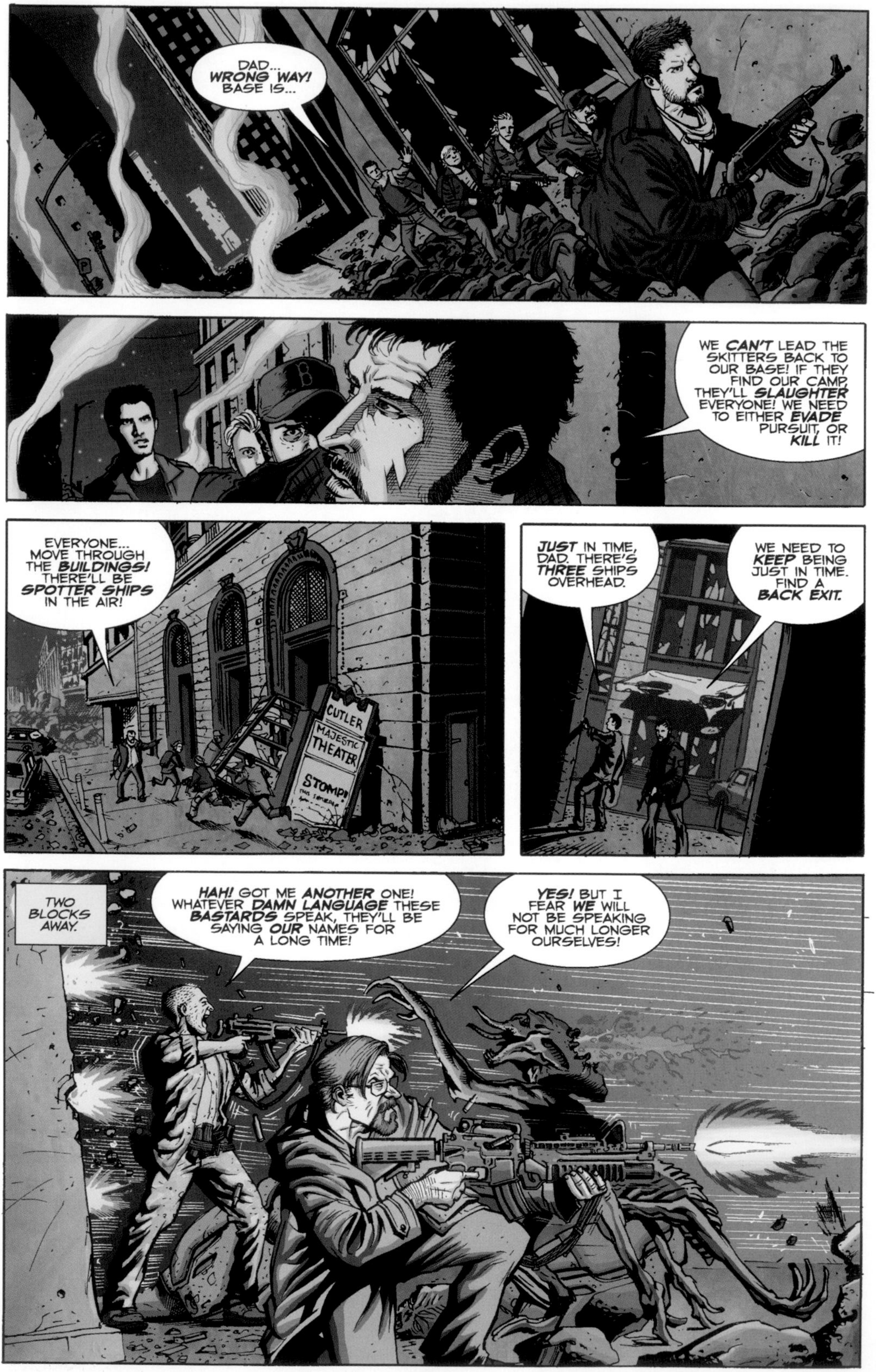

DAD... WRONG WAY! BASE IS...
WE CAN'T LEAD THE SKITTERS BACK TO OUR BASE! IF THEY FIND OUR CAMP, THEY'LL SLAUGHTER EVERYONE! WE NEED TO EITHER EVADE PURSUIT, OR KILL IT!
EVERYONE... MOVE THROUGH THE BUILDINGS! THERE'LL BE SPOTTER SHIPS IN THE AIR!
CUTLER
MAJESTIC THEATER
STOMP!
JUST IN TIME, DAD. THERE'S THREE SHIPS OVERHEAD.
WE NEED TO KEEP BEING JUST IN TIME. FIND A BACK EXIT.
TWO BLOCKS AWAY.
HAH! GOT ME ANOTHER ONE! WHATEVER DAMN LANGUAGE THESE BASTARDS SPEAK, THEY'LL BE SAYING OUR NAMES FOR A LONG TIME!
YES! BUT I FEAR WE WILL NOT BE SPEAKING FOR MUCH LONGER OURSELVES!

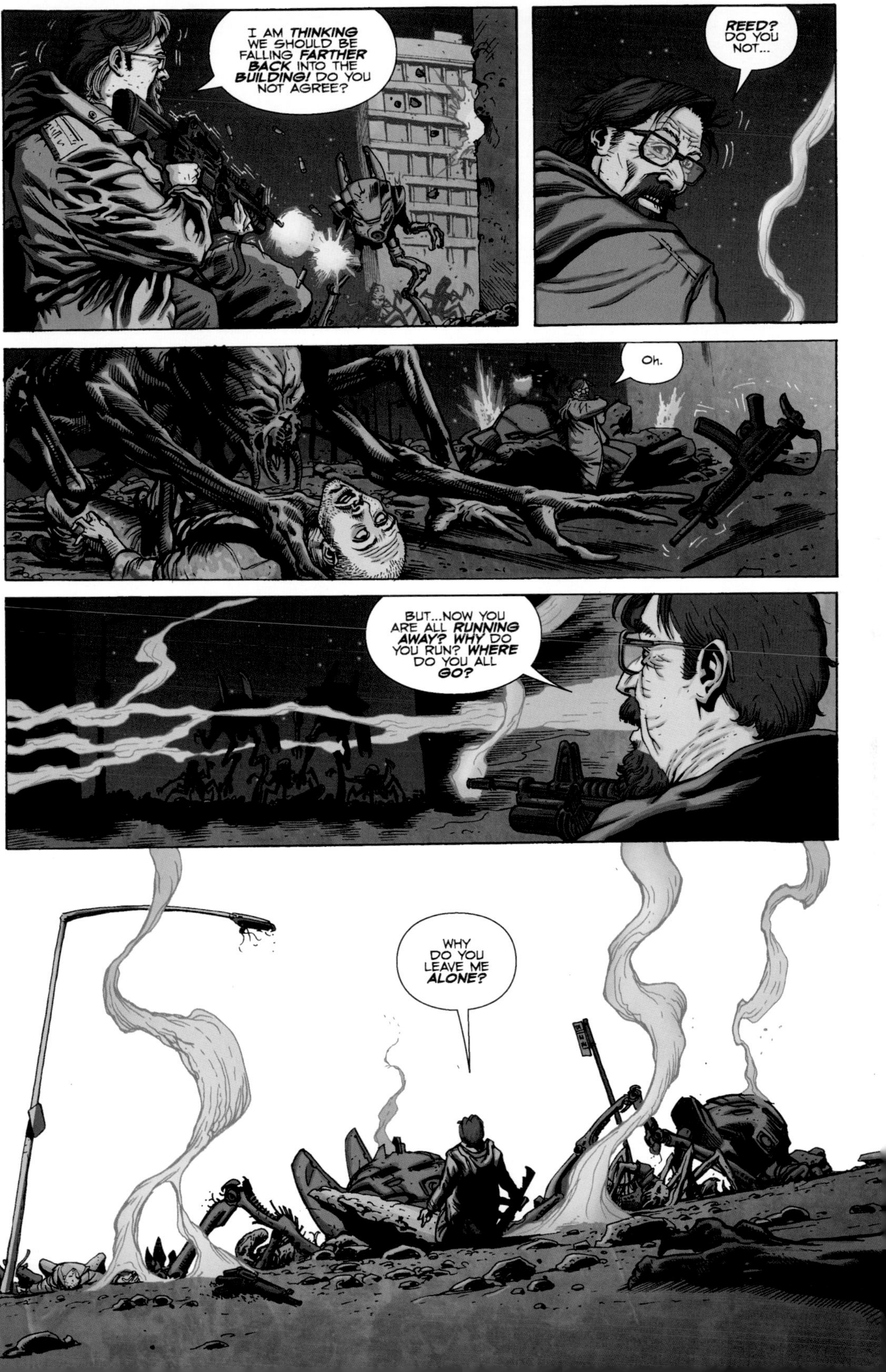
I AM THINKING WE SHOULD BE FALLING FARTHER BACK INTO THE BUILDING! DO YOU NOT AGREE?
REED? DO YOU NOT...
Oh.
BUT...NOW YOU ARE ALL RUNNING AWAY? WHY DO YOU RUN? WHERE DO YOU ALL GO?
WHY DO YOU LEAVE ME ALONE?

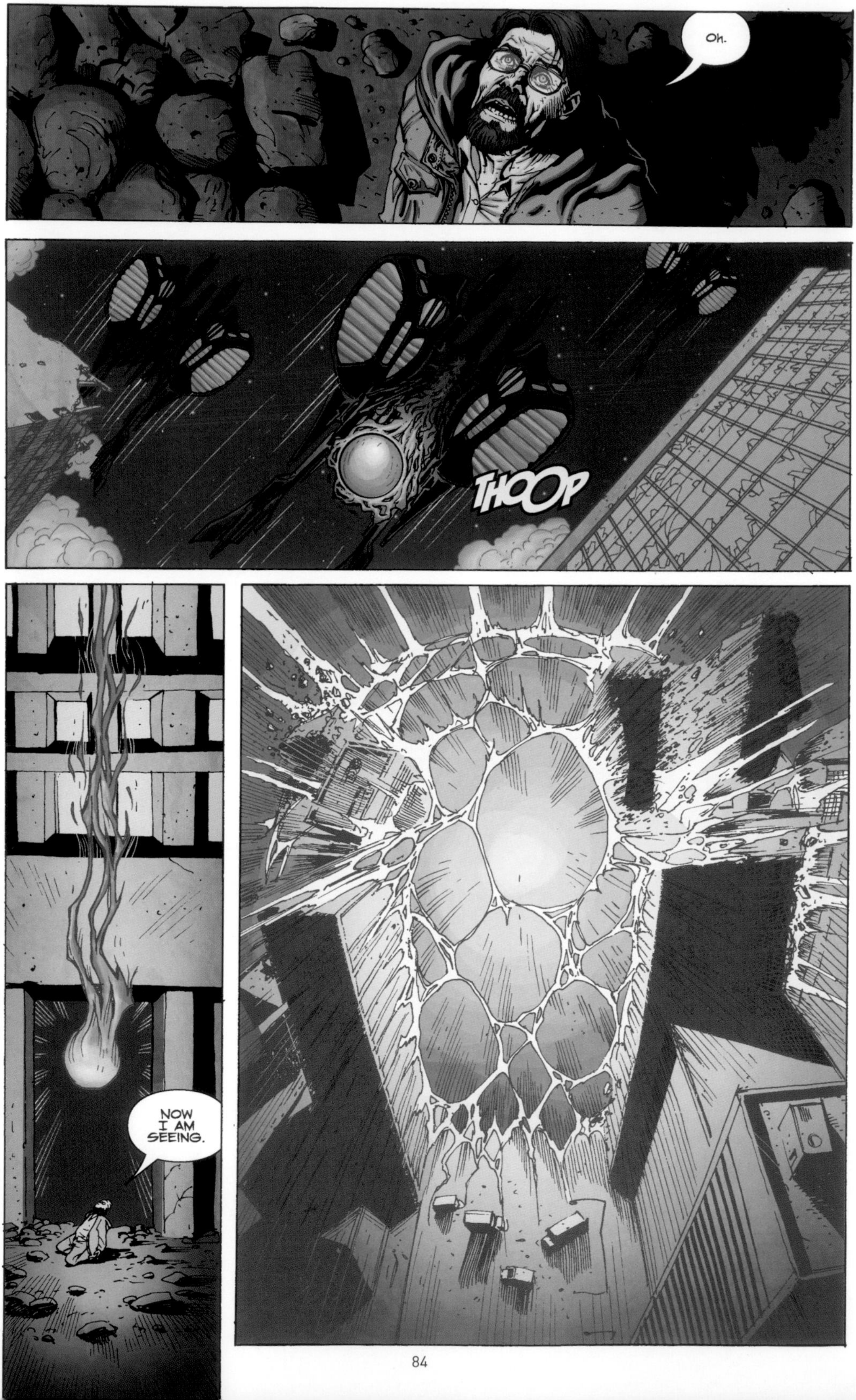
Oh.
THOOP
NOW I AM SEEING.

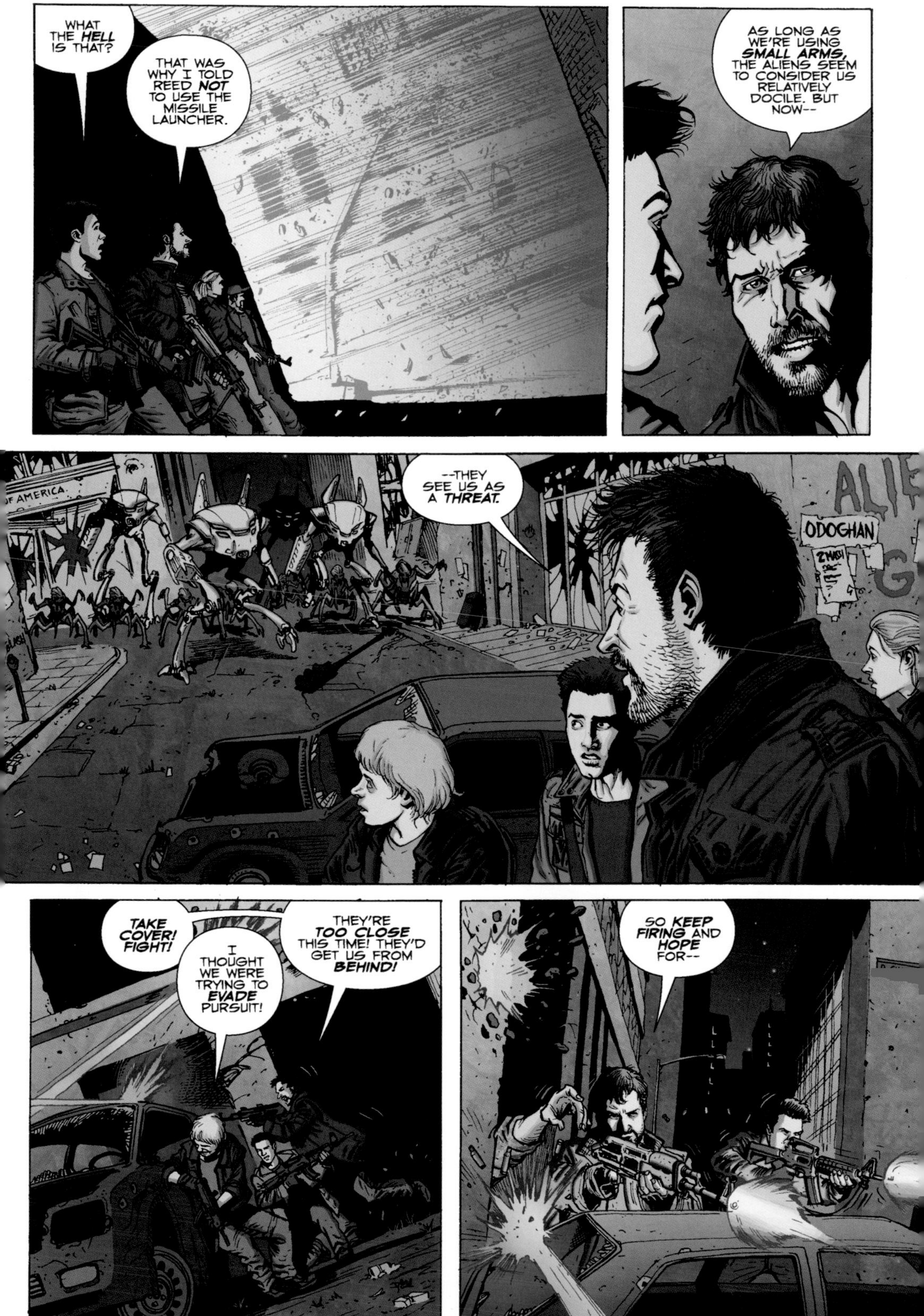
WHAT THE HELL IS THAT?
THAT WAS WHY I TOLD REED NOT TO USE THE MISSILE LAUNCHER.
AS LONG AS WE'RE USING SMALL ARMS, THE ALIENS SEEM TO CONSIDER US RELATIVELY DOCILE. BUT NOW--
OF AMERICA
--THEY SEE US AS A THREAT.
ODOGHAN
TAKE COVER! FIGHT!
I THOUGHT WE WERE TRYING TO EVADE PURSUIT!
THEY'RE TOO CLOSE THIS TIME! THEY'D GET US FROM BEHIND!
SO KEEP FIRING AND HOPE FOR--

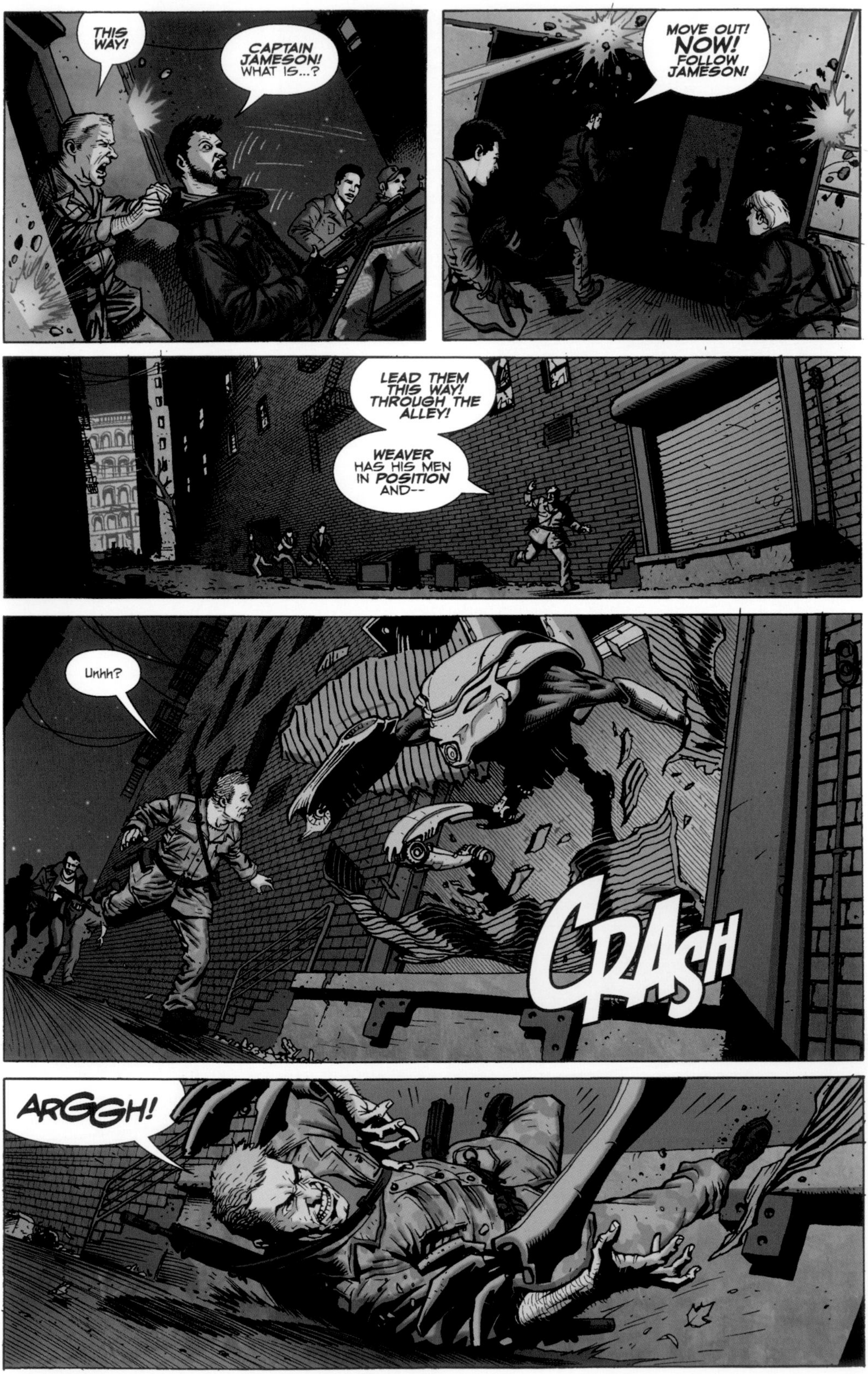
THIS WAY!
CAPTAIN JAMESON! WHAT IS...?
MOVE OUT! NOW! FOLLOW JAMESON!
LEAD THEM THIS WAY! THROUGH THE ALLEY!
WEAVER HAS HIS MEN IN POSITION AND--
Unhh?
CRASH
ARGGH!

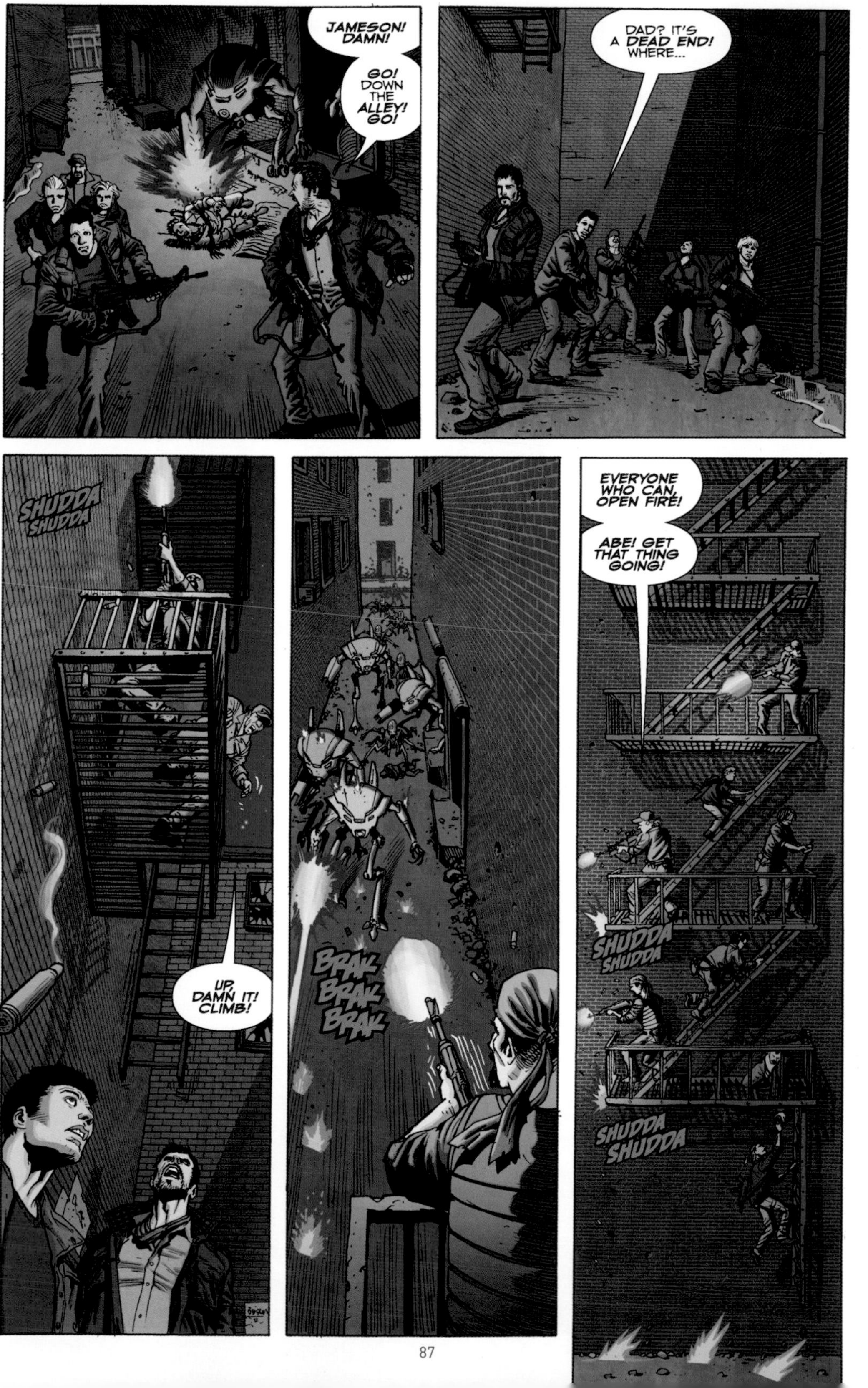
JAMESON! DAMN!
GO! DOWN THE ALLEY! GO!
DAD? IT'S A DEAD END! WHERE...
SHUDDA SHUDDA
UP, DAMN IT! CLIMB!
BRAK BRAK BRAK
EVERYONE WHO CAN, OPEN FIRE!
ABE! GET THAT THING GOING!
SHUDDA SHUDDA
SHUDDA SHUDDA

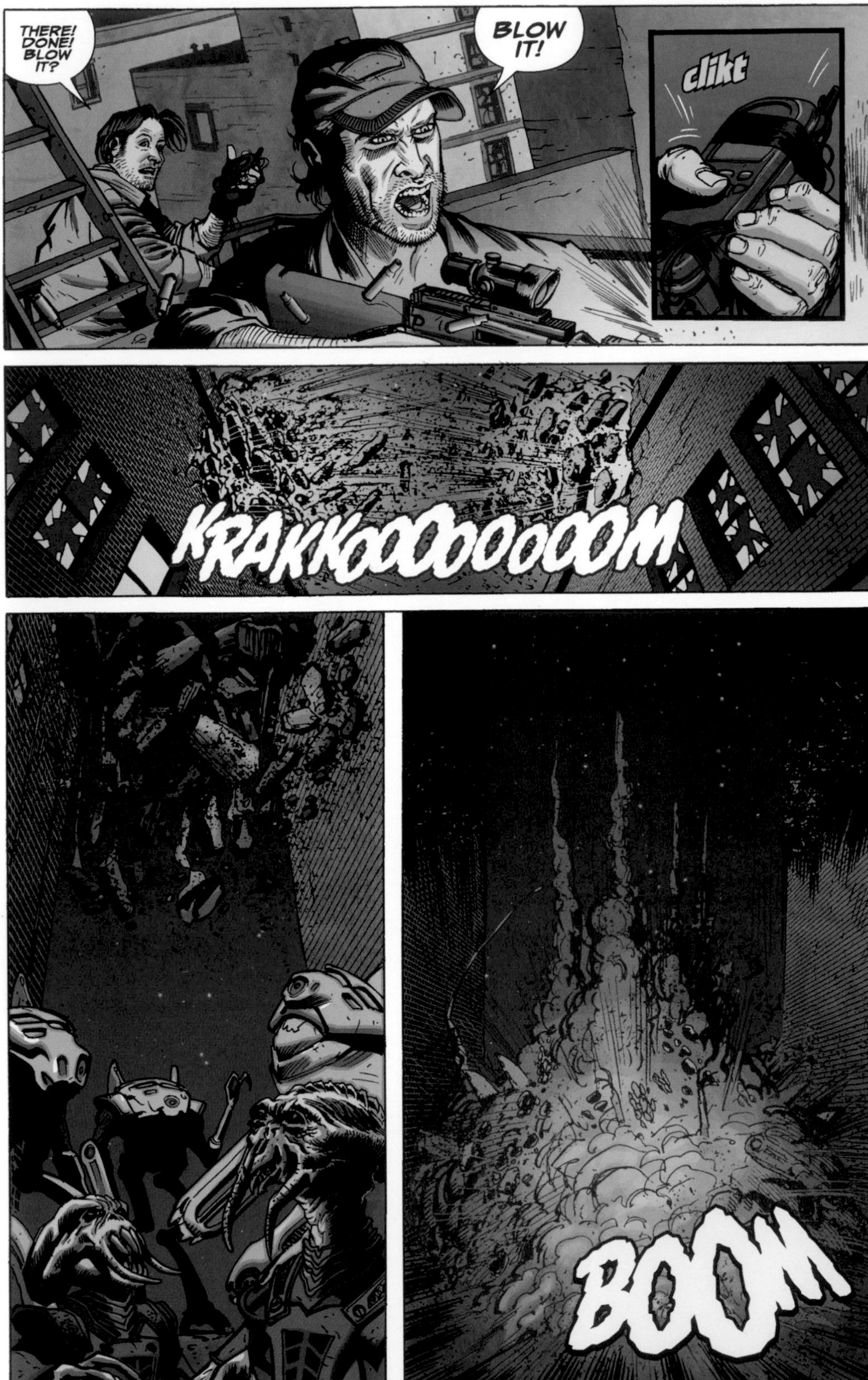
THERE! DONE! BLOW IT?
BLOW IT!
clikt
KRAKKOOOOOOOOM
BOOM

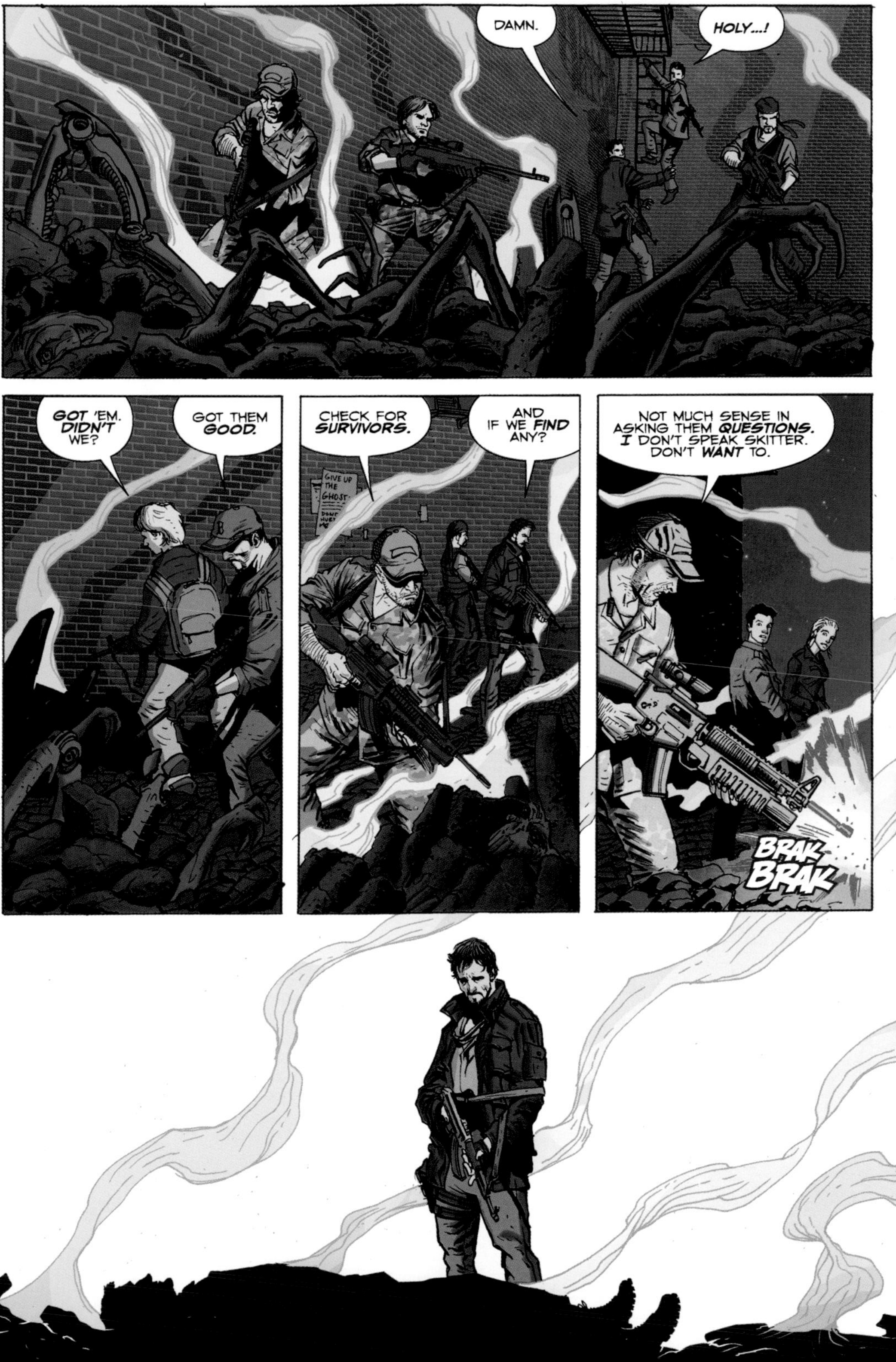
DAMN.
HOLY...!
GOT 'EM. DIDN'T WE?
GOT THEM GOOD.
CHECK FOR SURVIVORS.
GIVE UP THE GHOST
AND IF WE FIND ANY?
NOT MUCH SENSE IN ASKING THEM QUESTIONS. I DON'T SPEAK SKITTER. DON'T WANT TO.
BRAK BRAK

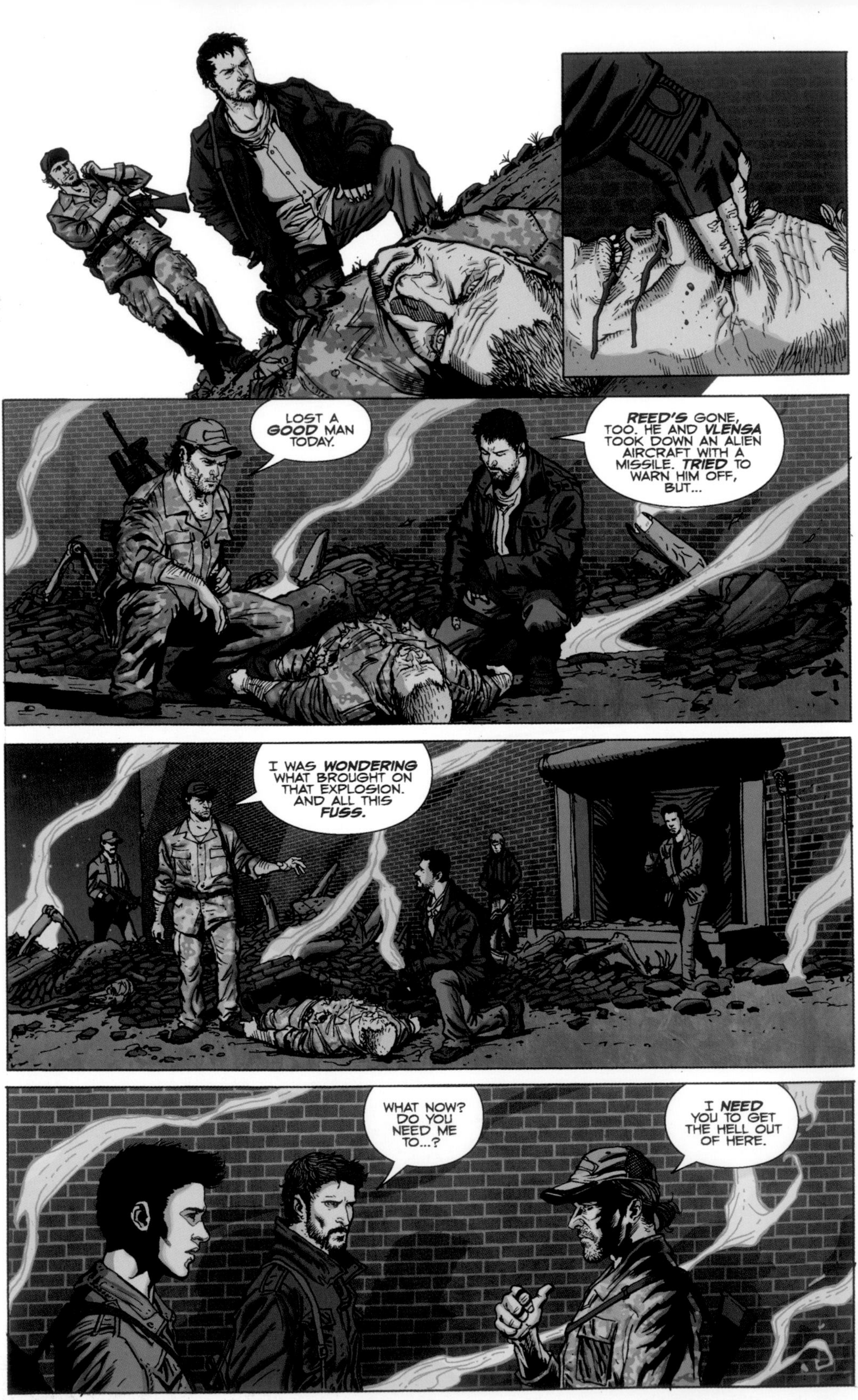
LOST A GOOD MAN TODAY.
REED'S GONE, TOO. HE AND VLENSA TOOK DOWN AN ALIEN AIRCRAFT WITH A MISSILE. TRIED TO WARN HIM OFF, BUT...
I WAS WONDERING WHAT BROUGHT ON THAT EXPLOSION. AND ALL THIS FUSS.
WHAT NOW? DO YOU NEED ME TO...?
I NEED YOU TO GET THE HELL OUT OF HERE.

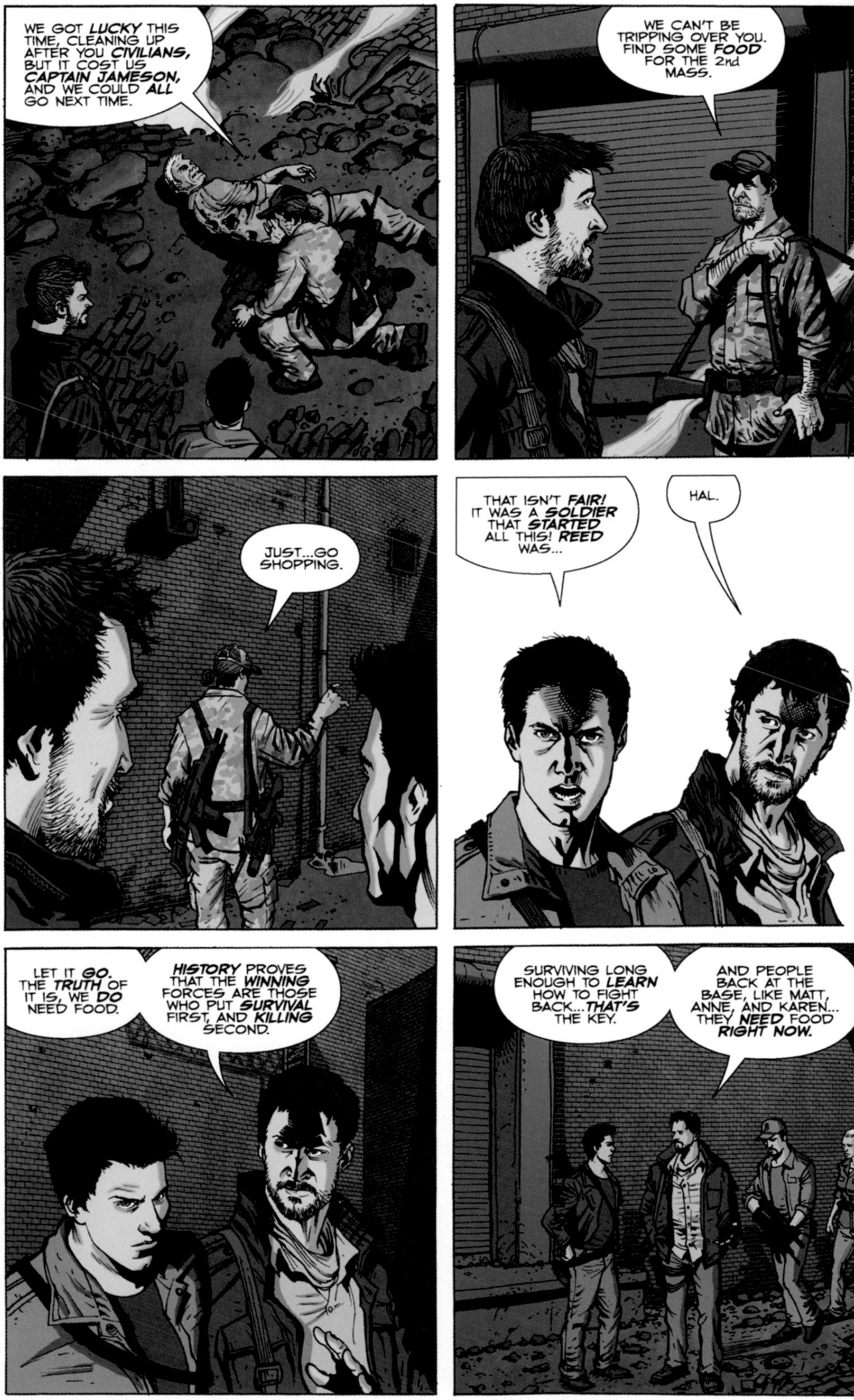
WE GOT LUCKY THIS TIME, CLEANING UP AFTER YOU CIVILIANS, BUT IT COST US CAPTAIN JAMESON, AND WE COULD ALL GO NEXT TIME.
WE CAN'T BE TRIPPING OVER YOU. FIND SOME FOOD FOR THE 2nd MASS.
JUST...GO SHOPPING.
THAT ISN'T FAIR! IT WAS A SOLDIER THAT STARTED ALL THIS! REED WAS...
HAL.
LET IT GO. THE TRUTH OF IT IS, WE DO NEED FOOD.
HISTORY PROVES THAT THE WINNING FORCES ARE THOSE WHO PUT SURVIVAL FIRST, AND KILLING SECOND.
SURVIVING LONG ENOUGH TO LEARN HOW TO FIGHT BACK...THAT'S THE KEY.
AND PEOPLE BACK AT THE BASE, LIKE MATT, ANNE, AND KAREN... THEY NEED FOOD RIGHT NOW.

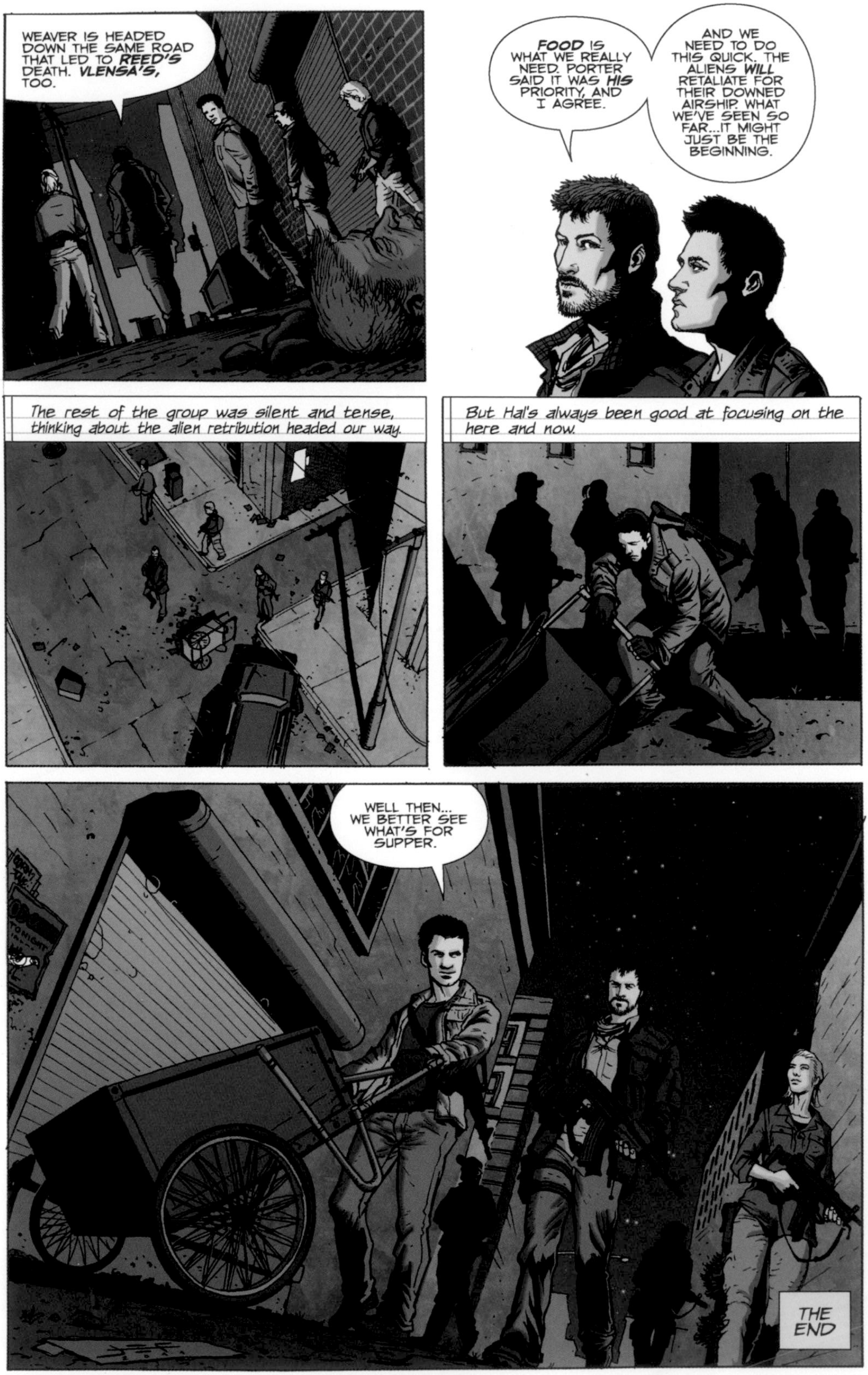
WEAVER IS HEADED DOWN THE SAME ROAD THAT LED TO REED'S DEATH. VLENSA'S, TOO.
FOOD IS WHAT WE REALLY NEED. PORTER SAID IT WAS HIS PRIORITY, AND I AGREE.
AND WE NEED TO DO THIS QUICK. THE ALIENS WILL RETALIATE FOR THEIR DOWNED AIRSHIP. WHAT WE'VE SEEN SO FAR...IT MIGHT JUST BE THE BEGINNING.
The rest of the group was silent and tense, thinking about the alien retribution headed our way.
But Hal's always been good at focusing on the here and now.
WELL THEN... WE BETTER SEE WHAT'S FOR SUPPER.
THE END

FALLING SKIES SKETCHBOOK

BY JUAN FERREYRA

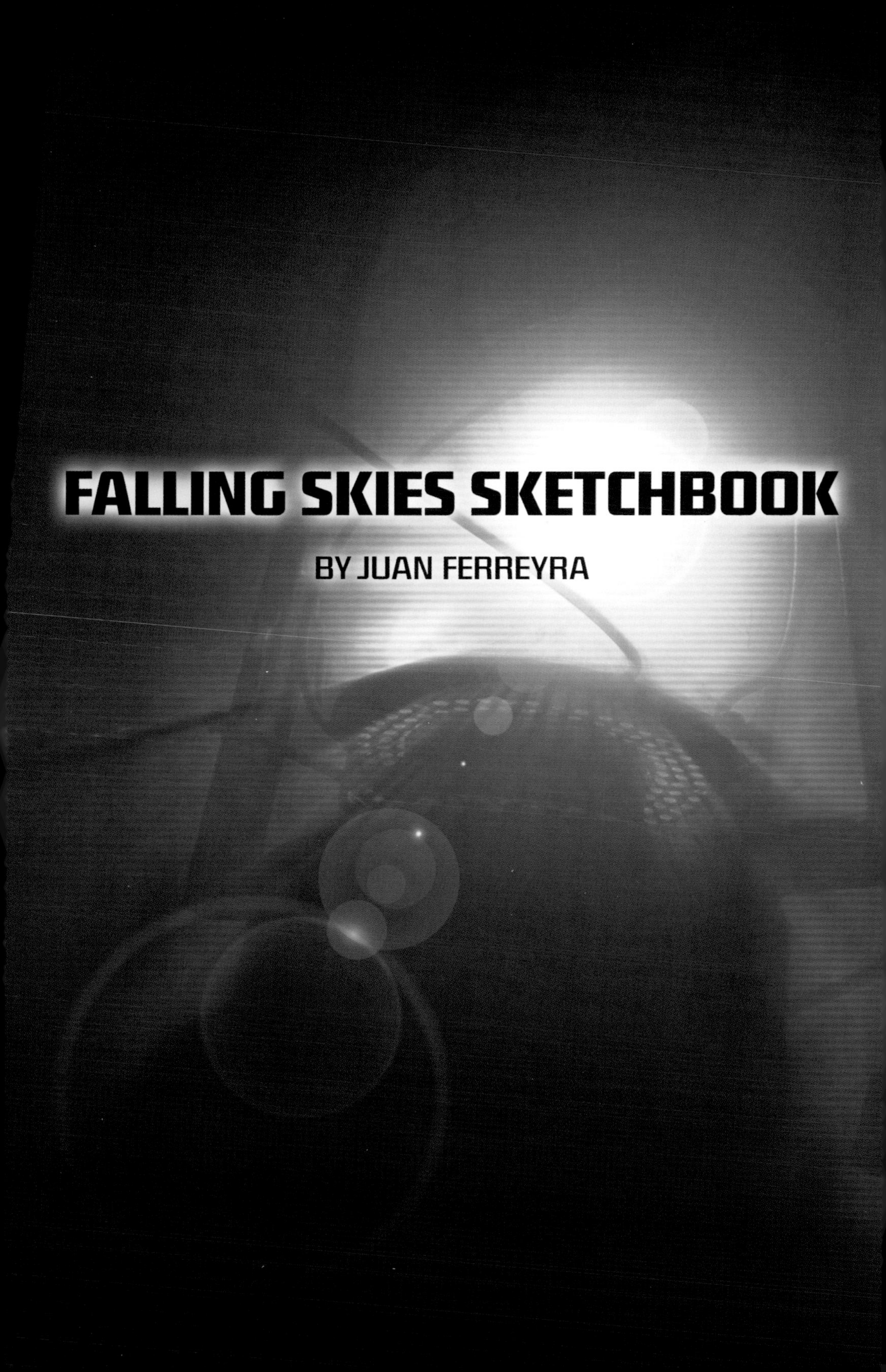

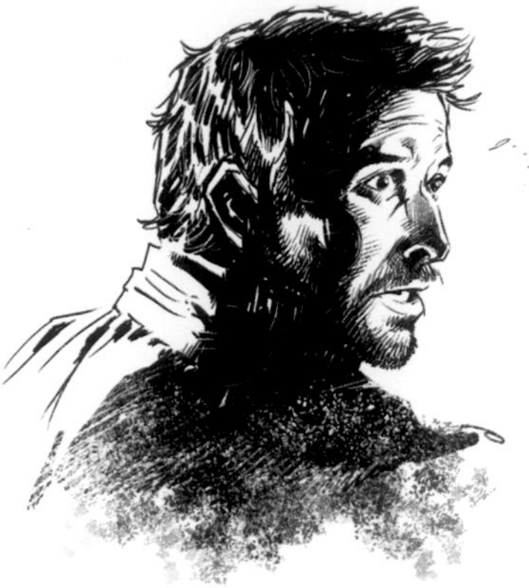
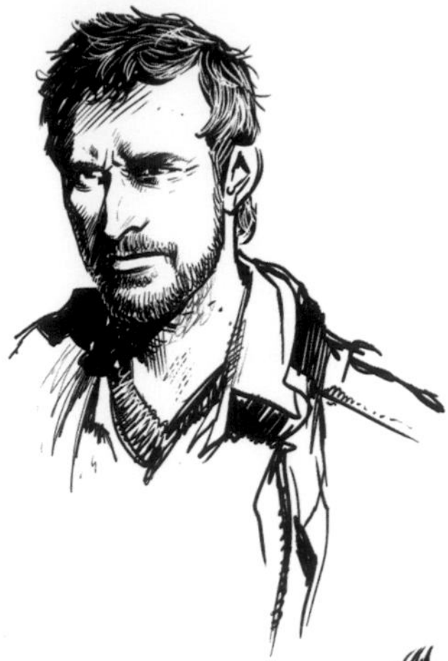
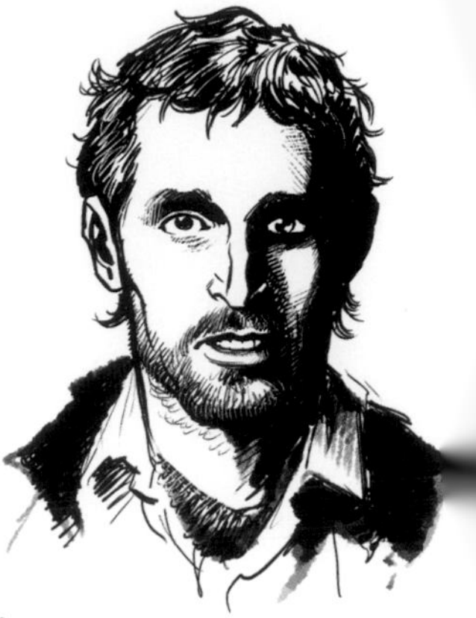

Because *Falling Skies* is based on a TV show, I needed to draw the characters to look very similar to the actors. This was the first time I had to do something like that. The first character I worked on was Tom, played by actor Noah Wyle. I like the first version of Tom, above. The third one, to the right, now that I look at it, is pretty weak. I wonder now why Scott gave me this job.

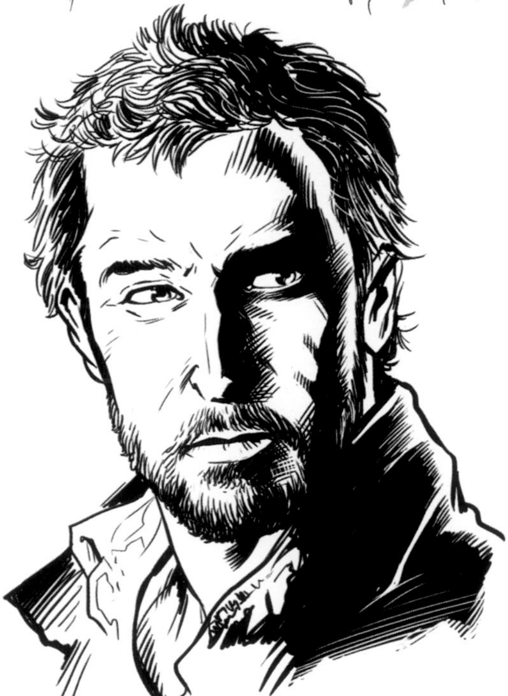
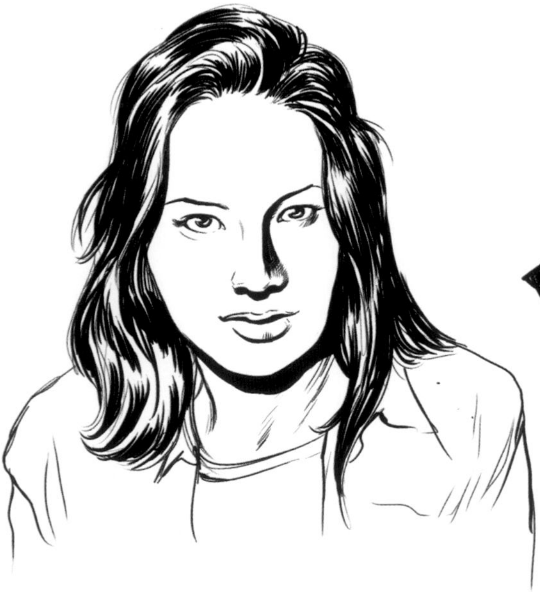

I like this version of Tom, too—serious, really thoughtful about what Anne's holding in her hand on the opposite page.

Drawing Anne was even more challenging. Moon Bloodgood is beautiful, and it was very hard to get her face right. It's really easy to end up with her looking like a Caucasian woman instead of having more Asian features.

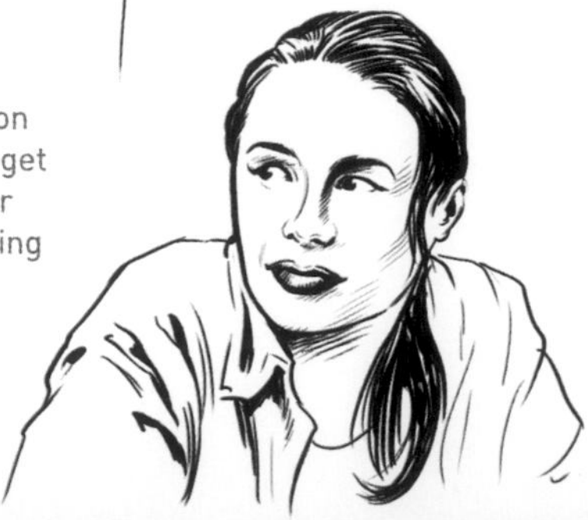

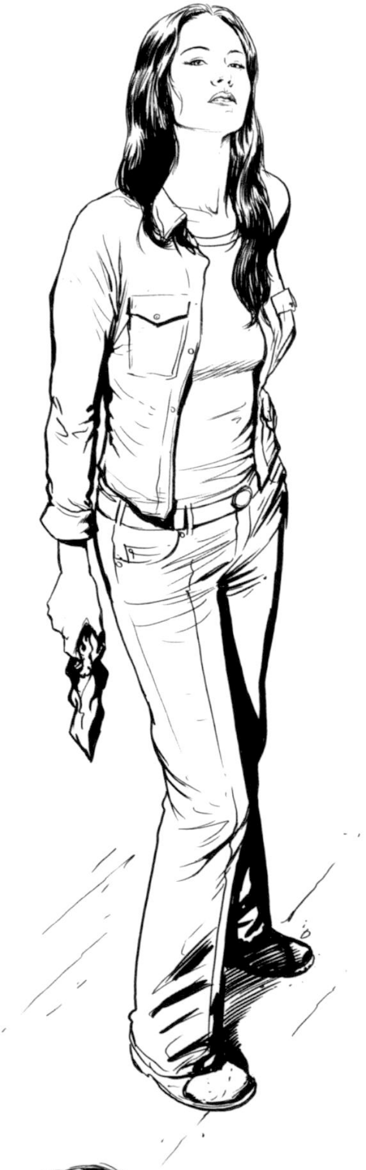

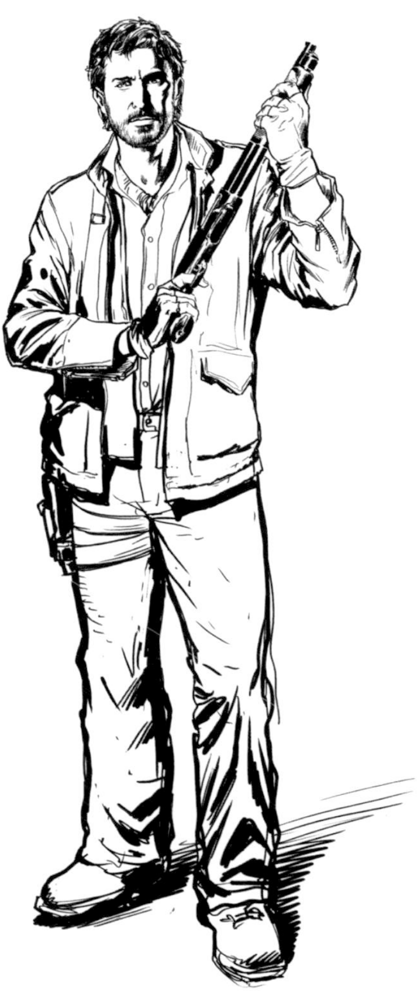

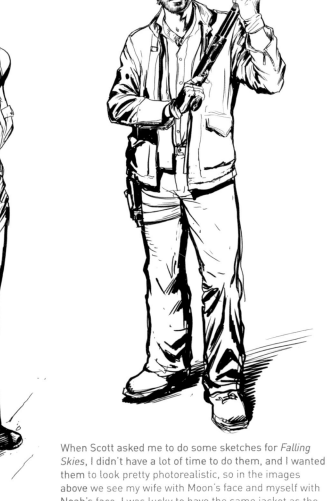

When Scott asked me to do some sketches for *Falling Skies*, I didn't have a lot of time to do them, and I wanted them to look pretty photorealistic, so in the images above we see my wife with Moon's face and myself with Noah's face. I was lucky to have the same jacket as the one Noah wears in the show.

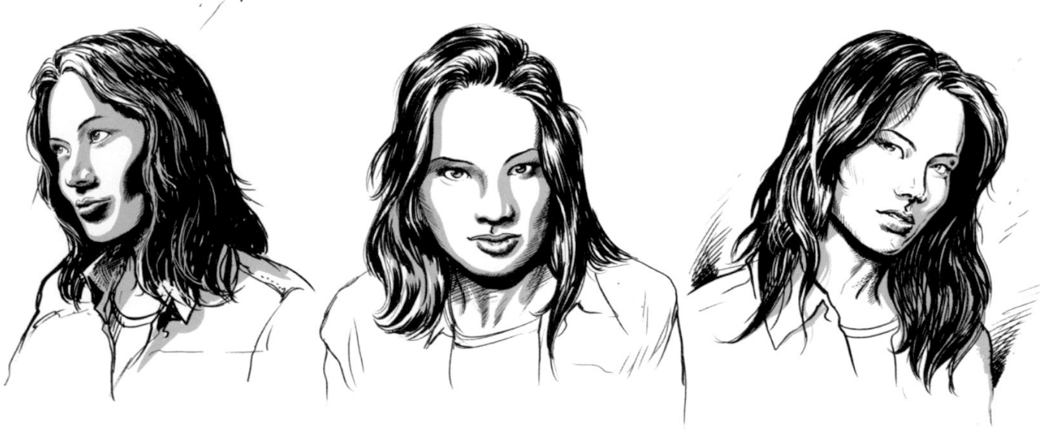

Yes, I had fun drawing Anne. Here I added some tones to the drawings.

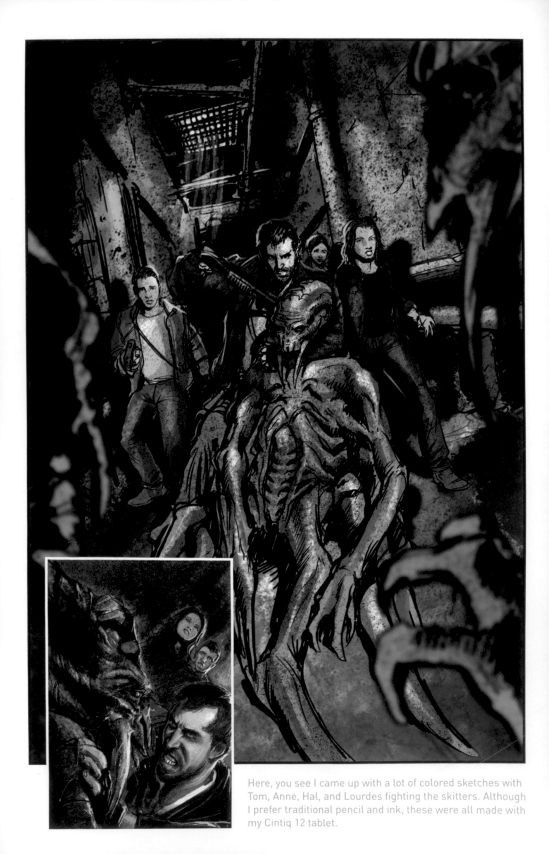

Here, you see I came up with a lot of colored sketches with Tom, Anne, Hal, and Lourdes fighting the skitters. Although I prefer traditional pencil and ink, these were all made with my Cintiq 12 tablet.

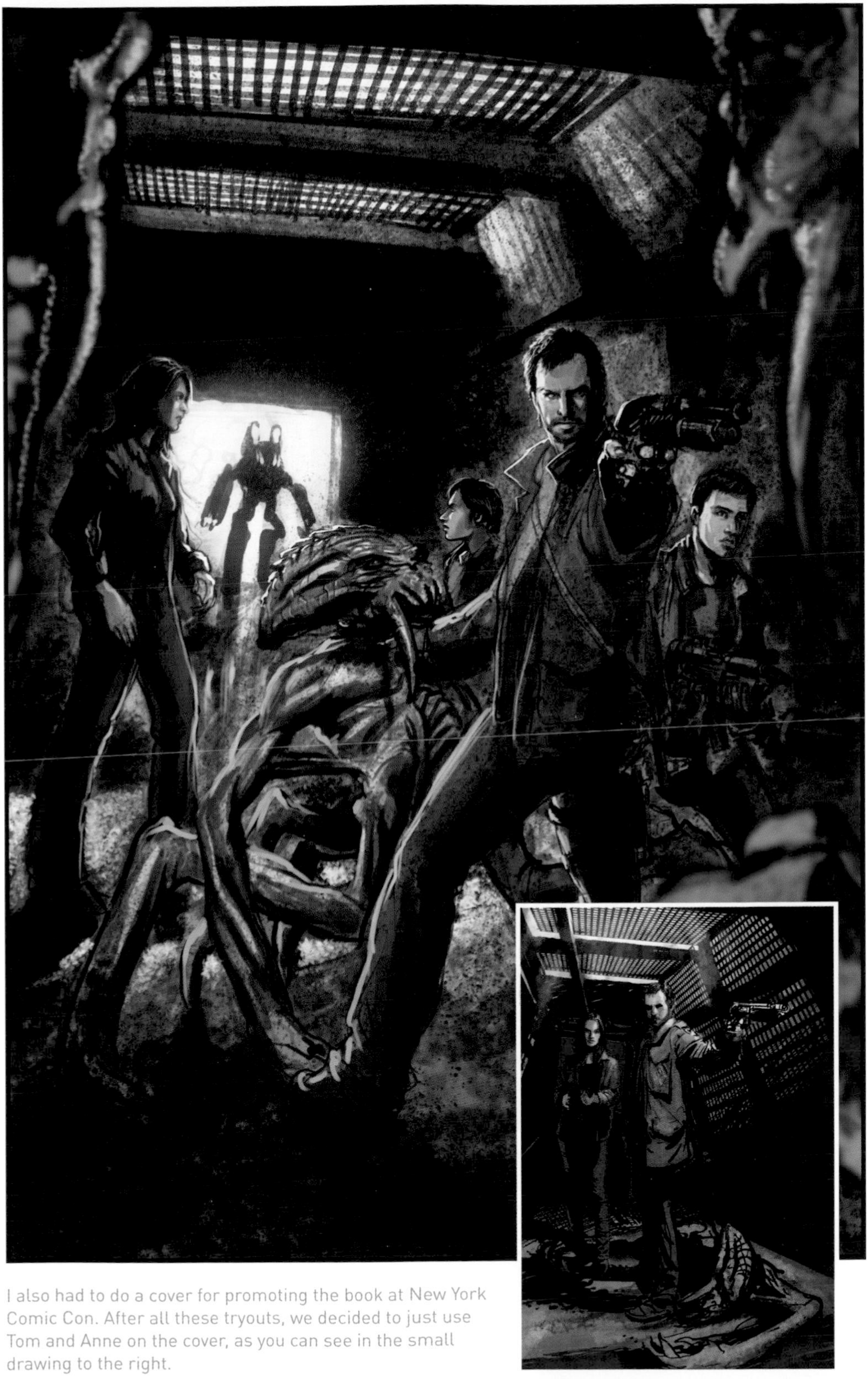

I also had to do a cover for promoting the book at New York Comic Con. After all these tryouts, we decided to just use Tom and Anne on the cover, as you can see in the small drawing to the right.

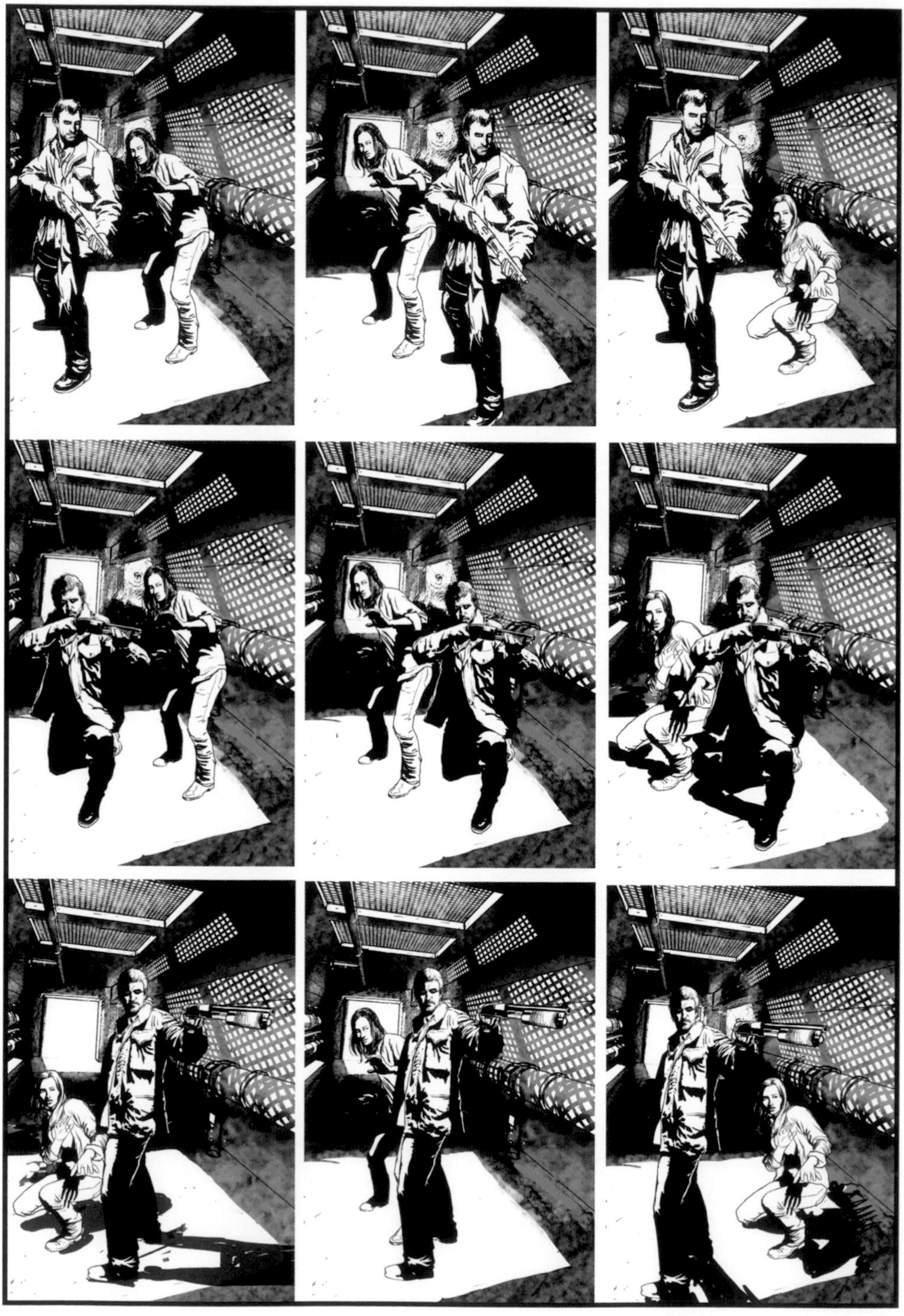

Wow! Look at all the different poses for this version of the cover, which we ended up not using! My editors, Scott and Daniel, told me the licensors felt we needed a different approach, so we decided not to use this cover. I still secretly believe Scott and Daniel used "the licensors" to make me change things the way they wanted. Not shown here is the background for this cover, fully painted with a lot of detail. I'll probably draw Darth Vader on top of it, print it, and hang it on my wall.

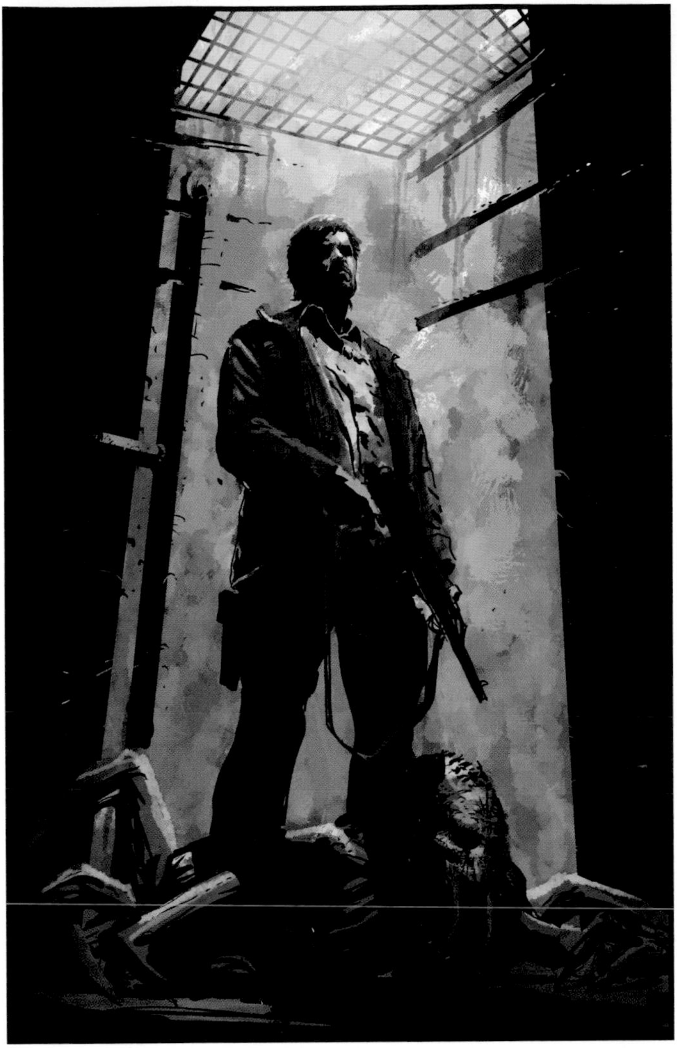

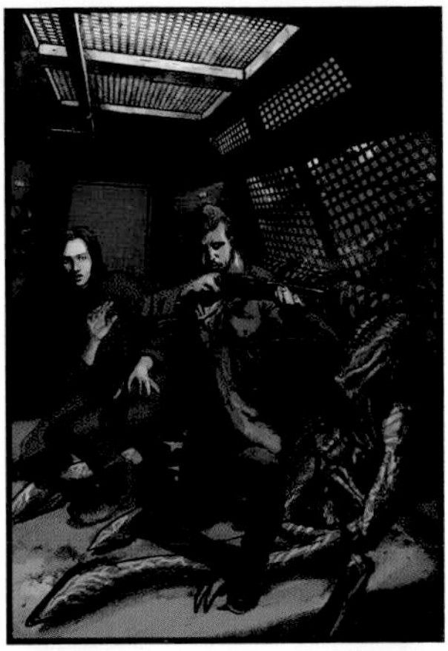

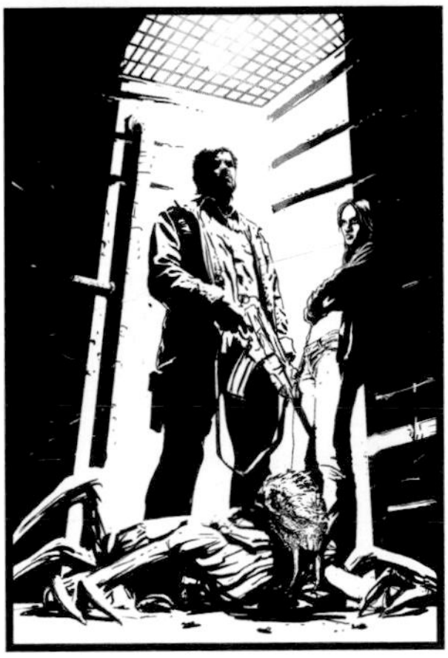

Then I came up with this option for the final cover. These versions are very "Tim Bradstreet," and the final one has a more painted look.

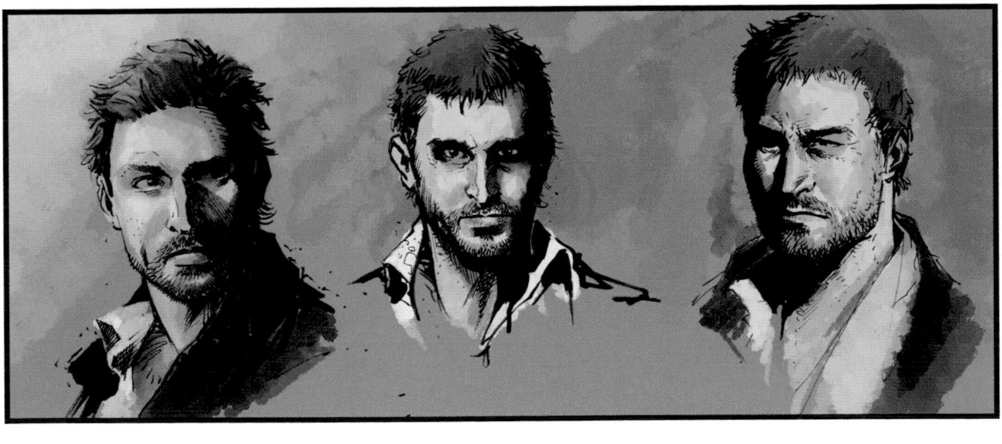

These were the very first Toms I drew. I would like to say that at the time I did these Noah Wyle hadn't been cast yet, but that wasn't the case. These just came up awful—trial and error at its best!

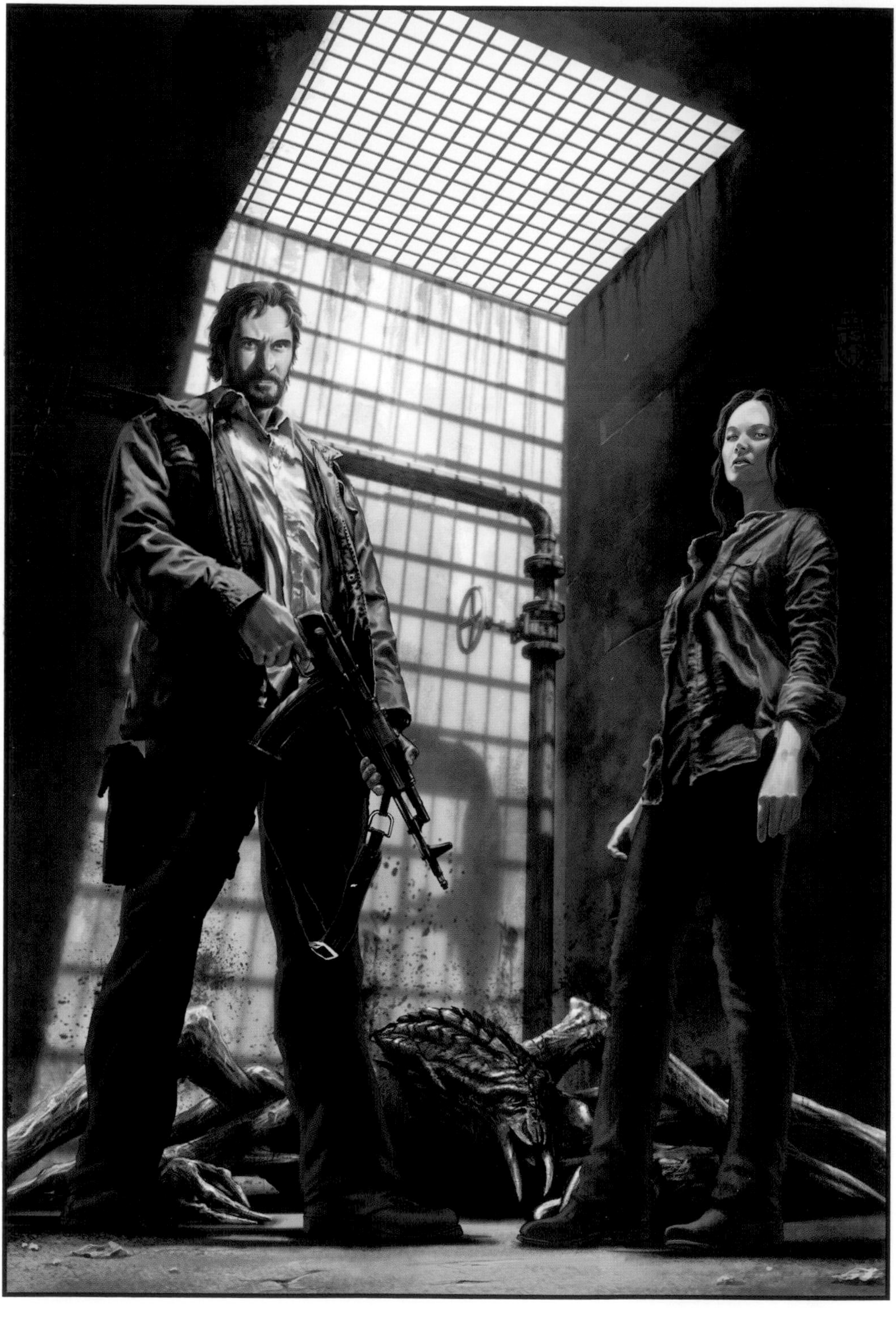

Two versions of the final cover, one with Moon, one without.

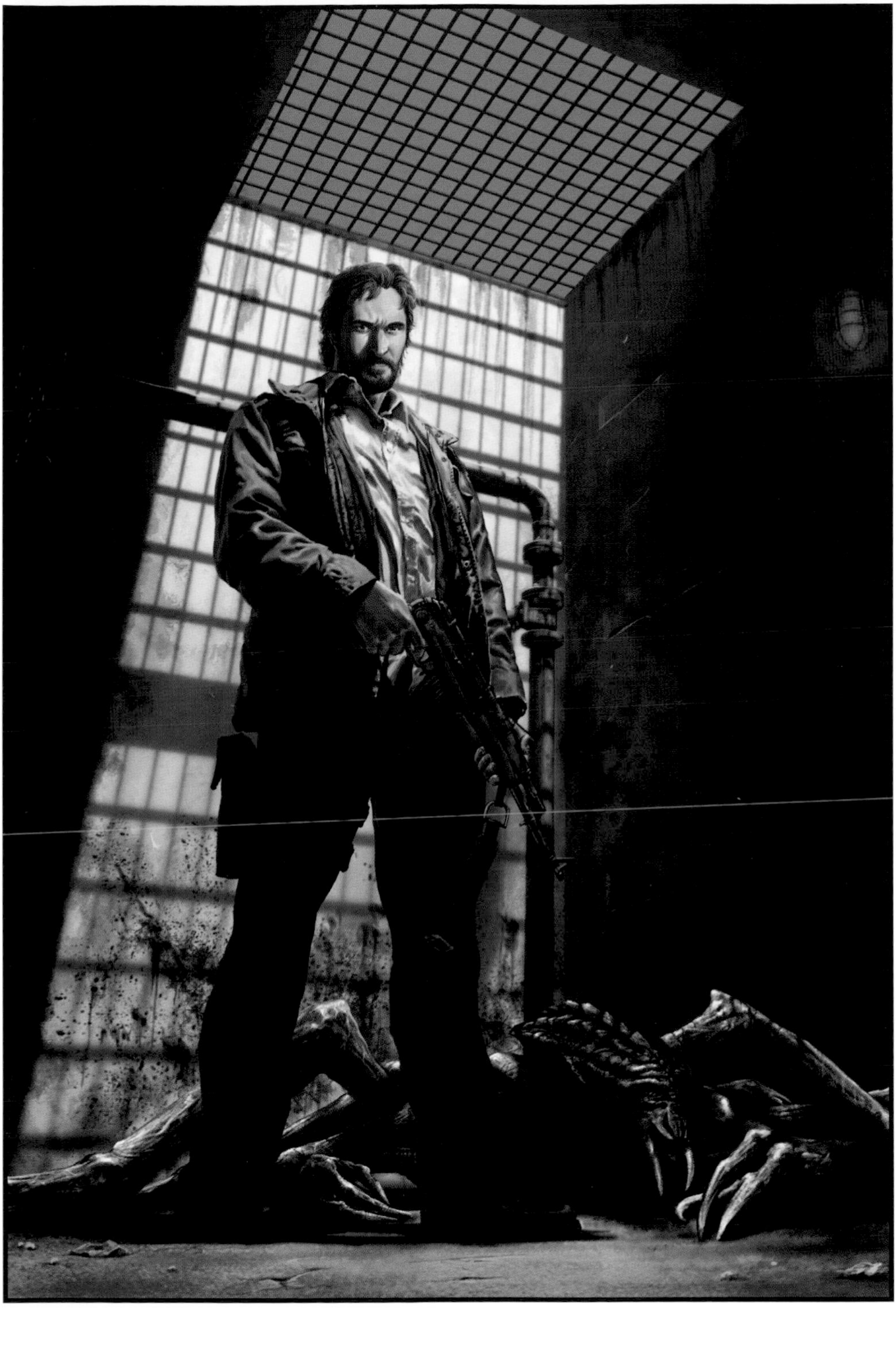

This is the one we used for New York Comi Con. Note the grate has been darkened so the white logo would read over it.

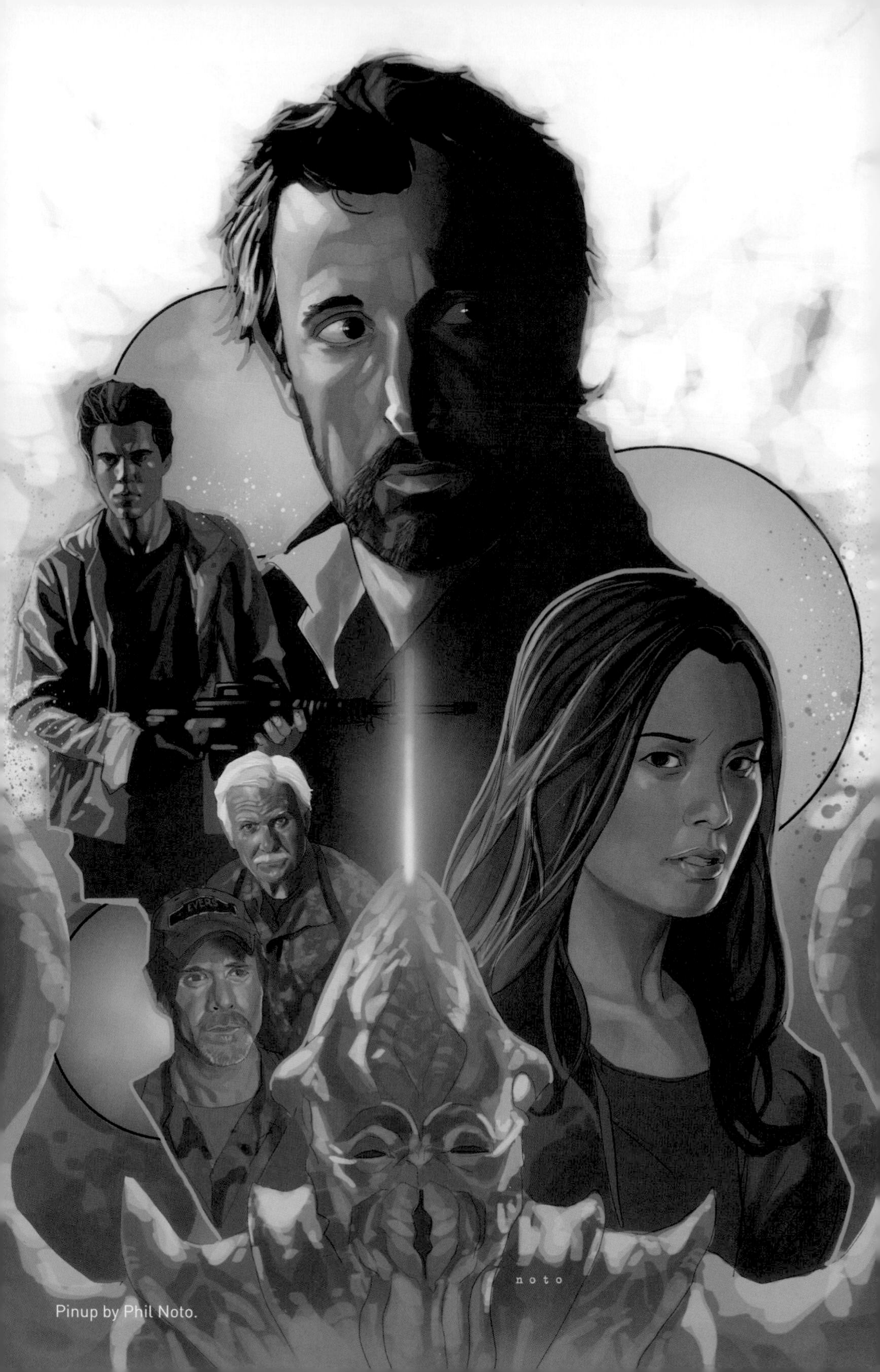
EVERS
noto
Pinup by Phil Noto.

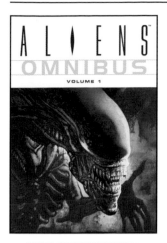

OTHER BOOKS FROM MARK VERHEIDEN

ALIENS
OMNIBUS
VOLUME 1

ALIENS OMNIBUS VOLUME 1

Mark Verheiden, Sam Kieth, and others. The first three Dark Horse *Aliens* series: *Outbreak*, *Nightmare Asylum*, and *Female War*, are collected in a value-priced, quality-format omnibus, featuring nearly four hundred pages in color. Written by television scribe Mark Verheiden (*The Mask*, *Battlestar Galactica*) and illustrated by Mark A. Nelson, Den Beauvais, and Sam Kieth.

978-1-59307-727-3
$24.99

THE AMERICAN
MARK VERHEIDEN

THE AMERICAN

Mark Verheiden and others. He's the ultimate American hero. Since the fifties, he's been a symbol of hope for the entire nation, an indestructible one-man army standing tall for the American way. When reporter Dennis Hough is assigned to cover a story about his boyhood hero, he begins to see cracks in the legend.

978-1-59307-419-7
$14.99

FEATURING SAM RAIMI'S CLASSIC CHARACTERS!
THE EVIL DEAD
MARK VERHEIDEN
JOHN BOLTON

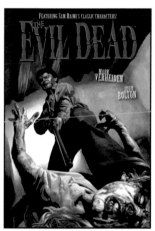

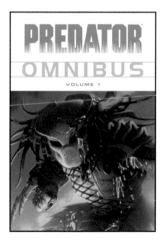

THE EVIL DEAD

Mark Verheiden, John Bolton. Writer Mark Verheiden *(Battlestar Galactica, My Name Is Bruce)* and illustrator John Bolton *(God Save the Queen, Harlequin Valentine)* present an exciting expansion on the classic horror film that introduced us to the powerful Book of the Dead, the relentlessly violent deadites, and Ash—one resilient, blood-soaked survivor.

978-1-59582-164-5
$12.95

PREDATOR
OMNIBUS
VOLUME 1

PREDATOR OMNIBUS VOLUME 1

Mark Verheiden, Ron Randall, and others. The three core Dark Horse *Predator* graphic novels: *Concrete Jungle*, *Cold War*, and *Dark River*, and several other chilling *Predator* tales, some never before reprinted, are collected together for the first time, in a value-priced, quality-format omnibus, featuring over four hundred explosive story pages in full color.

978-1-59307-732-7
$24.99

ALSO FROM DARK HORSE BOOKS!

MASS
EFFECT
REDEMPTION
MAC WALTERS
JOHN JACKSON MILLER
OMAR FRANCIA
FROM THE LEAD WRITER OF THE
BLOCKBUSTER BIOWARE VIDEO GAME
MASS EFFECT 2

MASS EFFECT VOLUME 1: REDEMPTION

Mac Walters, John Jackson Miller, Omar Francia, and others. The sequel to the blockbuster science-fiction epic, *Mass Effect 2* begins with the disappearance of Commander Shepard. The story of what happens next—exclusive to this graphic novel—will have the commander's companion, Dr. Liara T'Soni, undertake a mission in the Milky Way's lawless Terminus Systems.

978-1-59582-481-3

$16.99

PREDATORS

PREDATORS

Paul Tobin, David Lapham, and others. Sets up Robert Rodriguez's reboot of the *Predator* film series by showing how the characters fought for their lives and arrived on the Predators' alien planet. Then, after an adaptation of the film itself, find out what happened to the surviving characters after the movie!

978-1-59582-628-2

$19.99

REX MUNDI
BOOK SIX
Gate of God
ARVID NELSON
JUAN FERREYRA

REX MUNDI

Juan Ferreyra, Arvid Nelson, and others.

Volume 1:	978-1-59307-652-8	$16.95
Volume 2:	978-1-59307-682-5	$16.95
Volume 3:	978-1-59307-651-1	$16.99
Volume 4:	978-1-59307-824-9	$16.99
Volume 5:	978-1-59582-192-8	$17.95
Volume 6:	978-1-59582-403-5	$17.99

SERENITY
THE SHEPHERD'S TALE
JOSS WHEDON ZACK WHEDON CHRIS SAMNEE

SERENITY: THE SHEPHERD'S TALE

Joss Whedon, Zack Whedon, and Chris Samnee. Who was Book before meeting Mal and the rest of the *Serenity* crew, and how did he become one of their allies? Answers to these and more questions about Book's past are uncovered in this original graphic novel.

978-1-59582-561-2

$14.99

AVAILABLE AT YOUR LOCAL COMICS SHOP OR BOOKSTORE! • To find a comics shop in your area, call 1-888-266-4226. For more information or to order direct visit DarkHorse.com or call 1-800-862-0052 Mon.–Fri. 9 A.M. to 5 P.M. Pacific Time. Prices and availability subject to change without notice.

DARK HORSE BOOKS
DarkHorse.com

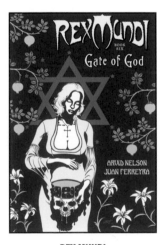